# Inside-Out Liturgy

## The Liturgy of the Church
## and the Liturgy of the World

By
**Robin Morrison**
**Copyright Easter 2022**

# With thanks and dedication to

Fr Andrew and the community of worshippers
at St. Mary's, Sunbury on Thames,
who made Linda and I so welcome,
Fr Simon who prompted the theme of this book,
the Reverend Dr Stephen Brian,
who urged to me speak about these things,
and the many, inspirational others
who taught me to look in the direction of these things,
by their own writing, or conversations with them,
including Metropolitan Anthony Bloom,
Archbishop Rowan Williams, Rev Professor Dumitru Staniloaie
(Theological Institute, Bucharest University),
particular nuns and monks in Romania,
Professor Nicos Nissiotis at Bossey,
Rev John Moyer formerly Director Frontier Internship in Mission, Geneva;
Kristin Roaldseth, formerly Regional Representative for Central America,
Executive Officer for Latin America and the Caribbean,
Norwegian Church Aid;
and the Rev Canon Dr Michael Hereward-Rothwell.
In addition, gratitude for all I have experienced through participation
in Orthodox Liturgies, mostly in Romania, but also Canterbury Rd Oxford,
Ennismore Gardens London, Zagorsk, Kiev, Moscow,
Geneva, and elsewhere.

*Whether we "spiritualize" our life or "secularize" our religion, whether we invite men to a spiritual banquet or simply join them at the secular one, the real life of the world, for which we are told God gave his only begotten Son, remains hopelessly beyond our religious grasp.*

Alexander Schmemann.
*The World as Sacrament.* Darton Longman and Todd. 1966.

*The paradox of salvation is that the more we become like God through the gift of grace, the more human we become. Our humanisation takes place in direct not inverse proportion to our divinization. Our humanity is not diminished by the gift of God but becomes more and more what it is meant to be; the place where the world and God become fully and personally present to each other.*

Michael Skelly S.J. *The Liturgy of the World; Karl Rahner's Theology of Worship.* A Pueblo Book, The Liturgical Press, Collegeville, Minnesota. p 55.

# TABLE OF CONTENTS

1 A CONTEXT FOR THE TERRITORY OUTSIDE-IN ..................................................13
2 WORSHIP OUTSIDE-IN AND INSIDE-OUT ......................................................29
3 DAILY MYSTICISM, INSIDE-OUT ..................................................................38
4 SOMETHING MORE OR SOMETHING LESS ....................................................58
5 WAYS OF SEEING OR MISSING WHAT ALREADY IS.......................................73
6 HOW THEN, DID SOME OF THIS BEGIN? ......................................................93
7 SACRAMENT OF THE LEAVEN AND THE WHOLE LUMP ...............................124
8 HOW THEN SHALL WE PUT IT, TO DESCRIBE IT? .......................................142
9 WHAT'S THE TIME AND WHERE ARE YOU? ...............................................153
10 LESS OR MORE THAN THE TOTALITY OF THINGS .....................................176
11 SACRAMENTS OUTSIDE-IN AND INSIDE-OUT ..........................................187
12 THE LITURGY OF PUBLIC WORKS .............................................................223
13 INCARNATING THE MESSAGE ...................................................................293
14 TOWARDS A CONCLUSION - BACK TO THE BEGINNING .............................311

Note

It has been good to reread Alexander Schmemann's book, *For the Life of the World*, also published or republished as *The World as Sacrament*. One of the joys of retirement is to rediscover and reread things that have meant a great deal at an earlier stage in one's life. This, for me, is one of those books. I don't give page numbers because there have been different editions, not least under those two titles. I first read it at about the time I was ordained in 1970 and was working as a young and naïve, Anglican curate in Hackney. I have shared it with many people and once led a retreat on it in the Deanery of Hackney, sometime in the early 1970s. It said so simply and profoundly what I'd learnt from the Orthodox during a year's study in Romania in 1967–68 and occasional conversations with the Orthodox ever since. I write as an Anglican priest and  hope I have not offended any Orthodox readers in what I have included or left out in my interpretation of their theological understanding of Liturgy.

I found Karl Rahner's writing on the *Theology of Worship* and "daily mysticism" only recently, and include some quotes from him, or about him, which seemed relevant to this work. Having spent much of my life working on Church and Society issues[1], it was important to me, at least, to find ways of bridging that gap. The early mystic writers have a great deal to offer, but I resisted the temptation in this book to include more than just the minimum of references to them. They represent a vast corpus of writings and experience from which to mine some of the great spiritual treasures of the early church, particularly the Eastern part of the Church. Not being a scholar of that era (or any other), I recognise how hard it can be to find their texts in a helpful translation and an affordable edition. It would be a shame however if contemporary Christians weren't reminded of their existence and significance.

I also want to honour the work of T. S. Eliot in his *Four Quartets*, a book that has stayed with me since university, and, later, when attending Helen Gardner's lectures in Oxford, and from which Linda and I chose a passage at our wedding in 1970.

Then I must record my gratitude to Anthony Bloom for all he taught me before he died in 2003, and to Rowan Williams, not only for his inspiration and some of our conversations when we overlapped for a time

---

[1] I was a Principal Social Responsibility Officer for the team in Derby Diocese and later Church and Society Officer for the Church in Wales, having also been an Industrial and University Chaplain and an Assistant Head of a Community School.

in Wales, when he was the Archbishop there, but for his latest book *Looking East in Winter. Contemporary thought and the Eastern Christian Tradition.* (Bloomsbury 2021). So many of his books have referenced the influence of Eastern Church theology and spirituality. I know of no other, living theologian who could write in this way, and cover so much profound territory. He mentions several authors that have meant a lot to me, including Christos Yannaris, who I remember from a conference of young Orthodox and Protestant theologians on Crete. I think I first met Rowan Williams at an annual conference of the Fellowship of St. Alban and St. Sergius, when I was foolish and naïve enough to facilitate an outdoor workshop on *Creation and Body Spirituality* in which he generously participated. This happened at some point in the early 1970s, again back at the enthusiastically naïve beginning of my priesthood.

I have included references to the Russian invasion of the Ukraine and the tragedy of that action in the stark realities of the life of the world. Perhaps this was inevitable, given the timing of this book and its references to Orthodox theology. It is indeed tragic that Patriarch Kyril has so discredited the reputation of that Church by his support for the ideology behind Putin's self-justification of that "special military exercise", which, it was repeatedly claimed by Russian State media, didn't target any civilians, and wasn't responsible for the horrors of their loss of life and homes in displacement and destruction! In writing about worship and Liturgy, it was impossible not to think of them.

In the history of the world, including our present times, not least because of the Russian invasion and destructive forces in the Ukraine, it is hard to talk about religion at all. The Orthodox Christian Church in Russia has legitimated that invasion, even though it meant the death and displacement of fellow Orthodox Christians in the Ukraine, just across their border. Even though it meant the denial, not just the distortion of truth, as large parts of the Russian population accepted at face value what they were told by the Russian, media. This kind of denial shows how powerful cognitive dissonance can be in the refusal to accept new facts which undermine basic beliefs. In the Russian Orthodox case, their beliefs tie them to a nationalised and patriotic spirituality of the Russian land, and its sense of a divine purpose or place in history. In addition, schools are already being given a new history curriculum to inculcate the official view that the military operation was to de-nazify and de-militarise the Ukraine to prevent their invasion of Russia as well as to reassert Soviet boundaries. History will also show that the official News channels insisted the Russians hadn't invaded the Ukraine, so it must be the Ukrainians themselves who had destroyed their own cities. All of which makes any sensible peace talks impossible - why would the Ukraine seek peace with the Russians, if the Russians haven't done anything? History will surely reveal how deep the lies and denial have gone, embedding themselves in the famous Russian "soul", so beloved of many nineteenth century Russian writers.

So, we are still living out the horrors of history in our times. The 20th century is usually thought of as the most violent of all, with its horrific two world wars and many surrogate wars, as well as the appearance of conservative, extremist Islam which only increased in the 21st century. So, yes, because of all that and more, it is hard to talk of Liturgy in as positive a way as I do, whether in the context of the Liturgy of the Church, or the Liturgy of the world. Surely both are charged with their part in the horrors of history, even if they also claim to prophetically challenge violence, and provide support and care for its millions of victims. But I dare to write these worlds about Liturgy in the hope that they will still make some kind of sense, even within that horrific truth about the human condition as evidenced by history.

So, it would be naive of me to think in a simplistic, or any other way, that what I propose about a "maximal" understanding of Liturgy can function in anything but the real world. The real world isn't just the world of the contented and comfortable in different societies. We hear from at least one Gospel account of the resurrection, that the disciple Thomas needed to know the risen Christ had something to do with the suffering Christ with holes in his hands. The two truths go together, however contradictory they may seem. If our understanding of the Liturgy of the World has any meaning, it must be earthed in the realities of the real world. This is particularly so, if we are to talk about a maximal understanding of its meaning and reference points.

History teaches us to look back, in order to understand the present through the perspective of history, even as we repeat its worst mistakes as well as its best achievements. These mistakes can be linked to a sense of fear and misunderstanding that morphs into paranoia, anxiety that morphs into aggression, defence that morphs into attack. Whatever the causations and correlations, we have failed in our struggles to avoid our mistakes, sometimes interpreted as intrinsic to the human condition and sometimes to particular systemic failures on one side or the other. And perhaps these mistakes and distortions of our nature will stay with us, way into the centuries that lie ahead, such that any future, visiting species attracted by our technological progress, may find them still present within our societies, and conclude that we are an intelligent but savage species. Or perhaps, in distant centuries to come, we will export our distortions and dangerous behaviours with us, as we search out other, inhabitable planets. In future centuries, a new woke generation may look back and want to cancel the culture of our times, but, if they are not careful, they will be cancelling the conditions which still infect their own culture, so ignoring its real warnings.

RM Laleham Easter 2022

# MAPPING THE TERRITORY INSIDE-OUT

In bringing into the same focus the *Liturgy of the World* and the *Liturgy of the Church* am I, in fact, negating the legitimate distinctiveness of each, as claimed by the advocates of each, from within their own diverse and often divided spheres of influence? There is a continuing risk of that, in any attempt to avoid the kind of dualisms which undermine central, Christian beliefs. My aim is not to dilute or negate a sense of the proper areas of distinctiveness, not least in perceptual terms from the inside out and the one to the other of both those realities, but to advocate the possibility that both can be true at the same time; both can cohere and connect at the same time. And, in addition to that, I want to understand more about the meaning and nature of Liturgy, in and of itself, as something which includes and transcends both the Liturgy of the Church and the Liturgy of the World. This will the central focus of Chapter Twelve as the climax that is pivotal to the whole argument of this book and probably its greatest surprise.

This approach to Liturgy, I believe, broadens the territory within which we perceive the Liturgy of the World and the Liturgy of the Church. It opens up a new way of understanding each in relation to the other, and, at the same time, expresses how, theologically, the one cannot be understood without the other. And if this is in any way true, then it hints at an underlying, ontological truth, right at the heart of the nature of things in themselves. The story of how this came to be is long and complicated. And, of course, others will have completely contrary views, and others will have expressed it with more knowledge and precision than I could ever do. I just hope I have not over-simplified it in the way I have pursued this understanding of the relationship between the Liturgy of the World and the Liturgy of the Church. So, let's begin on a journey to map out some of this territory....

*Just suppose*, for a moment, that "Liturgy"
isn't just a big word for a service of worship in Church,
but has everything to do with what happens in the world,

in our daily lives and work, our relationship experiences,
and the important moments and events that happen to us,
and all around us.

*Just suppose* then that the Liturgy of the Church
was a part of the wider Liturgy of the World,
a focal or pivotal point for it, certainly,
but always moving in the direction
of a wider horizon which involves and includes
every thing within that bigger part of nature
we call "creation", and the part played
by humans within it, in their purpose,
identities and relationships.

*Suppose,* then, that this Liturgy of the World
took us into the very heart and life of the world
as being, in and of itself, "sacrament",
the sacrament of God's presence within it.

*Suppose,* then, that the sacramental significance
of ordinary things, ordinary life, and work,
could be re-discovered and encountered
as being part of the mystery of God in creation,
part of the very nature of things,
or the being of their "ontology".

*Suppose,* then, that this mystery, this 'mysterion'
was in the nature of God's Otherness
moving in our direction,
and in the direction of other others,
and in the direction of the otherness
of the whole world, in what we believe
about creation and incarnation,
as expressions of the self-giving
emanation of God's love.

*Just suppose* that, sometimes, in our natural,
human attempts at being "religious",
in the religious movement
of beliefs and rituals directed towards God,
we missed that deeper mysterion,
moving in the opposite direction.

*Suppose,* then, that while we learn about mystery
from the Eucharistic "mysterion"

in the Liturgy of the Church,
that learning turns us around to learn about mystery,
God's mystery, in the Liturgy of the World.

> *And, therefore*, are we not called to be
> consciously part of that mystery
> of the Liturgy of the World,
> through a new way of discovery
> and fulfillment, through self-offering
> for the wellbeing of others?

*And having supposed* some of these things,
imagine then, if any of this were true,
how it might re-orientate our thinking
about the world and our part in it,
about the Church and its inside-out meaning,
and how it might change our understanding
of the meaning of the central beliefs of Christianity,
their relevance to, and presence within,
the Life of the World.

> *And supposing, just supposing,*
> if this maximal understanding of Liturgy were offered
> to those responsible for any kind of Christian worship,
> as an extra dimension of their experience of its meaning,
> their worldview about it, their orientation because of it,
> might it then become an active bridge
> between worship experience and life experience,
> straddling and transcending the usual divisions
> of the sacred and the secular?

*Supposing* all this,
might it then enable fresh connections to be made
between the Christian community's sense of identity
as a gathered, worshipping assembly, and their involvements
in the needs of other others in local communities,
or even national and international ones,
and their concerns in daily life and work,
because the Liturgy of the World isn't divided
into neat categories of boundaries and divisions?

> *Supposing and imagining* all this
> might then the Liturgy of the Church
> point us to join in the Liturgy of the World

as if we are contributors to, and collaborators with,
the ongoing work and value of creation?
*And might* this not be the vocation of all,
worked out in many different ways
because nature and our nature are like that?
*And might* all the different ways
add to something
then of value in creation,
as the variety of ways stretch beyond
any normal understanding of religious vocation,
for we dare not under-value anything that God has made.

*But a second time the voice answered from heaven,*
*'What God has made clean, you must not call profane.'* Acts 11. 9

# CHAPTER ONE

## 1    A CONTEXT FOR THE TERRITORY OUTSIDE-IN

### SECULARITY AND MODERNITY

This book began with a challenging quotation from the Orthodox priest, Alexander Schmemann[2], about a choice between an invitation to the spiritual or the secular banquet. This encourages us to examine a perceived dualism which seems to have infested much religious language, certainly since the Enlightenment. It is now surprisingly common to find religious people using the word "secular", as if it referred to everything that wasn't religious or sacred in the real world, or in the nature of reality. Perhaps this comes straight out of the culture of modernity, based on the achievements of the Enlightenment, with all the questions it begs. Many religious people associate that culture with "secular", value assumptions which need to be challenged or rejected. And they are right in one important sense. Modernity itself seems to have rejected many traditional, religious assumptions about the possibility of knowing something transcendent of human experience and rationality. In this sense, the post-Enlightenment world spawned a "secular" way of thinking that was diametrically opposed to much traditional, religious belief and thought. It also appeared to close down certain questions, in order to circle the intellectual wagons around a defensive and then aggressive rationality. To some extent, modernity is a natural development and projection from that crucial Enlightenment juncture in human thought and history.

This goes against much in this book, which draws upon the opposite point of view – that human perception and rationality can be and are the locus of a transcendent experience of the mystery of what we call God. Religious people can, therefore, applaud much in the ~~Enlightenment project and~~ inheritance in Western societies, as being

---

[2] 1921–1983, born in Estonia to émigrés from the Russian Revolution, educated and taught in Paris until 1951, when he immigrated to New York to teach at St Vladimir's Orthodox Theological Seminary, where he was made Dean in 1962.

something of a huge achievement, even as they continue to assert and explore the possibility and potential of this sense of mystery hidden within it. Many religious people welcome the development of rational, scientific questions and pursue intelligence-based enquiry and explanations for traditional beliefs about how the world works. They welcome the best of the latest science and its technological and human contribution to contemporary life, even if they join with others in asking questions about its less noble and less beneficial implications and use. Where it is, or generates, a reduction in a fuller understanding of knowledge, there is clearly a problem, as shown in the dominant ideology of "data" as the descriptive constituent of everything. Such an ideology ends up being its own reduction of our understanding of the many different kinds of perception and knowledge. At the same time, many religious people believe the pursuit of truth from whatever source, can never be the enemy of God, and that spiritual intelligence plays its part alongside, and within, other kinds of enquiries, experience, doubts and questioning. And for this and other reasons, they hesitate to dismiss that dimension of the "secular" which appears to include all that is important in understanding human experience and knowledge for its own sake, using its own, self-critical epistemologies, whether from within a religious framework or not.

So, when we hear everything that is not included in the religious sphere of understanding being summarily dismissed as "secular", we need to pause and challenge some of the assumptions and attitudes involved. As soon as experience of the world is divided up into religious and non-religious spheres, boundaries, and language, we may be creating a dualism that doesn't, in reality, or the nature of reality, really exist. In the religious perception of the world, this may have always been a factor, not least for convenience in talking about the world. But that which is central to Christianity contains a radical challenge to such religious worldviews. And yet, paradoxically, many who see worship as a defining aspect of Christianity, view Liturgy as something separate from the secular culture of the world. This book will offer quite a radical alternative to that point of view, turning it, as it were, Inside-Out.

So, we need first to delineate different understandings of the meaning and reality of the "secular". If it becomes a shorthand term for everything rejected or deplored about the non-religious world, because it stands over or against religious belief, then I suggest that, while this may be a common religious perception, it will not be an essentially Christian one. In the early history of Christianity, this was an important question, and caused many tensions because much was seen to be at stake with profound implications for central Christian beliefs, particularly Christology and the nature of the Trinity. However much Christians challenge certain ideas and trends in the "world", they cannot but embrace it as including the whole of created nature and all humans within it. In this way, they dare not call it secular, in ways that divide up or reduce what God has created as part of the same reality. They dare not talk of an ontological division between what is not of God, and what is of God, even though they might be highly sensitive to what kinds of beliefs, behaviours and values appear to harm and mar, block and distort the things which are of God. If on the other hand, the idea of the "secular" is used to stand for certain trends or fashions within the culture of a particular age, then surely it is right for questions to be raised and certain assumptions challenged.

Christians, from all traditions, have a radical belief in the reality of sin, although they also disagree in the way they understand it. But to speak as if "sin" flows from, or equals the nature of the "secular" per se, is to distort basic Christian beliefs about the world. Early Christianity emerged in an era when certain, current religious beliefs divided up the world rather neatly into that which was good and that which was evil. Zoroastrianism was widespread in the ancient Near East, and it influenced basic ideas about good and evil, light and dark, just as some Jewish sects talked of the children of light and the children of darkness. As we shall see, briefly, later on, certain forms of Gnosticism or more particularly Docetism and Manicheism proposed such a dualistic world in ways that made early Christians cautious and nervous about the implications.

So, in this book on Liturgy, I am suggesting we must be on our guard in the way we talk about the "world", and the way the idea of the "secular" is used rather negatively about everything that isn't found in religion, or the church. I say this not just because there are things found in the church which should concern us all, but because there are ways of understanding the so-called secular world that are not the opposite of every thing we believe to be spiritual. A priest friend of mine has made it part of his mission to challenge everything that is "secular", by which I think he means all the trends and fashions of contemporary thought that are borrowed from managerial or technological culture, or which rely entirely on post-Enlightenment ideas of human rationality and competence in ways that marginalise, or dismiss, Christian belief, or indeed mis-read the nature of Christianity in itself.

I believe there is a way for Christians to perceive the reality of "everything" as part of a sacramental communion with God, and as having liturgical significance in an inclusive, or what I will call a "maximal" sense and way. If any of that is true, then it doesn't help if we divide reality rigidly into two separate categories of the sacred and the secular, and then the "church and the world". Such a division would not only block the dynamic interrelationship between the two, but would miss the possibility that the "church" is part of the world, that the "material" is a vehicle for the spiritual, and that there can be epiphanies of the "sacred" in the heart of what we think of as the secular. If Christians fall into the habit of rigid, dualistic distinctions, then it might be they are missing something of the nature of God as Love and, through that, what God sees in the world and God's "presence" in creation and Incarnation.

In saying this, I realise that many Christians will think I am underplaying or under-estimating the reality of sin in a fallen world, a world from which they wish to withdraw, or a world they wish to reject or condemn as being under the influence of the "Devil" as a kind of personal anti-God[3]. One would have to be blind to ignore the reality of this "fallenness", however it is described or understood. The reality of wickedness is all around us and within us, as the writers of the Old Testament psalms were acutely aware.[4] But there

---

[3] A view arguably more influenced by Milton than the Bible

are other ways of looking at it, and trying to understand it, which still insist on its latent potential to be a place where the presence of the mystery of God can be implicitly sensed and indirectly experienced. And it is to that latter orientation that my thoughts on Liturgy will turn.

While I will draw heavily on the insights of Orthodox theology from the Eastern Church in what follows, from my brief reading of recent Roman Catholic documents and books it seems a rediscovery has been happening amongst many priests and theologians. This emerged partly because of, and after the Second Vatican Council, although, of course, there was then a backlash against it. For example, *Gaudium et Spes, the Pastoral Constitution on the Church in the Modern World,* is one of the four constitutions resulting from the Second Vatican Council in 1965. It was the last and longest published document from the Council, and is the first constitution published by a major Church Council to address the entire world. It seemed to warn of the danger of emphasising and over-emphasising the distinction between the sacred and the secular. It asserted or implied that our attention to God in worship is related to and perhaps depends on our attentiveness to God in ordinary things. Commenting on it, Fr. Donal O'Leary, a priest in Leeds, said,

*Before church worship can be an explicit experience of God, daily life must be seen as a potential and implicit experience of God.... the poisoning effect of a deadly dualism between grace and nature is one of the main causes of people's disillusion with the Church today. We can find God in all the moments of our day, even those that seem furthest from God. All our experiences of pain, confusion and even evil can be implicit occasions of grace. There is nothing in life so secular or so sinful that we cannot find God in it.... The weekend Eucharist is not then about inviting God into the secular lives of our parishioners. Rather is it the reminder, the sacrament, the celebration and purification of the way that the Christian God of the Incarnation is already at the heart of our week-day lives, loving and healing us, forgiving and encouraging us at every hand's turn, whether we know it or not...This*

---

[4] See Psalms 5 and 7 for example which read in the context of the Russian invasion of the Ukraine suddenly make a lot of sense and recall what the writers must have felt about geo-political tensions and violence in their times.

*Christian humanism, this celebration of our humanity needs constant emphasis in our catechesis and preaching...*[5]

In this kind of theological orientation, the implicit becomes explicit and the idea of sacrament is linked to the implications of the Incarnation in everyday life, with ever new implications for the way we understand the relationship between the church and the world, in a re-evaluation of the significance of all that is captured by that word "secular". Clearly this "Christian humanism" turns us around. It points us again and again in the direction of human experience as being the locus of the incarnation and the continuing love of God's presence in a created world. And that "presence" is perhaps better described as the creating source of a world that "makes itself" through cosmological and evolutionary processes. Donal O'Leary, like so many others, believes this vision of the world requires a paradigm shift to take place in the churches,

*We are dealing here with mystery. We are called to explore it, to work the vision. The more we try to renew and refresh our whole approach to Liturgy and theology, to surrender ourselves to this mystery of the implications of Incarnation for our own lives, the more resonance, presence and power will we bring to the celebration of the sacraments... It may take some time for us to be convinced and comfortable with this theology of liturgy. For many of us it carries a profound challenge of imagination. You could call it a paradigm shift of the greatest significance.*[6]

In the introduction to this article, O'Leary quotes that great teacher of spirituality in relationship to, and from within, the realities of daily living, Thomas Merton,

*The Liturgy is the great school of Christian living, the transforming force which reshapes our lives and our characters in the likeness of Christ. Christ embraces all things, the divine and the human the spiritual and the material making himself all things to all in the liturgy revealing himself at the heart of our lives.*

There are many ways of exploring the idea of Inside-Out Liturgy. Sometimes we have to talk about the spiritual and the

---

[5] *A Vision of Liturgy – the Old Tradition and the New Translation.* The Furrow, Vol 60. No 12 (December 2009) p 651, 652

[6] Ibid p 652

material by using separate words, with separate and oppositional meaning for each, in the same sentence. And sometimes our vision of Christ in all things, draws them so close together that we are back at the centre of the meaning of Liturgy itself, so that, whether it is the Liturgy of the Church, or the Liturgy of the World, that which is implicit, becomes explicit in our experience of its significance. And we look to our Liturgical experts and to each act of worship not so much for greater clarity about liturgical rubrics, language or detailed choreography, but for a re-orientation in our basic understanding of our life in the world – which I will call the "Liturgy of the World". We don't necessarily need more liturgical commissions on the detail of different sacraments, the authority for their efficacy and validity, but on our understanding of a sacrament view of our life in the world per se. We don't necessarily need more self-conscious missions of evangelism from the world *to* the church, the material *to* the spiritual, or the secular *to* the sacred, but a rediscovered understanding of how God is already present in the lives we wish to convert or transform, or learn from, help to develop and support.

Some, in the Roman Catholic Church, have put this even more starkly. Professor John Baldovin SJ in his *"Reforming Liturgy"*[7] reminds us that liturgy must never separate the sacred from the profane, *Giving attention to the liturgy for the liturgy's sake alone, is not Christian faith; it is narcissistic obsession.* I will be suggesting that the Liturgy, in its maximal and earlier meaning, is much "more" than the way it is often understood. By its very nature and meaning, it cannot operate authentically and credibly within narrow church boundaries. It doesn't just spill over into the Liturgy of the World, but frames its circumference of meaning and reference points. The Liturgy of the Church may be seen as the generative, starting point for the Liturgy of the World, but, equally, we might say the Liturgy of the World is the context within which the Liturgy of the Church emerged and found its own meaning, reference points and implications.

---

[7] Liturgical Press (2008)

It is therefore appropriate and helpful for the church to look for signs of spirituality in the Liturgy of the World. The Benedictine Rule is a source of refreshed, ancient spiritual ideas, and contributes to our understanding of the meaning of the liturgy. In the Rule, we find reference to the cellarer being expected to pay as much attention to the pots and pans in the kitchen as to the chalice and ciborium on the altar. Mark Hederman, a former Abbot of the Benedictine community at Glenstal Abbey, saw *liturgy as the movement towards the infinite, without damaging one tissue, without spilling one drop of what it means to be fully human, to be fully alive as men and women.*[8] Liturgy is the *eternal yeast in the dough of humanity.*

In its maximal meaning, I believe the orientation of the meaning of Liturgy, waiting to be rediscovered, translated, and used much more commonly, is a movement from the mystery of God, in the "infinite", *towards* us, and with us. This might be a better understanding than talking about it moving in the other direction. Of course, the very idea of "directions" here might be unhelpful, and certainly both are involved. But when it comes to those central beliefs of Creation and Incarnation, the movement is, as it were, in the direction of God towards the other, which is the cosmos, and our human existence, rather than the other way round – our movement towards "the infinite". Perhaps the Orthodox have the most helpful understanding by talking about it as "theosis", a dynamic, circular movement of God to us in creation and in Christ, and then, in Christ, we and our humanity moving closer in the direction of communion with God. Spatial metaphors are an understandable reference point for a meaning that is beyond language. If we use the idea of two directions at once, or separately, overlapping perhaps, we are hardly doing justice to the eleven, or so, claimed dimensions in the physics of the cosmos itself, let alone anything applied to the nature of God. So perhaps "circular" is a better metaphor for the movement of theosis, so long as we realise the limits of that and any other metaphor.

---

[8] In his book *Symbolism*

O'Leary references the Benedictine monk, Daniel McCarthy, a teacher of liturgy in Rome. He says that, *because of the incarnation, the sacraments enable us to reflect on and interpret the whole of our lives and within them to find the experience of communion with God mediated in ordinary and daily ways.. the divine mystery is revealed in ordinary and human ways through a shared meal, through another person. The mystery of this exchange gives insight into the deeper reality of our daily lives so that even our everyday interactions with others may mediate our sharing in this communion of divine mysteries.*[9]

It is a useful and insightful article for many reasons, and is a good example of how something significant is happening and being re-examined, albeit not everywhere in the Catholic Church, because we could quote many counter-movements and statements. But there seems to be a bubbling up realization that there is something profoundly significant in the idea of sacraments, or rather the meaning of "sacrament" per se, that holds the world, humanity and the "secular" in its grasp. Much of this came from the inspiration of the Second Vatican Council and its drafters, including of course Karl Rahner, to whom we will refer on several occasions. Much of it emerged from a generation of monks and nuns who were committed to more action on behalf of the poor and oppressed.[10] It was as if two great insights were emerging together at about the same time – the first that the church needed to be more active in human rights and the liberation of the oppressed, in, and for, and on behalf of, the concerns of the world. The second, that the most central act of worship and

---

[9] O'Leary. *A vision of Liturgy* p 649

[10] I was once lucky enough to spend time with Sr Joan Chittester OSB in her monastery in Eirie, USA. I had invited her over to do a lecture tour in Britain and this was her return invite to me, spending Holy Week with them giving talks and even celebrating the Eucharist. Some from her community had spent time on the Nicaraguan border with Honduras, supporting the liberation movements there. Others were involved in the work of Pax Christi. A close friend was and still is Sr Terri McKenzie CHCJ who I first met at a UN meeting in New York when she invited myself and Dom Helder Camara (Archbishop of Olinda and Recife) to one of the community houses. He was the liberation theologian, quoted as saying "When I give food to the poor, they call me a saint. When I ask why they are poor, they call me a communist."

liturgy was the exclusive business of the priesthood and the church; that everything else was an addition, a seductive distraction, or an expression of some kind of lefty politics. In some cases, perhaps too many, it was as if one part of the church stood its (radical) ground in the territory of the former – and the other part of the church stood its (conservative) ground in the territory of the latter. In that great division, perhaps it was natural for the one to become even more radical and the other to accrue around it even more conservative ideas and representatives. And, usually, the centralizing instinct of the Vatican chose to control the former more whole heartedly than it did the latter. The tragedy was that, in the process, as the decades passed, those at either extreme of the division forgot how much they needed the other, or could have been part of the same orientation and understanding, based on what was an emerging perception of the wider significance of the Liturgy. I will be suggesting that the Liturgy could become the source of a new engagement with society, giving us a new perception of the significance of the world and therefore of all that needs to be transformed in it, as well as all that needs to be affirmed and valued in it.

Meanwhile, several recent, public pronouncements by Conferences of Catholic Bishops included references, here and there, to how these two themes might influence one another and respond to recent cultural shifts. They were at pains to affirm the way God is all in all, including in and through the ordinary things of life, a theme we will return to later in a section on the way Liturgical Time is part of the movement of time itself.

*The Liturgy is the routine inscription of eternity in time, the continual action of Christ who is Lord of time. By its very "routine" and "ordinariness", the liturgy writes us into time; in its rhythm and seasons it celebrates our finitude and embodiedness. It is not an escape to eternity from the contradictions of our finite temporal existence, but a way of seeing them within the greater horizons of God's eternal life[11].*

---

[11] The English and Welsh Catholic Bishops' Conference document "*On the Way to Life*" 2005 quoted by O'Leary p 649

Drafters worked behind the scenes of these documents to explore and examine contemporary cultural assumptions about modernity, post modernism, and its dominant narratives, with their sub narratives and counter narratives validating certain ideas like freedom, rationality and objectivity. Modernity was a self-grounding idea, they said, free from any sense of external transcendence from another narrative. And within modernity, came the positive virtues of secularization, including differentiation, specialization rationalisation, and worldliness, with the natural order understood as something autonomous functioning within its own natural laws.

Religion had been, in most Western countries, separated off into the private sphere of personal beliefs, in stark contrast to the "secular" which relied on post-Enlightenment rationality with the object of creating more social/economic progress and individual freedom, ideally both at the same time. In post-revolutionary France and America, religion was formally separated off from the political sphere, and the theocentric from an anthropocentric world. Scientific rationality replaced belief as the authoritative source of true knowledge. As in the European Constitution of 2003[12], equality, respect, freedom, civil and human rights were values set by a new humanism, with conscious disregard for any background those values might have had in Christian history, a disregard explained in part because of religion's involvement with violence and wars on that continent, and in part by the values of equality emerging slowly in a new world order, after WW11, in a more multicultural (and pluralistic religious) world. The agenda for the future was economic and social progress with its underlying optimism, if not idealistic, technological assumptions about the linear, automatic enhancement of public wellbeing, once certain policies and structures had been put in place. Education and social mobility would guarantee human progress (presumably as compensating forces for poor parenting, a subject hardly ever mentioned) and these would function in their left-wing

---

[12] I was part of a group of Anglican Social Responsibility Officers in Brussels working on this document and the reasons for its drafters not including any reference to the contribution of Christianity in Europe.

version through more state intervention and subsidy, and in their right-wing manifestation by a smaller state, encouraging more individual freedom of choice as the route not only to personal fulfilment, but the public good.

That conflict of worldviews, a hangover from previous ideologies of left and right which came dramatically to the surface during the Cold War years, could only be overcome by moving to the central ground of politics, where economic and social liberalism met together and the State was seen as neither a nanny, a governess, nor as an absent father or moralising judge, but more as a dynamic partner in a grown-up relationship. But into that world crashed the realities of 9/11 in a global reality which was far from being some kind of modernist or post-modernist paradise, but a place vulnerable to Islamic and other kinds of terrorism, where religious extremists rejected all ideas of modernity, democracy and individual freedom, not least in life-style choices like dress, education and moral values. Modernity[13] considered such religious ideas as being irrational and traditional in a repressive sense. But there were clearly serious cracks in any political and social system that allowed this kind of religious eccentricity and extremism to percolate through, and disrupt stability and security. The shock was that such acts broke the rules of Enlightenment rationality and the political world order as taken for granted by the West.

Leaders of democracies and their media were suddenly on a steep learning curve into the values of a theocracy which devalued democratic assumptions about political representation, the rule of law and order, individual freedoms and equality. The only response the West had in its armoury against such disruptions and threats was more vigilant secret service measures and military invasions on training camps and regimes which supported Islamic extremism. But

---

[13] I realise this coded word isn't always a helpful way of describing a much more complex social/political set of attitudes which have an oscillating presence within human history, at least since the Enlightenment. Here it seems to refer to a particular era in the history of human thought, but I wouldn't want to be too prescriptive or limiting in the way it is understood.

this response only fuelled the fires of individual Muslims committed to the cause of using violence against kafir- unbelievers. And many of them were already living within plain sight in Western societies, somehow hiding their anti-Western beliefs in the process.

So, modernity found it hard to defend modernity, using its own value systems. Liberalism didn't seem capacious or strong enough to defend liberal values. Western democratic, and modern "secular" values clashed with traditional, conservative Islam, and many such Islamicist countries were oil exporters to the West. The world of modernity was no longer a safe place from which to pursue liberal ideas. Fences had to be erected to protect civilised society from the barbarians at the gate or already inside it. And while that was happening, "civilized" society was having to face some of its own uncomfortably, un-civilising enemies and questions from within. Its modernity project was being shaken and challenged to the core, not least by the way some capital-based processes imploded on themselves in the economic crash of 2007/8.

*Guadium et Spes* had opened with these words, back in the middle of the twentieth century before the first Islamicist, terrorist bombings had happened[14] in Europe or America,
THE CONDITION OF HUMANITY IN THE WORLD TODAY

*Hope and Anguish. In every age, the church carries the responsibility of reading the signs of the times and of interpreting them in the light of the Gospel, if it is to carry out its task. In language intelligible to every generation, it should be able to answer the ever-recurring questions which people ask about the meaning of this present life and of the life to come, and how one is related to the other. We must be aware of and understand the aspirations, the yearnings, and the often dramatic features of the world in which we live. An outline of some of the more important features of the modern world forms the subject of the following paragraphs.. Ours is a new age of history with profound and rapid changes spreading gradually to all*

---

[14] Often dated as the 1990s onwards, although in Bangladesh, Muslims massacred and raped Hindus in the Noakhali riots of 1946 with a complicated history of tensions going back to the 1905 division of Muslim and Hindu Bengal by Viceroy, Lord Curzon, well before the horrors of the partition of India in 1947.

*corners of the earth. They are the products of people's intelligence and creative activity, but they recoil upon them, upon their judgments and desires, both individual and collective, upon their ways of thinking and acting in regard to people and things. We are entitled then to speak of a real social and cultural transformation whose repercussions are felt at the religious level also. A transformation of this kind brings with it the serious problems associated with any crisis of growth. Increase in power is not always accompanied by control of that power for the benefit of humanity. In probing the recesses of their own minds, people often seem more uncertain than ever of themselves: in the gradual and precise unfolding of the laws of social living, they are uncertain about how to plot its course.*

*In no other age has humanity enjoyed such an abundance of wealth, resources and economic well-being; and yet a huge proportion of the people of the world is plagued by hunger and extreme need while countless numbers are totally illiterate. At no time have people had such a keen sense of freedom, only to be faced by new forms of social and psychological slavery. The world is keenly aware of its unity and of mutual interdependence in essential solidarity, but at the same time it is split into bitterly opposing camps. We have not yet seen the last of bitter political, social, and economic hostility, and racial and ideological antagonism, nor are we free from the spectre of a war of total destruction. If there is a growing exchange of ideas, there is still widespread disagreement in competing ideologies about the meaning of the words which express our key concepts. There is lastly a painstaking search for a better material world, without a parallel spiritual advancement.*

*Small wonder then, that many of our contemporaries are prevented by this complex situation from recognizing permanent values and duly applying them to recent discoveries. As a result, they hover between hope and anxiety and wonder uneasily about the present course of events. It is a situation that challenges and even obliges people to respond.*

Yet, our contemporaries were part of a culture of late modernity and post-modernism which had worked well enough within their own orientations and self-definitions. They facilitated or created those definitions as part of their own value system. They gave to contemporary culture a sense of power and liberation over the past, where the past stood for a lack of progress and freedom, hindered as much as challenged by certain forms of establishment religion. It was a past undermined or complicated by the internal and implicit dangers of even its best achievements, as for example the scientific and Industrial Revolutions, and Colonialism.

Later generations would look back and congratulate themselves in understanding and articulating these dangers more fully, in having the kind of perspective that could not only list the limits of history but do so from an ideological filter as well. We were slow to learn that history was the history of history, and that was always about perception of one kind or another. For our human nature was on both sides of our human perception, but also capable of freeing ourselves from the distortions of self-justifying assumptions contained within that perception.

This, too, was part of the implications of the freedom and individual autonomy which modernity gifted onto its high priests and acolytes or disciples. And those followers easily adopted its creeds of diversity and differences, not always seeing how the affirmation of individual or group difference could lead to real, cultural divisions, many of them seriously conflictual. One vote, had slowly become one person's rights, which so easily became, one person's rights to exploit or ignore or look down on another person's ideas. For international institutions, like the United Nations, had fashioned the charters of human rights without proper consideration, or at least mention of human responsibilities. In a democratic society, addicted to the values, spoken and unspoken, of individual rights, it is all too easy for beliefs and behaviours to become broken, fractured, and undermining of their own rhetoric and ideas, or at least incompetent in sustaining them in the face of real division and tensions. When the individual is positively encouraged to become the author, judge, agent and representative of their own beliefs and life-style choices, there is little to guarantee this will lead to a real recognition of the value of the other, or any kind of wider mutuality and commonality, unless the State increases its regulatory framework to minimise risk and protect others from the attitudes of other others. Legal codes may be able to enshrine the best of rational attitudes and assumptions, but they can be a blunt instrument when it comes to managing dysfunctional, emotional intelligence and irrationality, or the fraudulent power plays behind the scenes of the very powerful.

As an alternative form of salvation, secular modernity has had to come to terms with its own limits or struggles to cope with internal contradictions, or respond to global crises and extremist attacks. And meanwhile, many traditional, as well as new Christians continued to use a religious language system about salvation that was individualistic and boundaried in its own frame of reference, and equally lacking in communicating any of the profundity and breadth of its relevance or reach. And the more the hierarchies of formal religion introduced programmes of evangelism to conversion within its own frame of religious reference, and on its own terms, the more it had to accept that it wasn't touching the values of modernity, or those affected by it. It seemed that something else was needed that crossed the barrier between the religious and the secular; something deeper, something more inclusive, something more sensitive to peoples' lived realities, which took their daily situations more seriously, and their human experience as having implicit, if not explicit transcendent or spiritual value; something that could be seen as having the kind of profound quality that spoke to them in a new and transformative way of the mystery of life and then of God from within their cultural and scientific worldviews.

And strangely, that something had always been available in the life of the Church. And that something was worship, or rather a kind of worship that could be experienced as a vehicle of mystery at the heart of life. And that kind of worship had always moved in and out of the history of the church, sometimes obscured and sometimes waiting to be discovered or rediscovered as that which the church, or parts of it knew as *Liturgy*. But not the worship or the Liturgy that locked itself into its own religious ghettoes, protecting itself as a defense against, or escape from, a creeping secularisation looming up all around it.

# CHAPTER TWO

## 2    WORSHIP OUTSIDE-IN AND INSIDE-OUT

*Divine self-communication means, then, that God can communicate himself in his own reality to what is not divine, without ceasing to be infinite reality and absolute mystery, and without man ceasing to be a finite existent, different from God. God remains the holy One who is really accessible only in worship.* Karl Rahner [15]

There are so many ways to worship and to think of worship. Most religions include an element of worship, as praise, confession, gratitude, self-offering, dedication or an expression of a relationship with God. The central act of Christian worship has always been the 'Eucharist", which comes from a lovely Greek word, ευχαριστώ. It is still used in common Greek conversation. Thank you for this. Thank you for that. Thank you for passing the salt, or the wine. Praise comes from gratitude, and gratitude comes from the deepest part of our being.[16] Charles Wesley's hymn describes it as an experience of being "lost in wonder, love and praise".[17]

This sense of "lostness" can happen for many reasons and occur in many different situations. For some it's gazing up at the Milky Way and the contemplation of cosmological statistics. For others, it's looking at micro-organisms through a microscope. For others it's a passage in the Bible, a sermon, or a word of prayer. For others, it's a very personal experience of the Holy Spirit or Jesus in their lives. For others it's a relationship, a poem or painting. For others it's a sublime landscape or tree. For others, it's good news about their health, or the strength to carry on with bad news. Light glimpsed in the darkness, hope in despair. For others, it can be a sense of profound awe and wonder that just comes unexpectedly into their lives. A sense of something beyond; God's presence, overwhelming, gratuitous, unmerited, humbling, beyond our

---

[15] *Foundations of Christian Faith.* p 119-120, quoted by Skelly p 56

[16] I think it was Oscar Wilde who said something like, God couldn't be a gentleman because no gentleman would expect such praise, but I can no longer find the quote.

[17] *Love Divine all loves excelling.* 1747.

understanding, and yet, somehow glimpsed, as if within our understanding, our spiritual intelligence, or senses. A sense then of gratitude, praise, thanksgiving, (ευχαριστώ), which overflows into other aspects of worship, springing from a sense of wonder, a numinous enounter with something outside us that touches something within us; the mystical I-Thou epiphany that the Austrian Jewish philosopher Martin Buber (1878-1965) spoke about, so powerfully[18].

In different parts of the Christian tradition, worship is seen both for its own sake, and to overspill into a life lived and well lived, for the sake of others. In that sense, social engagement and social responsibility flow naturally from the spirituality which emanates from what we say and do in worship; from the experience of God that we have in worship. It is, one might say, the Liturgy outside of Liturgy, that gives Liturgy its larger meaning, an inside-out meaning as it were. And it is from that "outside" world that we enter into the "inside" world of worship only to discover that both in-form and stretch each other's meaning and boundaries. And that will be the theme of this book with a focus not so much on a detailed history of parts of the Church's liturgy, or a practical outworking of Liturgy in social justice terms, but in its own right as inside-out sacramental holiness.

Working with colleagues as a Principal Social Responsibility Officer in one Diocese, and then the Church and Society Officer for the Province of Wales, it was a privilege to discover how involved in social need many local churches were and are. It was also sad to discover how many weren't. Some colleagues, in those kinds of social policy and action networks, used to think that we should, as it were, shout louder about the need for social justice across a range of economic and social areas as a form of Christian witness. And there were and are enough causes and issues to inspire such shouting out and engagement, internationally and at home. And often it was those who didn't go to church who were leading the way. But, sometimes, a few notable church leaders and others would put their heads above

---

[18] In his book "I-Thou" 1923

the parapets and join in, making their own distinctive contribution from a Christian perspective. And that was and is a fundamental Christian witness about the importance of making connections between what we know of from *Church*, and what we know of from *World*.

Shouting out and then acting in creative, caring ways, certainly attracts networks of support from many within the churches. My own view has been that, in addition to this kind of witness and practical engagement, we should return to the nature of worship, in and of itself, rather than leave it behind as a kind of poor cousin. Whatever else Christians did or didn't do in their working or volunteering lives, we all have worship at the centre of our belief as the source of a spiritual, mystical connection which can then naturally evolve or overflow into effective and loving service. But for the connection to really work well, clergy, in particular, in their role as formal (and identifiable) representatives of the Church had to minister on both sides of the connection – the Liturgy within the Church and the Liturgy in the World.

In my working years of ministry, I've seen many move from the former into the latter, and, in the process, been accused of selling out to a social Gospel (a strange and dismissive way of talking about the Gospel), or to the influence of some kind of Marxist, leftist agenda. And yes, at one point I was on the receiving end of such opprobrium in a rather painful way. But because of resource issues and other pressures, or a different theological focus, or a lack of training confidence and capacity, there was often an absence of clergy in the places where decisions were being made about the working of social and economic justice, social care and the creation of wealth and wellbeing as a source of distributive solidarity and altruism. This absence was often seen and interpreted as a lack of interest, or a negative criticism by the relevant agencies. Time and again, I heard or sensed this observation and it inspired me to reflect more on what was happening within the Liturgy of the Church that reduced its involvement in the Liturgy of the World. And while many Christians use the language of mission and evangelization as their way of connecting with the "world", one suspects that this too might be a reduction, although they would never see it like that. Meanwhile, the parables and stories of Jesus, or at least many of them, seemed to imply that the continuing danger was for our religious priorities and purpose to override the real needs of those in trouble.

So, in this attempt to look at the connection between the Liturgy of the Church and the Liturgy of the World, or what I have called Inside-Out Liturgy, let's start with worship and focus on what we think it is, or does, and let's pursue the idea of worship as a vehicle for a relationship with God.

One might say that any belief or claim that such a relationship is made possible by worship is extraordinary in itself. How can we humans, as individuals or in groups, believe that, somehow, worship enables us to talk of a relationship in which God communicates or participates with us, in our human lives? Does this belief and this spiritual experience, which seems to be ubiquitous across human history and cultures, tell us something about our human condition, that we are somehow wanting or capable of some kind of encounter with God? But does it also show that we believe God can really enter into whatever we mean by that encountering experience and by spirituality or worship? As Rahner asks, can *God communicate himself in his own reality to what is not divine?*

On the other hand, many mystics, of different religions, have asserted that humans are made for worship; that there is something embedded in our evolutionary or human development that calls us to go deeper, because the mystery of God is implanted in our very being, however anonymous it feels, or hidden, or beyond us. And this mystery would, in some cases, explain, they say, that illusive sense of un-fulfillment we experience from time to time, which seems to have no direct cause or explanation. It may come from an orientation towards God that is itself an expression of a glimpsed presence of the transcendence of God, immanent within us. A presence that seeks fulfillment in spirituality and spiritual practise, in admiration and wonder, which can lead to a degree of contemplation that may, in turn, become a platform for worship in an orientation towards the *spirit* and the *truth* of our human condition. For *God is Spirit: and they that worship him must worship him in spirit and in truth.* John 4.24

When we dare to think or talk of God, by definition we are talking about a being or reality that/who is absolutely transcendent of our human condition and experience. Whatever Christians say about Jesus as the incarnation of this God, in knowable form, if God is transcendent of our humanity and therefore of our knowledge of what is true and real, how can we pretend we can relate to this transcendence? If God is the wholly Other, as a transcendent, incomprehensible, and unknowable mystery, how can anything we do or say bring us into relationship with him/her/it, or, in other words, that which is beyond those things? If God is not transcendent in this way, then how we can go on thinking of God as being God? Can a God who is knowable and comprehensible be transcendent of our human reality and grasp? How much dare we take away from the nature and being of God in order for him/her/it to be reduced into the sphere of our human knowing and capacity for relatedness? And would we then want to worship such a God?

It is obvious that we are entering more than just the horns of a dilemma here. This takes us into the territory of metaphysical paradoxes. It also takes us close to the heart of the great Christological problem. How can God be, or remain as, a transcendent God, and yet be "in Christ" in first century Palestine? We need sometimes to face this stark question head on, and not brush its difficulty under the table. It's all very well to say that we humans naturally solve it by projecting a smaller, more manageable, even domesticated image of God onto the reality of a transcendent God. But how far dare we allow this "domestication" to go? The honest answer must be, quite simply, that we allow it, we collude with it, to go a very long way indeed, often without realising what we are doing.

For example, there are many who think of God in terms of a particular gender, look, colour, culture, even age, partly because of this domestication projection, and partly because they argue, strangely, that, for example, if Jesus was male, then God must be male, especially if he is the Son of God! And especially if we assume that "Abba", the word used by Jesus himself about God, literally means "Father" as well as Teacher. But wait a minute, if Jesus' maleness means God must be "male", does Jesus's Jewishness also mean that God must be a Jew, and so on? Does this mean that God only speaks a combination of Aramaic and a little Hebrew and Greek?[19] After all, Muslims claim that Allah speaks in Arabic! Do we really think there is a physical maleness, or any other kind of gender or physical attribute in God?

Well, yes, apparently, we do. The evidence is clear in the language some have used in, for example, the argument against ordaining women because they said, a woman could not re-present the maleness of Jesus/God at the altar! And some who argue that, have done their degree in theology, and must have met the counter point that God is transcendent of everything we know as humans, including gender! A God with gender must have other characteristics that are human, and then we are very quickly slipping into a reduction, making God less than God and more human than God can be.

It is tempting though, because we keep coming back to the Incarnation, where we assert our belief that, in some way, Jesus is God in human and knowable form. But it's one thing to say, as the Church has said, that, with the Ascension the humanity of Jesus is taken up into the Godhead. It is another to say that the divinity of God is taken down or reduced into the nature of our humanity. And while that latter statement contains a truth in the person of Jesus, we dare not allow it to imply a reduction in the full nature of a transcendent God who is, in the true sense, "super-human".[20]

The 5th/6th century Pseudo – Dionysus was perhaps the first theologian to use the descriptive "super" and apply it to the nature of God, the names of God, the characteristics of God, including that of "super-essence," and "super-being", and "super-good". This is how

---

[19] It is hard to know what languages Jesus spoke. He would certainly have known some Hebrew and perhaps some Greek and Latin. He would certainly have spoken Aramaic.

[20] And even in the 21st century we seem to find "super - man" type myths attractive enough to be a commercial success at the cinema. Perhaps like the ancients, we like to believe, or need to believe, in super-human, semi divine figures.

he put it, from within the thinking frameworks of his times.

*TRIAD supernal, both super-God and super-good, Guardian of the Theosophy of Christian men, direct us aright to the super-unknown and super-brilliant and highest summit of the mystic Oracles, where the simple and absolute and changeless mysteries of theology lie hidden within the super-luminous gloom of the silence, revealing hidden things, which in its deepest darkness shines above the most super-brilliant, and in the altogether impalpable and invisible, fills to overflowing the eyeless minds with glories of surpassing beauty. This then be my prayer; but thou, O dear Timothy, by thy persistent commerce with the mystic visions, leave behind both sensible perceptions and intellectual efforts, and all objects of sense and intelligence, and all things not being and being, and be raised aloft unknowingly to the union, as far' as attainable, with Him Who is above every essence and knowledge. For by the resistless and absolute ecstasy in all purity, from thyself and all, thou wilt be carried on high, to the superessential ray of the Divine darkness, when thou hast cast away all, and become free from all.*

His point, in his *Mystical Theology* and the *Divine Names*, was that we can only think of God in terms that are descriptive in a human way, and we must be careful that we do not equate the nature of God even with all the positive adjectives we use about God. Our language is limited by it being knowable in a human sense, even when we try to use it of God. By definition, he says, we cannot equate the meaning of any human words with the nature of God. God, therefore, must always be transcendent or "super", over and more than the meaning of those words, including goodness, perfection, all-knowing.

This is how St Basil the Great addressed the same problem.

*God is without structure and simple Do not imagine a shape in regard to him ... Do not enclose God in bodily concepts nor circumscribe him according to your own mind. God is incomprehensible in greatness. Consider what a great thing is, and add to the greatness more than you have conceived, and to the more add more, and be persuaded that your thought does not reach boundless things. Do not conceive a shape; God is understood from his power, from the simplicity of his nature, not greatness in size. God is everywhere and surpasses all; and God is intangible invisible who indeed escapes your grasp. God is not circumscribed by size nor encompassed by a shape, nor measured by power, nor enclosed by time, nor bounded by limits Nothing is with God as it is with us ... the shape of a body is corruptible. The incorruptible is not depicted in the corruptible, nor is the corruptible an image of the incorruptible.*[21]

*Although human cognition can only operate within the laws of circumscription, it is not considered enough to receive only the gifts of God. The believer must also believe in that God is, in spite of being unable to fathom God's divine, Un-circumscribable and in-comprehensible ontology. It is within this context of belief that the meta-image operates. To strengthen my argument, I refer to Gregory of Nyssa:*

*"Just as when a small fragment of glass happens to be exposed to a ray, the entire circle of the sun is seen in it, not appearing in it in conformity with the sun's size; as the smallness of the fragment receives the reflection, so, in the smallness of our nature, the images of those ineffable peculiarities of the Godhead shine forth ... the image is not the same as the archetype. Therefore, just as through the unspeakable wisdom of God appearing in all things we do not doubt that there is a divine nature and power in all being, so all things remain essentially themselves, and yet, if anyone should demand an account of the divine nature, the essence of God would be very far away from what is demonstrated and known in each thing in created nature, and yet it is agreed that the divine nature is present in these despite the difference".* [22]

Yes, to all of that, so the challenge remaining for those of us committed to worshipping God, is, firstly, to make sure our vision of God is not too small in the projections, metaphors and images we use, and, secondly, to focus it in the incarnation as the revelation of God in human form. Somehow, we have to find our way of doing both at the same time, believing that both can be true at the same time! There are so many ways of understanding what the incarnation of Christ means, and we can struggle with positioning our personal belief within the context of what the church learnt to say about this, both as part of its Trinitarian belief, and all that it says about the birth, life, death, resurrection and ascension of Jesus. Many <u>Christians seem perfectly</u> comfortable now in talking about God in

[21] *On the Human Condition* quoted by Anne Karahan, p 99 in her *The Image of God in Byzantine Cappadocia and the Issue of Supreme Transcendence.* Papers presented at the Sixteenth International Conference on Patristic Studies held in Oxford 2011. Studia Patristica LIX, vol. 7 (2013): 97-111. Eds. A. Brent and M. Vinzent. Leuven: Peeters Publishers, 2013.

[22] Ibid p 110

terms of a very personal, sometimes disturbingly intimate relationship, and, in so doing, they seem to be certain about what God is doing, or working at, or causing to happen, or even thinking! It is now commonplace to hear such statements as, "God works this way," or God has told me that..." or "God decided differently..." or "God did this or God did that". And presumably this is the same God who is the source of a universe we are only just beginning to understand, with its billions of stars in each of its billions of galaxies, and at least one planet where the simplest of organic life evolved from inorganic life, and then into more complicated forms including hominids and hominines, and finally homo sapiens from homo erectus and other variants, when, just two or three hundred thousand years ago, the kind of people we now seem to be.

When some Christians speak so confidently about their knowledge of what God is doing, I am in awe at their capacity to be so intimately involved with God, or to speak so apparently casually about God's nature and will. How different that is from the spiritual advice given by the mentors, mystics or staretz, or abbots of those early Christian hermits, monks and nuns, and the people who came to see them. Those guides in the spiritual life would have cautioned anyone most severely when making such easy assumptions, even when experiencing profound spiritual visions. There is of course much more to say about the assumptions behind our worship of God, and some of those will appear in what follows. But it's worth pausing, from time to time, in order to ask ourselves, and each other, as Christians, what we think we are talking about, or doing, when we use terms like "worship". This was perhaps as good point as any to ask that question, before we move on from worship to Liturgy, let alone Liturgy *within* Liturgy, or Liturgy outside of Liturgy, where Liturgy means something *more* than just worship.

# CHAPTER THREE

## 3     DAILY MYSTICISM, INSIDE-OUT

*It must be made intelligible to people that they have an implicit but true knowledge of God – perhaps not reflected upon and not verbalized; or better expressed, they have a genuine experience of God ultimately rooted in their spiritual existence, in their transcendentality, in their personality, or whatever you want to call it.   Karl Rahner*[23]

Most religions have evolved spiritual practices to enable worship and prayer in their communities and individual lives. Some of those practices have developed in their own rights, sometimes by people not involved in worship or religion per se. "Spirituality" has been recognised as a dimension of human experience, with or without a particular religious framework or reference point, and, has become popular in our modern world as a kind of therapy for mind or body. People will pay good money to go to yoga or mediation classes. "Mindfulness" is taught in many schools. Meanwhile, religions have developed their own rhythms and rituals of spirituality and worship. A Muslim might pray five times a day. A Christian monk or nun may do the same. Clergy and many Christian lay people say a daily office. Many may go to a weekday, as well as Sunday Eucharist. There are many forms of spirituality practiced by Christians now.

The Jesuit theologian, Karl Rahner[24] took very seriously "every day" mystical experience. This is, at first sight, a radical view of the spiritual significance of ordinary living within the grasp of every human, but it was in fact a restatement of some ancient teaching inspired by the implications of the Incarnation. He was convinced that what he called the "transcendentality" of God, holy other and

---

[23] *Faith in a Wintry Season; Interviews and conversations with Karl Rahner* edited by Paul Imhof, Harvey D.Egan and Hubert Biallowons. New York; Crossroads, 1990, p 115

[24] 1904 –1984. A prolific writer and teacher and an adviser at the formative Second Vatican Council, considered along with Henri de Lubac, Hans Urs von Balthasar and Yves Congar as one of the most influential Catholic theologians of the 20th century.

incomprehensible, was, through grace given as a self-communication by God within the latent experience of every human being, even in their rejection of that knowledge.

*We are inescapably and fundamentally oriented toward the absolute holy mystery of God. This transcendental orientation to God is the a priori condition of possibility for every act of knowledge and freedom, and so is an inescapable part of human experience and a fundamental element of human nature. Every human experience is a transcendental experience in which we reach toward the unlimited horizon of the holy mystery of God. We always live in the presence of, and are related to, this absolute mystery even when we are not directly conscious of it, and even when we are absorbed with the particular and comprehensible realities of everyday life....* [25]

It was within that framework that he talked about the place of worship but also the ordinary business of being human, whether or not a person went to church, or even consciously responded to God through their formal declarations of belief. Many theologians have talked about ordinary living as being transparent to something "more". The idea of "transparency" might be more helpful than using the word "transcendency" of that experience. Something that is transcendent of human experience isn't usually seen to be accessible through human perception, however spiritual or mystical it might be. On the other hand, there is no doubt that mystical writers have talked about the higher levels of contemplation which take us closer into the transcendent.

Rahner splits this up into levels of "acquired", then "infused", then "awakened" contemplation. The mystics, themselves, talk about states of mystical love and altered consciousness, which may well be present in everyone, but often remain dormant, inaudible, distorted, unnourished, misunderstood, or ignored. In the mystics and saints, this experience becomes amplified, enhanced, and simplified at the same time, well beyond the complexities of different types of prayer and ritual. Some have talked of prayer beyond prayer, prayer that doesn't need prayer, when a relationship has replaced the words of

---

[25] Karl Rahner's Theology of Worship. Michael Skelly. SJ. The Liturgical Press, Collegeville, Minnesota. p 50

prayer. And it's quite possible that many who go to church are living a life of holy prayer, without ever having read a book about it, or even receiving advice from a spiritual director.

A story was told me by an Orthodox monk that a Bishop was concerned about a certain monastery. He'd heard that the community was really quite ignorant. Most of them couldn't even read. So he went to visit it himself, crossing a sea to do so. Sure enough, he was surprised to find that they weren't even saying the Lord's prayer correctly, let alone the psalms. So, he spent some days teaching them the correct way to do these things. Then he left, confident that things would be better. He hadn't gone very far in his boat when he heard a voice shouting after him. He turned to see one of the monks walking across the top of the water, saying, "please, tell us again Father Bishop. We're not sure we are saying the fifth line of the Lord's prayer correctly".

Apparently, the same Bishop heard that the singing in another monastery wasn't going very well. He went to visit and discovered that indeed it wasn't at all good. None of them seemed to be able to sing in tune. So, he went back and asked one of the best singers he knew to spend some time with them. This man went and joined the monastery and his singing was so superior the monks stopped singing all together. A month later, the Bishop had a dream in which the Angel of the Lord appeared to him and said, "how is it that in heaven we haven't heard any singing coming from that monastery in the past month".

There are many reasons why people go to church. For some, the words matter most; for others it's the music, and for others the sense of community. And, sometimes, many forms come together and inform each other. In any particular congregation, using the same rituals and words, we cannot easily tell what worship might mean to particular individuals, because there is something intensely personal about this. And the personal spiritual experience can be so close and real that people can't find enough of the right words to talk about it. In some churches, it would seem strange if we asked that question, as if we were prying into a private as well as a personal area of life. We can look around at a congregation, and try to see from their eyes and hands and voices, which part of the worship seems more important for them. We need to show great respect for diversity and different stages, as different parts of the meaning of worship affect and involve them. For some, it will be through the words in a verse of a well-known hymn, or the associations of a hymn tune they had sung at their wedding or a funeral they'd been to. For others, it might be a silent pause in which they can bring to the surface of their concentration, the things which matter most, because they are most on their minds. We may move at the same pace through the same rituals and words of the liturgy, but that movement includes waves of intense or less intense moments of concentration, focus, liberation, inspiration wonder and awe for particular individuals.

And, sometimes, the clergy will never be sure what means most or why, because individuals themselves aren't sure, or couldn't put this into words. And that is true of the clergy as well. Sometimes, individuals might be reticent about saying or sharing any of this. Some might be shy, spiritually. Others might be struggling and afraid to admit that they have been bored, or can't engage, or disagree profoundly with something said, but just come to support someone else. Others will clearly be moved and inspired by the Spirit, so that their thoughts are taken up as if into heaven, even though their feet are still on the ground. After all, people come to church for many different reasons and some are as so hidden or deep within their personal experience, that they cannot easily be articulated. Some would want a shorter service, and some a longer one. Some come for the sermon and may often be disappointed.

I knew a very impressive person who was the C.E.O. of a leadership and management organisation. After organizing a conference or two together, he told me he had once been a churchwarden. For ten years, he had waited for a sermon to have anything to do with the Monday to Friday world of work. He was disappointed, and for that and perhaps other reasons, stopped going to church and felt it had so distanced itself from real life and work place realities that it no longer spoke to anyone but itself.

## INSIDE-OUT AND OUTSIDE-IN

The theme of this book is about the Liturgy of the Church over-spilling into the Liturgy outside of itself, in the Liturgy of the World, where "Liturgy", in and under God, means something more than worship alone. But there is another truth, and this is a shared part of the circular relationship between these things. The Liturgy of the World has often infused itself into the Liturgy of the Church, informing it and supporting it. This happens sometimes without our appreciation of its significance. There are some indeed who reject anything of the world penetrating into that which has been separated off as "religion". It often seems they want to huddle in a church building, or their own inward-looking worship, as if behind closed doors. But it is obvious that individuals bring themselves and their concerns from their daily lives to be offered to God in the Liturgy of the Church. This isn't just about the gifts brought for example at Harvest festivals, or the skills people offer to help in the running of the church, but about who they are and what they want to give and share.

I once knew an Assistant Chief Constable quite well. I'd been working with the senior team on various issues. He was responsible for team training and was involved in community relationships. He told me he went to Church and mentioned the name of the priest. In conversation, he told me that the only thing he'd ever been asked to do to help out in that church was to give out the hymn books as people arrived at a service. I then met the priest concerned and mentioned the name of the policeman. "Ah yes, he's something in the police, isn't he?" I smiled and thought to myself, "yes he is and he has all sorts of skills you could use in this church and congregation, if you but got to know him better or even visited him at work."

Bringing the Liturgy of the World into the Liturgy of the church is also about every session of intercessions, in every service of worship in the world. That is where the real concerns of people are brought into worship and articulated. This is where those concerns meet the re-membering of the words and actions of Jesus, which were so earthed in the lives of the people of his times and more. And pre-eminently perhaps, this is where we bring into the Liturgy of the Church, the very complex processes which give us bread and wine to place on the altar.

These are ancient processes which now include the complicated supply lines of agriculture, land use, technology, production, financing, management, advertising, distribution, and then the purchasing choices and consumption of bread and wine. These are economic and social processes, which represent both rural and urban realities. They involve and affect the working lives of many people, right up to the point that we, as customers, visit the local baker or supermarket, or send to the specialist supplier for wafers and altar wine. This is the hinterland backstory of bread and wine in the Eucharist, into which we have threaded various theological stories and themes, and, we have to add, many disputes over the centuries. This is a landscape of involvements with a much larger horizon in the Liturgy of the World than internal debates about transubstantiation, transformation, epiclesis, and memorial. It is also a landscape that is largely hidden or unmentioned in the Liturgy of the Church, as it takes of bread and wine, ordinary things from nature and human work as if they haven't travelled through that human hinterland. No doubt in the time of Jesus, the relationship between wheat and grapes, and wine and bread was more direct and obvious. Now it is certainly more complicated, as any farmer knows.[26] There are many layers to the complexity of human work and human nature. Several of the parables of Jesus spoke of these things.

In other words, we are bringing, symbolically, things of creation and human transformation into the arena of the Liturgy of the Church, but their journey starts outside of that, in the Liturgy of the World. This is an outside-in movement that then should become, in our spiritual imaginations, an inside-out part of our faith, returning us into the Liturgy of the World to understand its

---

[26] One of my roles as the Church and Society Officer for the Church in Wales was to coordinate the work of the Rural Life Officers from each Diocese. Meeting at the Royal Welsh Show at Builth Wells we reflected on the issues raised by farmers, unions and rural communities. I got to know some of the civil servants from Rural Affairs department in the Welsh Assembly Government and listened to their stories about Brussels and Westminster over e.g. the bureaucracy in the Single Farm Payment scheme.

significance in a new way. This is a liturgical drama that no-one should find irrelevant, or just "churchy". And nor should we domesticate its meaning, significance and power, for the meal of the Eucharist is right at the heart of the crossing point between the Liturgy of the Church and the Liturgy of the World where meals are a daily occurrence in all their different forms and economic and aesthetic circumstances.

At that intersection point, the symbolic signpost of Liturgy points in both, no, in all directions at once. It stands there like a cross, solemnizing the meaning of those directions. Just as we look in one particular direction, wondering if that is what is truly important and the way we should go, then we notice its balancing signpost pointing us in another direction. And this happens at every point in the compass of these signposts. So that if we could, for a moment, stand as it were, in that still point at the centre of the signpost, we could sense and see how inclusive they truly are. Wherever they point, they seem to making connections we could, or should have seen. They take us into the heart of nature itself, and the human gift and responsibility of fashioning something good out of its bounty through human work, something that will gladden the heart of men and women, young and old. Something that brings a new sense of fulfillment in the workplace of creation, which takes raw materials and turns them, transforms them, through the work of human hands into something that we can speak of as the holy in their midst. The holy that has been restored to us by that simple meal on the night of betrayal; a night possibly filled with Passover themes of suffering and liberation made new, set in a new and everlasting covenant of meaning. In so many churches now, all over the Western world, Catholic and Protestant, we might hear these words or something similar to them setting the scene for the Eucharistic prayer which follows. This is the moment when the Liturgy of the World enters the Liturgy of the Church and visa versa. They are words that vividly communicated something very precious and important.

*Blessed are you, Lord God of all creation. Through your goodness we have this bread to offer, which earth has given and human hands have made. It will become for us the bread of life. Blessed are you Lord God of all creation, for through your goodness we have this wine to offer, fruit of the vine and work of human hands. It will become our spiritual drink.*

They are words which weave through the meaning of that intersection point in all directions. We know we are in the presence of much history and interpretation, in the presence of the divine made human, and the human called to enter into that divine Kingdom where God's *will be done on earth, as in heaven,* made possible in the self-giving of God in Jesus. It is a simple meal this morsel or crumb bread, and this sip of wine which is so easily spilt and carries so much re-presentative and symbolic meaning. This meal has been celebrated in prison camp huts, in battlefields, in the slums of great poverty and oppression, in homes and great cathedrals, at simple kitchen tables[27], and magnificent altars, at first communion and on deathbeds. It may be the most simple meal we can imagine, and, because of that, it is accessible to everyone, even if wine is not available. And there is a more in it than ever meets the eye, because of this simplicity which gives a glimpse or reflection of the heavenly banquet itself. For as we sit around the meaning of its profound simplicity, we are conscious that the whole world could be there with us, as a sacrament of communion with God, in all the places and times of God's continuing presence, transcendentally and immanently there, in the suffering and resurrecting realities of the life of Jesus, given as the life of, and for the whole world.

In the Liturgy of the Word within the Liturgy of the Church, a good sermon will come out of real circumstances, experiences and stories from the Liturgy of the World, locally and internationally, providing a context within which the Gospel can engage and involve itself in the opportunities, suffering and needs of the world. For the Gospel in the Liturgy of the Church, as it is deconstructed for

---

[27] I was once at a religious community in Scotland, where the Eucharist happened in what they said was a chicken hut they used as their chapel. One had to bend down very low to get inside and sit just off the ground on very low benches. One of the community, still wearing his working overalls, had just come in from a job in a factory to celebrate the Eucharist. There was evidence of a dirty job still on his hands, as he took the bread with the simplest of words, in their simple liturgy. It was a humbling experience indeed.

different situations, touches real lives and real events, just as God, through the reality of Jesus, has touched everything in the world by his presence. That incarnational movement of God in the direction of the world is the source of truth and inspiration from which we draw our understanding of what we experience, whether we do it consciously through the Liturgy of the World, or the in Liturgy of the Church. And the Word and Wisdom of God that/who is the source of all creativity from the beginning of the world, can inspire by the Spirit new ways of interpreting and teaching the Gospel of the Word make flesh, which incarnates itself in our words and the meaning behind our words, as they attempt to flesh out its reference points in the experiences people live with, and know, in the Liturgy of the World.

When we come to talk about the meaning of "Liturgy" per se, which affects both of these axes in a similar way, I hope the integrating connection will become clearer. I hope I will then be able to draw out more explicitly the etymology of both, as understood by early Christians and incorporated into their worldview because of their understanding of Liturgy.

But, meanwhile, there is more to be said about how we enter into the Liturgy of the Church bringing with us our experience of the Liturgy of the World. All of us, who attend worship, bring our experiences of the world as we perceive and experience it, into our participation in a service of worship. All of us, lay people and priests, old and young, cannot but do this, whether or not we intend to consciously do it. And some of those experiences will be shared in families, or amongst friends, or work colleagues, and so small or larger community realities fill the space within and between the words of the Liturgy of the Church. And that "filling" touches what is already there in the re-presentation of the transforming experience of Jesus's life as the incarnate life of God *in the world*. We note the NT does say that the incarnation was given *for the life of the church*, but *for the life of the world*. The church is the response to that life and attempts to re-present it in the Liturgy of the Church so that it can be affirmed in the Liturgy of the World.

So, that which was already in the world, as part of the Liturgy of the World because of creation and human nature's part in creation, is taken up into the Liturgy of the Church because of God acting in Jesus, revealing himself in his birth, life, suffering, death and resurrection. And then the connection, which is already there, is made again, and in a new way in Christ as the Life and the Light of the World where the darkness has not overcome it.

And as we, in our small but significant ways, bring the Liturgy of the World into the Liturgy of the Church, so we see the latter bouncing back with its own unique message for the life of the world. In the shining of a light of insight and interpretation on things in the world, the liturgical intersection is significant and powerful. The light reveals what is already there often in the shadows, as part of what we call the ontology of creation in the nature of how the world has been created. And, so, it is part of Liturgy in both directions, and at the very heart of the meaning of that word, as we shall see later.

Liturgy, understood in this way, can be sensed and glimpsed by those who inhabit either the Liturgy of the World or the Liturgy of the Church, or both. And sometimes, and sadly, we who inhabit both do not realise that is the case. We inhabit one, as being more natural or explicable, or important and relevant than the other, and so we turn away from the other. And this happens in both directions, in the attitudes and lives of those who inhabit either side to the exclusion of the other, and even sometimes, in those who inhabit both sides, but haven't as yet made the connection. And, sometimes, either side will turn against the other and paint pictures of it as being harmful and dangerous to what they believe and where they stand. But the Holy Spirit, who brooded over the void at creation, is the same Holy Spirit who inspires those present in the Liturgy of the Church to grow closer in their worship and their lives to the presence of God in Jesus everywhere present in the world. And when we hear that the Spirit leads us into all truth, presumably we must include "all" truth as referring to truth about "all" things, not just the kind of things that happen in church or figure on internal church agendas. And presumably those that talk most about being inspired by the Spirit in their discipleship are thinking broadly about inspiration of all kinds, certainly as it affects all kinds of roles and responsibilities, activities and actions in the Liturgy of the World.

So, as Paul hints in the New Testament, we must keep our horizons broad when we talk of the gifts of the Spirit in teachers and administrators and in every other work and role which contributes to the good of others, not just to roles within the life of the church, but everywhere. Even as I say this, I sense eyebrows being raised and many Christians wanting to disagree with me. For there are many Christians who still think of secular jobs as being just that, having nothing to do with Christian discipleship and vocation. And according to them, if a church activity doesn't "make" disciples, then it is of little or no importance. If a life lived is just "in the world" without any conversion to explicit discipleship, it is inferior or even to be put aside as not being worthy of Christian attention. I remember sitting with one evangelical priest in his study when he insisted that was the case with such dogmatic surety that it disturbed and frightened me.

Then when we hear that doorstep question, "you don't have to go to church to be a good Christian do you?", we think we understand, and yet we sense the reduction involved. It's not the going to church, but the being church that constitutes the nature of church, and that requires some self-aware commitment and openness. And when people say they sincerely believe that not going to church can equally inspire a good, moral life, it may be an understandable reaction to the failures of the church itself, particularly the hypocrisy or Pharisaism which tends to be one of the sins of religious people. For, indeed, there is often more moral goodness in the lives of people who don't go to church, than in those who do. And that moral goodness is also part of the Liturgy of the World and speaks its own truth within it. Jesus himself often pointed out the goodness in people, whatever their synagogue or Temple-going record or religious belief and background! He even sometimes held up unexpected individuals as examples of faith. In Luke 7. 9 (and Mathew 8.10) we find this example. *When Jesus heard this, he was amazed at him (a Roman centurion), and turning to the crowd following him, he said, "I tell you, I have not found such great faith even in Israel.*

Many people are searching for ways to express or develop a spiritual dimension to their lives. It may even be something innate in our evolution. We could use the analogy of music. It appears that we are hardwired to listen to music and be moved by it, even if we know nothing about it technically, and can't play an instrument. Apparently, our brains are capable of "listening" to patterns and tones and colours in music, and even of anticipating them for the pleasure or interest they stimulate. We can absorb musical "movement" as an emotional experience that lifts or calms our spirits. Music can express what we can't usually put into words, or even feel through our intellects alone. It can be in the background, or in the foreground of our attention. It can be a piece we've heard many times before, and which is now embedded in our consciousness. It can even be a piece we've never heard before, and yet it totally absorbs and fascinates us as if it engages a gear in our listening brain. Our musical tastes develop and change over time, as does our spirituality and prayer life. It may be that these are in some ways a natural dimension of being human, part of our hardware, or even our software.

Sometimes, as with computers, our hardware becomes out of synch with developments in software or vice versa. At that point, at least in computing, nothing seems to work because the one thing isn't capable of driving the other which has now become out of date. That is the crisis point when one is forced to seek for help (and spend more money). That can also be the point in our spiritual lives when it helps to turn to someone who understands the way something is out of synch in our spiritual listening ear, or lives.

People searching to train or develop their spiritual sensitivities don't always find, in formal religion, an opportunity to do this, and so they turn elsewhere, looking for spiritual practice and guidance of different kinds. Many people live in ways that speak of the values the church stands for, without using its language or beliefs in any direct way. It may be they are searching for a spiritual home, but already live a good life with high standards as part of their understanding of what it means to be human within their own kind of "faith" values, based on their experience, as in the example from

Mathew above, which Jesus takes so seriously. And surely Christianity, perhaps more than other religions, is about being human in the fullest sense of that word, not least in the way we treat other people in organisations or relationships, to say nothing of the way we treat the environment.

This is what Rahner called the "mysticism of everyday life". He wrote extensively about divine grace appearing in the ordinariness of everyday life. Surely, that goes to the heart of the radical claim of the Incarnation. That was certainly the focus of many of Jesus' parables and actions. But that grace may be blocked or lost within the detritus of our ordinary lives, or in the way we turn away from reflecting on its implications, particularly if we've decided that religion is an irrelevant, or dangerous, or empty thing in the first place.

Some people live their non-church lives in ways that appear to be very close to living a church life, and what it represents. This can happen when, for example, people touch an experience of the grace of being forgiven, or the sacrificial act of forgiving others, or a profound sense of gratitude for ordinary things, or know the unmerited kindness of others that can be an enrichment of their humanity and an example to others. And when those who represent what the church represents, find a way of affirming and then engaging with those who have turned against the church, or, more likely, ignored it, then perhaps the words and meaning of the Liturgy of the Church can come alive in the Liturgy of the World.

Perhaps the Liturgy of the Church contains surprising connection points with that Liturgy of the World, albeit sometimes hidden within church references, culture and language. Yet, as values express themselves in actions, so values come from beliefs. In the Liturgy of the Church, those beliefs are sometimes communicated only subliminally, as people grow up with, and continue their church going commitments. Sometimes, the style of the Liturgy obscures. Worship that turns away from any sense of the holy and the mystery in Liturgy, might have many other good things to say, but might also be a reduction to something less. And that would be a shame. We might argue that all worship can be a "reduction" in different ways.

That is often the case, and it can be hard to live with the compromises involved, or the sense of boredom or dissatisfaction that may result. But we have to be careful we are not imposing on communal worship our own ego needs or sense of spiritual superiority. We have to find ways of participating that respect the ways of others, but also allows for questions to be asked and positive suggestions made.

Sometimes, those who claim, somewhat defensively, that they don't need to go to church to be a good Christian, may be saying something profound, whether they realise it or not. There is a sense in which being fully part of the Liturgy of the World is a way of touching what is latently the Liturgy of the Church, but not yet clothed with the cultural habits and assumptions of church experience about what matters most. And if those who represent the Liturgy of the Church, listen hard enough to what is being said, underneath this defensive and rather rhetorical claim, we may hear an echo of something more significant, if not profound. It may be disturbing. It may teach us something new about something old or taken for granted. It may ask of us something more than we have reached for before, in order to truly meet the person behind this statement. For they may have a truth to tell which shames us, if their experience of "going to church" has never convinced them of the meaning underneath what they have seen on the surface at least. And what is on the surface doesn't always lead into what it symbolizes, or means at a deeper level.

We, who go to church to "be" the church, can and often do let it down, let down what it could be, what it is called to be. We have too often failed to live what we proclaim to be true, and often we don't even realise that, so insensitively have we allowed the habit or the culture of the church to blur or blunt our senses. But the bigger issue is this. The church and the Liturgy of the Church is essentially about the human, and being human in the *image and likeness*, as it were, of the God who we claim took on human form. The Liturgy of the Church is given for the Liturgy of the World, and points us in that direction in order to meet the mystery at the heart of daily life, and perhaps in the heart of all human beings.

Meanwhile, in the church throughout the ages, there have been many kinds of worship, prayer and spiritual practice. There are still retreat houses and spiritual directors to turn to, but sadly these are not used as much as they could be, and once were, for which of us doesn't need spiritual guidance and help? The local church could be its own centre of spirituality as an open welcoming space for those seeking help to develop their inner lives. It could function as the local community retreat house, in order to support those seeking spiritual development, learning and workshops, as well as those who regularly come for worship. While prayer might be a "natural" need and activity, it doesn't always come easily or naturally, even to church goers. The central acts of worship inspire us to spend more time and care in prayer, during a Sunday service, but also every day of the week as part of the rhythm of our lives.

Paradoxically, it seems there is little direct teaching about prayer and spirituality flowing from mainstream, church life. In some Anglican contexts, it is assumed that people don't need it, because they are catching its presence in informal, unspoken ways. There is a shyness to talk openly about something considered to be so "private", or personal. And yet the church has vast and often untapped resources of spirituality and prayer to draw on and share. It is a pity to keep these too quiet for the sake of respecting individual "privacy" when it comes to something so basic a part of the corporate, worshipping life of the church, as well as something so intensely personal in our relationship with God. It is true that corporate worship can, of its self, inspire patterns of personal prayer in the week. It is also true that some church goers hesitate to ask for help or speak openly of their difficulties and a sermon on other kinds of teaching on prayer can be very rare indeed.

In the monastic practice of spirituality, one key tradition of prayer and worship has been to set special times or "hours" aside to be with God, using set forms of "office". This was a commitment to focus only on God through a cycle of daily, weekly and yearly prayer. The day was divided up so that whatever else was being done, monks and nuns could ensure worship would take place a certain number of times a day, as happens in Islam as well. For example, the rule invented by Benedict of Nursia (c 480-547) divided the day up into seven "hours" - lauds (dawn), prime (sunrise), terce (mid-morning), sext (midday), none (mid-afternoon), vespers (sunset), compline (retiring) and the one night time canonical hour of night watch. This gave the passing of a day, in ordinary time, a framework within which a life could be lived to the full in remembrance and praise of God. But Benedictine monasticism also spoke of prayer as the work of a monastery. *Orare est Laborare* and *Labore est orare*. Benedict saw prayer and work in partnership with each other as contemplation and action can, and should be. This was a lasting insight that developed over time. Of course, the balance between the two oscillated at different points. But it is a useful reminder of how the Liturgy of the World can overlap with the Liturgy of the Church.

The point is that work is what we all do in terms of energy used in daily living, with all the attendant questions about for whom, and for whose benefit and for what purpose. And, underneath all that, is the real liturgical point – that work is part of our human experience of creation, and our role and responsibilities within it. It is the self-expression of the human being in relation to nature and other human beings, and, through that, to the *self-communication* of the transcendence of God, to use Rahner's phrase. It has its own intrinsic value, whether or not we choose to perceive it as having spiritual significance. From the perspective of a maximal understanding of Liturgy, this value comes from the ontological nature of work, in and of itself, as an expression of the nature of human value in response to the work, the ergon, of divine value and presence through the emanating expression of God's Love in the world. For those who believe, this emanating expression of love isn't just an add on to what we believe about Jesus. It goes to the heart of our most central belief about the nature of all creation, in itself, as the expression of that emanating love, and "energeia" of God which we think of as revealed in the whole Jesus event. Christians can claim that this is not just something relevant to the Liturgy of the Church, but of the whole world. Therefore, it is something accessible to all through the ordinary experience of "work" as perceived as an expression of human value and meaning. *As it was in the beginning so it ever shall be, world without end. Amen*

Prayerful work brought order into people's lives, and into the disorder that seemed to be a built in, given, part of things, and the way things are handled by humans. The Cistercians applied the idea directly to farm work and agriculture. Other religious Orders applied it to the production of woollen cloth or carpentry, cooking and cleaning, mending and making, and others to icon painting. Sadly, it seems that the monastic understanding of spirituality, based on this kind of daily mysticism failed to keep up with the type of work developed in, and after the Industrial Revolution. Agricultural work and rural rhythms were one thing. Work in a factory quite another. And yet, all kinds of work, including domestic work in the household, are concerned with bringing order into disorder, useful things out of raw materials, in the shaping and organisation of our societies and daily lives.

Out of the church's reflection on daily work, came the insight that all parts of the day and all time are special, whether or not we are at work, or at prayer, or relaxing, or studying. The early church, at the time of the New Testament itself, talked about "prayer without ceasing". In 1 Thessalonians 5:16-18 we find these words, *rejoice always, pray without ceasing, give thanks in all circumstances; for this is the will of God in Christ Jesus for you.* Of course, the phrase could have meant many things, but certain spiritual traditions, particularly in the Eastern Church, took this phrase very seriously. But no one can pray ceaselessly in the sense of a formal set of prayers. So, they thought, this must mean something different which transcends that understanding of prayer. If, therefore, we take prayer as a relationship with God, that is something we can develop beyond the usual words and times of prayer. If our inner lives became so rooted in the presence of God, perhaps there is no need for such things. Perhaps we have moved beyond different categories or types of prayer (thanksgiving, confession, intercession...) to a relationship quality that stays with us all the time, sleeping as well as waking. In the Eastern church, they developed the idea of the "prayer of the heart" and the Jesus Prayer. Once embedded within us, the prayer could be there with one, all the time, because it had moved from the head to the heart, the relationship heart, where the presence of God dwelt nearer to us than we ourselves.

This implies something different, a different orientation, not to special times of the day, at least not those alone, but a continuing relationship with God that never stops in the Liturgy of the World. One doesn't have to stop the rest of life in order to pray, just as you don't have to stop praying in order to do something else in the living of ordinary life. The activity of a relationship with God can include all of life, and all that we are and do at work or at home. This is a maximal sense of prayer that comes out of a sense of the Liturgy of the World shot through with new meaning, based on an ancient mystical tradition.

So, there have been many ways of integrating, as well as separating prayer or worship from daily life, just as there are ways of living the Liturgy of the Church as inter-related with, or separated off, from the Liturgy of the World. There is a natural struggle and a joy in either way, or both ways, or in the relationship between them. There is a place for old and new forms of monasticism and mystical theology to structure our tangible sense of the presence of God in and through all the time we have in our lives. Even without a specific monastic calling, there is a place for break times in our daily and working lives, segments, and sessions or prayer adjusted to different categories of time. That happens already in the Liturgy of the World as we move through time for meals, time for work, time for sleep, time for relationships, time for worship, time for relaxation, time for holidays, and school terms, and the pattern of rotas in the working week. As Ecclesiastes 3. 1-9 puts it more comprehensively and poetically,

*a time for everything under heaven, a time to be born and a time to die, a time to plant and a time to uproot, a time to kill and a time to heal, a time to tear down and a time to build, a time to weep and a time to laugh, a time to mourn and a time to dance, a time to scatter stones and a time to gather them, a time to embrace and a time to refrain, a time to search and a time to give up, a time to keep and a time to throw away, a time to tear and a time to mend, a time to be silent and a time to speak, a time to love and a time to hate, a time for war and a time for peace.*

But supposing all time was time within the sense of the

presence of God, and suppose out of this came special times to acknowledge that presence with others, to develop it with others, and on our own. And supposing, in the Liturgy of the World, time itself has been redeemed and transformed, and supposing all work could be seen in the same way. Suppose our prayer life could morph into a new spiritual orientation, from within which, everything in the Liturgy of the World could be seen as if it were part of the Liturgy of the Church and vice versa. And supposing then, we could integrate what has been previously separated and still retain the usefulness and place of special times and special places and special rhythms and seasons in our lives, but all part of the same daily mystery given to us by God. And the God who was in Jesus lived that continuous relationship with the presence of the nature of God that was inside him, and outside him, presumably both equally and at the same time.

And that same Jesus had his own rhythm of prayer. There were times when in addition to that inner presence of his "Abba", he would draw aside, step aside from the pressures of activity all around him, in the demands and questions and doubts of others.  We are told that he went to the other side of the lake to be alone, or to be with God, or to be with others with God. He took just three disciples up the mountain of Transfiguration to enter more into the nature of the divinity that was the incarnation in all its shining glory seen in his human nature. He was sent, or drawn, or withdrew into the desert on his own to face the inner struggles of his human nature. On the night of his betrayal, he prayed alone in agony in the garden, hoping perhaps that those closest to him would keep watch with him, to share something of that agony he was going through. But because he drew aside from normal activity doesn't mean he didn't live totally "in God" in everything he did at other times, and at all times. Julian of Norwich (c 1343 –1416) who lived a strange life (during both the Black Death and the 1381 Peasant's Revolt) as an English Anchoress shut up in a cell attached to St Julian's Church, produced many lasting insights[28] inspired by her mystical spirituality about living in

---

[28] in her *Showings* or *Revelations of Divine Love*, probably the earliest surviving texts written in English by a woman. These were prevented from being printed

ordinary life itself, which she then described as something that could be offered to God as true worship. Here is just one of them, relevant to our purposes here.

*Our life is all grounded and rooted in love, and without love we may not live... Be a Gardener. Dig a ditch. Toil and sweat. And turn the earth upside down. And seek the deepness. And water plants in time. Continue this labour. And make sweet floods to run, and noble and abundant fruits to spring. Take this food and drink, and carry it to God as your true worship.* **Revelations of Divine Love.**

---

during the Reformation. The *Long Text* was first published in 1670 by the Catholic Benedictine monk Serenus de Crecy, reissued in 1843, and published in a modernised version in 1864. In 1901, a manuscript in the British Museum was transcribed and published with notes by Grace Warrack.

# CHAPTER FOUR

## 4    SOMETHING MORE OR SOMETHING LESS

*Lord my God, when your love spilled over into creation, you thought of me. I am from love, of love, for love. Let my heart, O God, always recognize, cherish, and enjoy your goodness in all of creation. Direct all that is me toward your praise.* St Ignatius of Loyola (1491-1556)

We can, all too easily, make assumptions about the meaning of "Liturgy", and Liturgical Time. They are, at first sight, words that come from, and are about, what happens in Church. But, paradoxically, at the same time, they are words that are only rarely used in Church, and only rarely understood as having any other reference points apart from what happens in Church. Of course, there are many different types of church, and many different words are spoken about and in worship, which may, or may not, have anything to do with "Liturgy", let alone Liturgical Time.

EXAMPLE

In the "new" and growing church movements of the West, those words, Liturgy and Liturgical Time are rapidly losing their currency, their relevance to how people think. In fact, if you look at the service sheets (I mean overhead screens) and websites of those movements, you will probably never find mention of them, as if they no longer exist. They have been relegated to the past as theological antiques, now stored in the back of the shop, where everything is gathering dust and only rarely asked for, let alone brought out to be displayed in the shop window, let alone be taken onto the streets, into homes and place of work. And those who occasionally come looking for them, asking for them, are probably seen as rather eccentric specialists, antiquarians, who no longer live in the real world as most experience it.

But perhaps those who've put these things back there, hidden away and forgotten, haven't had the chance to consider them more carefully. And that might not be their fault. For now, thousands upon thousands of new Christians have hardly ever been told about them. So, they now, quite naturally, disregard them as having no relevance to the way Christians worship, or talk about their worship, at least in those "new" church movements that seem so attractive to younger people. And it's as if those new movements set up their own new "shops", rather than change the use and look of old ones, to proclaim their new way of doing worship and make all comers feel welcome in the process. And, although so much is new, and, to older people used to worshipping in other ways, so much is strange, they are creating a new department, culture or movement of post-antiquities type newness, which claims to be in touch with the true meaning and presence of the source of all worship who is Jesus. And, sometimes, such claims are made with little apparent appreciation for what is being said or meant about the mystery of God. Somehow, it is easy and perhaps understandable for them to think that their way is the only way that is truly authentic and faithful to the Gospel message or at least part of it.

Somehow, in the process, they've lost the habit, or forgotten how to look in the textbooks of the old liturgies, or to understand what they might have meant, or why they were there. And that might not be there fault, if they've never been taught or introduced to anything else. To those who are creating something fresh and new, it is probably natural to think, if not say - who needs antique things of that kind anyway? Who needs liturgical frameworks, lectionaries, ceremonies and rituals of movement and understanding? They are for antique shops and their catalogues, and for antiquarians who write about those things. They are only for specialists and can be disregarded in the important task of creating new Christian disciples who will learn to worship in these new ways, with neon lights of inspiring experience and role models all around them, except, that is, the lights and role models of a theological past which failed to create enough "new Christian disciples" in their view of the world. So, they ask themselves, why should we take a second look at their old, discredited way of doing things, pushed to the back of the stage, or dumped in dark corners? Who needs it anyway? So, leave it there, box it up, or cover it over with something so that it won't get in the way.

And we can understand why "they" are starting afresh (a word that is much loved in new church movements) when they look at the smaller numbers and apparently smaller enthusiasm contained in old fashioned church going. And by this, and from this, they make certain assumptions – that such worship can't have been doctrinally correct, and wasn't sufficiently faithful to the discipleship/conversion calling of a "growth" based Christianity, or is too complicated for contemporary values and interests where young people (and others) want easy, quick and, above all, certain answers, even to questions they hadn't thought of asking. And anyway, it seems as if they are so caught up in the repetition of certain choruses that inspire their praise of Jesus, that they don't need anything more.

But the worship they were judging wasn't always as old, nor as traditional as they might have thought. Once it was the new living way, closer to the time of those who remembered and knew Jesus himself. Once it was part of a spreading outwards of Christian belief and worship in the Mediterranean area, in Syria, North Africa, and the equivalent of the modern-day Turkey. However much every generation has to find its own way, surely it can at least take a look at the best and deeper things of the past, especially where that past takes us back closer to the beginning, and particularly in the case of a different understanding of liturgy itself. For there are many ways of understanding liturgy, and some of them may have something truly significant to say to our contemporary world. Significance and meaning are always important to every generation. And it's just possible that Liturgy, in its "maximal" sense, has always known this. And, if so, then its maximal meaning might include more than we think religion or worship usually does, and that "more" isn't just about the quantity or quality of things within the worshipping community, but the significance of everything else.

Every now and again, someone goes into the theological antiquities department and asks to look at what has been disregarded, forgotten, or hidden away. And perhaps they've come across something in an old catalogue or read an old book, or a new book about older books. And perhaps they are excited, because what they have found, as far as they can see, is something new in a lasting way, something that might be truly valuable, if only it could be better known and more fully understood. Part of the surprise is that its newness is truly "fresh", as if it re-freshes the parts that liturgy hasn't traditionally been seen to reach. Surely, they say, people would be really interested if only they knew more, if only they would be willing to take a truly "fresh" look, and then have the courage to question some of their own prejudices, or even their own, understandable ignorance. And, so, they leave the theological antiquities shop with something new to think about, something that has come to them and their generation as a surprise, something that shed new light on a variety of things they had taken for granted before, or not even thought about before.

For this new, "old" thing, seems to have something surprising and refreshing to say about itself in relation to everything else. And it seems to show that, centuries ago, people were on to something important, that we might have somehow missed, or now forgotten, especially in modern, Western forms of Christianity. And this something may re-orientate our assumptions and our worship in a direction that is just as committed to God's presence in Jesus as we think ours now is, with its fresh new neon lights way of doing things. And a new orientation is perhaps what a maximal understanding of liturgy can most do, and what might be, after all, most important. For a new orientation can be a transformation of our most basic understanding, and that can include a new perspective on the things we thought we already knew and understood well enough.

And the more they think about it, those visitors from the future back into the past which was, back then, very present, and very relevantly present and real, the more it seems that this is worth considering, or reconsidering, as having some kind of significance, one that turns some assumptions around, or even upside down. And the more they think about that, the more it seems possible that this has less to do with ordinary church going, as they understand it, and more to do with everything else. And it might then occur to them, that, under the heat and energy of the neon lights in their new forms of "fresh" worship, and the certainties in their faith, somehow, they might have created a religious world that was more or less entirely preoccupied with their own religious feelings, forgetting perhaps that, back then, at certain special moments, Christianity grew to be less of an inspiring, inward-looking cult for the converted, and more about everything else as well. But how could that be, and how could they have missed it?

It is possible that, in many parts of the Church of England, particularly in large urban areas, this might well be the general direction and momentum of the future. If and when that happens, many might well say this is the best way forward and it is the future of Christianity in this part of the world. And if so, others might feel, if not say, that this is an ironic tragedy because knowingly or unknowingly it has created something new based on a "reduction" in waving the flag as the most popular and dominant form of Christianity in the 21st century. It is a possible scenario because it would take a very brave kind of church leadership to challenge the basis of such success, even though many parish priests, parishioners and academics might notice or point out the detail in the way the reduction is taking place, not least in the use of scripture and the type of worship. However broad and broad minded the Church of England thinks itself to be, it may come as a surprise to some that all sense of that breadth dissipates itself as forms of worship emerge which can hardly be thought of as having anything to do with the Church of England.

Of course, I may well be stereotyping, and certainly generalising on the basis of my own limited experience of such approaches. And it is true that many new Christian movements have much more about them than a kind of religious pop concert type, personal experience. Their converted discipleship often leads to a converted life-style with an active concern for those in need. And yet, it is sometimes hard for them to accept the value of existing Christian approaches from traditions other than their own. I have looked at several websites where a call is made for people to evangelise countries where there is already a deeply embedded church, particularly the Orthodox Church. Perhaps that attitude doesn't represent all new Christian movements. Perhaps, it is understandable that new Christians and new disciples find it hard to believe that there is any other way of believing than their own. Perhaps, in their zeal to share with others what they themselves have found, they have forgotten how to see what is already there.

## LITURGY; AN ENOUNTER WITH THE OTHER

But there is something more, which takes us back to the heart of early Church attitudes, particularly as they developed in an Eastern context of spirituality and theological attitudes. Whatever we recognize and feel, in ourselves, because of a conversion experience, or our ongoing open-heartedness to the presence of the Spirit, or of Jesus in our worship and lives, are we open to meeting a glimpse or reflection of this same presence in others, even or especially in others who may well not have anything to do with Christianity or any formal religion, let alone any conscious recognition or conviction about Jesus? It is one of the most impressive claims and experiences found in theology and spiritual guidance, that we can meet the Christ in unexpected people, places and ways, rather than just from within our own assumptions about Christ's presence in our own lives, based on our own personal experience. So, this is more than just moving away from our own self-absorption to see the needs of others in our attempts to respond to that need as an expression, or continuing rediscovery, of the best of our humanity in our human nature. It is the movement out of self-absorption, in all its narcistic and egotistic forms, to sense our relationship with what is most profound about the otherness of an-other person, which is, in its own way, a reflection of the *image and likeness* of Christ. The same Jesus who pointed the religious people of his day in the direction of different 'others', time and time again, and was heavily criticized for it, to say the least. This seemed to show that Jesus, as a reflection of the way God works, moved in the direction of not only the Otherness of this world in God's Creation, but of other others within that otherness; others who were profoundly different according to the judgemental categories of our prejudiced perception but not in God's.

Of course, that enounter may not be obvious. When the truth of this does becomes obvious to us, we only have to reflect that the *image and likeness* of Christ in us might only dimly, or never be obvious at all to someone else. But in our quest for recognizing the presence of spiritual significance in the Liturgy of the World, it helps to view other others in this way. We do this not just for some therapeutic reason to take us out of our own pre-occupations, though this it will certainly happen. We do it to discover that the world of others, in which we live and work and do the ordinary things of life, is a world containing its own Liturgical significance as a reflection and re-presentation of that which has sacramental transcendence and meaning in what Rahner calls the mysticism of ordinary life.

But there is more. For surely an encounter with the presence of Christ in others can be complimented by a more general experience of the presence of God, as creator or source, from within the things of God's creation. The other human may be a prime location for the presence of God, glimpsed in the humanity of the other, but so are the things and creatures of creation, in that they, too, are part of our basic belief in a Creator God, not because they are conscious of that relationship, but because we believe it exists. And if we don't believe this exists, then for us it won't exist, even though it does exist. For if this is true, it must be true in an ontological, as well as an existential sense. It is un-destroyed by the way nature is and works, just as that basic relationship with God as creator is un-destroyed however marred it is by the way human nature is, and works, and develops. If the Otherness of the nature of God, as holy mystery, manifested that nature as Love's energy, in the creative reaching out emanation of self-giving that made possible the existence of the otherness, which is the cosmos, and all its different ways of "making itself" within that otherness, then it becomes more important to develop our belief that we can recognize the Christ not only working in our own lives, but in the otherness of other others, within the Otherness of cosmic and evolutionary reality, which is gifted by, and in the Otherness of God[29].

Belief in such a God takes seriously the kenotic, ec-static nature of Love as shown in Christ. We believe that part of the mystery of the Trinity, in itself, is an inner perichoresis or movement

---

[29] This is, of course, only one way of articulating a belief in God as creator or source in a world where we understand more and more about cosmic and evolutionary reality. See my "Love's Energy" Trilogy for a development of this approach.

of love that enables each person to be fully a unique person, and at the same time fully part of the same society of persons in communion and complete and utter union with each other. There is no individualism within the nature of the Trinity. But, also, there is no society, or communion between the persons, which diminishes their full personhood. Like so many things in theology and life, we are asserting here that two things (at least) that look, or are, contradictory can be true at the same time. While human societies find it hard to ever achieve, in their political organization and behaviours, a balance between the corporate and the individual, so that neither diminishes or threatens the other, so, as we understand it, and dare to believe, the society of God models for us a perfect balance of what the Russians call the "Sobornost" or fellowship in the Trinitarian community of God. While discussing the thought of Sergei Bulgakov, Vladimir Solov'ev, Nicolae Berdjaev, Alexei Khomiakov, Georges Florovsky and Antonii Khrapovitskii[30], Rowan Williams comments on the idea of the "catholicity" of the Church as

*the transformation of the human self, the dissolution of a "mine" and "yours" mentality and the gift to the believer of the unity-in-communion of the Holy Trinity in which each subject possesses the wholeness of divine life...the trinitarian and pneumatological emphasis enables Florovsky to state clearly why the catholic consciousness is never a mere collective mind, and why, indeed, catholicity means the emergence of a truly personal mode of knowing, delivered from the prison of individualism, yet still free.[31]*

This dimension of the nature of God, as Trinity, is significant for our understanding of Liturgy, and what it invites us to model in the way we organise our relationships with each other in human organisations, as well as in the experience of the church at worship. It does this in ways that neither the instinctive, centralizing or legalizing authoritarianism of the Catholic Church, nor the instinctive individualism of the Protestant Churches seem to be able to reproduce. In the case of Catholicism and Protestantism, there are ecclesial/doctrinal reasons for the way they function organizationally

---

[30] Who became Metropolitan of Kiev
[31] Looking East in Winter. p 177

in those different ways. They don't exactly mirror their political equivalents, but there are similarities. Catholicism seems to have settled well in regimes with dictatorial leadership structures; Protestantism in more democratic cultures, but of course the parallels are more complicated, historically and sociologically, and the similarities are best understood as correlations rather than causations. In the case of the Orthodox, at least in the Byzantine era, the Emperor seems to have taken on theological controls and responsibilities in contrast to the Pope who took on political controls and responsibilities (not least over the appointment of Dukes and Princes in the various Italian States). There has been a tendency, or a temptation, for the Orthodox Church to espouse and spiritually legitimate the nationalist and patriotic ideals of the county in which they have their own autocephalous place, none more so than in Russia, as illustrated by the behaviour of Patriarch Kyril in supporting President Putin.

There are many examples we might choose, from political life, to illustrate the dilemmas of leadership and organizational structure. At the moment, the Russian invasion of Ukraine and the destruction of many of its cities is being seen as a war against "democracy" by its own people, and many in Eastern European countries that used to be part of the Soviet, Communist system. Indeed, Russia has been trying to stop the emergence of democratic structures and leadership in the Ukraine since well before its invasion into the Crimea, going right back to the beginning of the 21st century. There are of course conflictual interpretations of what democracy means, or rather how it is formed and practiced in different Western countries. America has often been criticised, even by some of its own people, for being far less democratic than its own rhetoric implies. But I'd like to quote at length from Benjamin Franklin's[32] famous declaration (read out by the Maryland delegate, James McHenry) in September, 1787 at the Convention on the American Constitution. This is a good illustration of how hard it is to fashion and defend a democratic constitution or

---

[32] The great polymath, scientific enquirer and inventor, printer, publicist, international diplomat.

state – perhaps its greatest challenge - when it has to take seriously a pluralism of views

*I confess that I do not entirely approve of this Constitution at present, but Sir, I am not sure I shall never approve it: For having lived long, I have experienced many Instances of being oblig'd, by better Information or fuller Consideration, to change Opinions even on important Subjects, which I once thought right, but found to be otherwise. It is therefore that the older I grow the more apt I am to doubt my own Judgment and to pay more Respect to the Judgment of others. Most Men indeed as well as most Sects in Religion, think themselves in Possession of all Truth, and that wherever others differ from them it is so far Error. Sir Richard Steele, a Protestant, in a Dedication tells the Pope, that the only Difference between our two Churches in their Opinions of the Certainty of their Doctrine, is, the Romish Church is infallible, and the Church of England is never in the Wrong. But tho' many private Persons think almost as highly of their own Infallibility, as that of their Sect, few express it so naturally as a certain French lady, who in a little Dispute with her Sister, said, I don't know how it happens, Sister, but I meet with no body but myself that's always in the right. In these Sentiments, Sir, I agree to this Constitution, with all its Faults, if they are such: because I think a General Government necessary for us, and there is no Form of Government but what may be a Blessing to the People if well administred; and I believe farther that this is likely to be well administred for a Course of Years, and can only end in Despotism as other Forms have done before it, when the People shall become so corrupted as to need Despotic Government, being incapable of any other. I doubt too whether any other Convention we can obtain, may be able to make a better Constitution: For when you assemble a Number of Men to have the Advantage of their joint Wisdom, you inevitably assemble with those Men all their Prejudices, their Passions, their Errors of Opinion, their local Interests, and their selfish Views. From such an Assembly can a perfect Production be expected? It therefore astonishes me, Sir, to find this System approaching so near to Perfection as it does; and I think it will astonish our Enemies, who are waiting with Confidence to hear that our Councils are confounded, like those of the Builders of Babel, and that our States are on the Point of Separation, only to meet hereafter for the Purpose of cutting one another's Throats. Thus I consent, Sir, to this Constitution because I expect no better, and because I am not sure that it is not the best. The Opinions I have had of its Errors, I sacrifice to the Public Good. I have never whisper'd a Syllable of them abroad. Within these Walls they were born, & here they shall die. If every one of us in returning to our Constituents were to report the*

*Objections he has had to it, and endeavour to gain Partizans in support of them, we might prevent its being generally received, and thereby lose all the salutary Effects & great Advantages resulting naturally in our favour among foreign Nations, as well as among ourselves, from our real or apparent Unanimity. Much of the Strength and Efficiency of any Government, in procuring & securing Happiness to the People depends on Opinion, on the general Opinion of the Goodness of that Government as well as of the Wisdom & Integrity of its Governors. I hope therefore that for our own Sakes, as a Part of the People, and for the Sake of our Posterity, we shall act heartily & unanimously in recommending this Constitution, wherever our Influence may extend, and turn our future Thoughts and Endeavours to the Means of having it well administred. On the whole, Sir, I cannot help expressing a Wish, that every Member of the Convention, who may still have Objections to it, would with me on this Occasion doubt a little of his own Infallibility, and to make manifest our Unanimity, put his Name to this Instrument.[33]*

Reading between the lines, one can see how this great thinker navigated between a need to affirm and caution the tendency of individuals to think they are "Infallible in order to manifest (our) Unanimity"! As late as 1996, the Vatican was still defending the doctrine of Papal Infallibility (1870) against what it perceived to be the "dogmatic relativism" of some clergy and people.[34] At the same time, the Vatican was supporting various Dictatorships, and senior Bishops, against clergy who were encouraging opposition through their liberation theology, writings and actions.[35] Many of these priests, monks and nuns were condemned by the Vatican at the time,

[33] Benjamin Franklin: Speech in Convention, 17 September 1787. Commentaries on the Constitution, Volume XIII: The Documentary History of the Ratification of the Constitution Digital Edition, ed. John P. Kaminski, Gaspare J. Saladino, Richard Leffler, Charles H. Schoenleber and Margaret A. Hogan. Charlottesville: University of Virginia Press, 2009.

[34] Particularly Rev. Dr. Hans Küng, a Swiss professor of theology at Tübingen University

[35] Including Gustavo Gutierrez of Peru, Leonardo Boff of Brazil, Juan Luis Sefundo of Uruguay, Jon Sobrino and Pedro Arrupe of Spain, Ernesto Cardinal of Niceragua, Fr. Tissa Balasurya of Sri Lanka, a friend of mine, who had his books condemned and banned.

or a bit later by Cardinal Ratzinger, soon to become Pope Benedict XV1.

If the Liturgy of the Church invites us to share in the communion of worshipping life in "Sobornost", then the Liturgy of the World can include parallel experiences of a common life, based on well thought out, and clearly expressed values, often hard won and hard defended. In large organisations, these, of course, have increasingly been articulated within a regulatory and legal HR framework that has become ever more complicated. Similarly, the record of Unions in protecting workers from negative conditions has sometimes morphed into other political agendas that have complicated the agenda of their value-based concerns. Some of the most efficient, well run and "happy" organisations, I knew as an Industrial Chaplain, have been those that transcended regulatory or Union frameworks for value-based standards in workplaces. Their leaders inspired loyalty, support, enthusiasm, creativity, innovation, openness and honesty coming to the surface amongst staff at all levels. Where that is the case, one might say that the Liturgy of the World has much to teach the leadership of organisations in the Liturgy of the Church.

The word "values" can mean many things, and it illustrates underlying beliefs and a certain spirituality. But it seems that humans, in all organisations, have a strong sense of when they are being treated fairly and supportively to inspire higher levels of cooperation and wellbeing, which, in turn, makes for both happier staff morale, and a more productive working atmosphere and results. Sadly, in too many organisations, this is not the case. The larger the organisation, in any sector, the more a regulatory framework seems to build up and intervene in between different, managerial levels. While such a framework begins with the most virtuous of intentions, it often breaks down or complicates communications, its over-heavy, bureaucratic structures failing to make life easier, and often blocking individual purpose and initiative. In such cases, any sense of "sobornost" is broken, or at least unbalanced. Either the working of the corporate diminishes individuals, or a strong sense of individual or group rights and power diminishes the corporate potential of the body concerned. In the case of the Trinity, Christians have believed there is something else at work, which flows from the inner life of the person-in-community "sobornost", as part of its very nature, as if its inner and outward dimensions were the same.

The inner movement of Love's union, and meaning, in the Trinity moves outwards, reaching out away from itself to be itself, or as an expression of its self. Love's Energy reaches out and moves away from God's nature in order to express and be God's nature, in creation and incarnation. This self-emptying of Love for the sake of the Other is modelled in Christ, so that we may learn to encounter it when we reach out to the otherness of the "other", as if we may meet something of God in every other other. The same is true when we choose to see creation itself as a place where holiness dwells as in a mirror, a sacramental mirror of the nature of the holiness which is in the mystery of God, and the way God's love moves in our direction. And when there is attentiveness to the kind of love which moves away from self, it seems that the "other" receives the gift of being taken seriously, spiritually, in their full autonomy, but also in their communal (organisational) life with other others, nurtured by that kind of self-giving love which creates its own experience of supportive mutuality. And wherever we find the fruits of the Spirit being allowed or encouraged to reveal themselves in human empathy, kindness, forgiveness, understanding and acceptance, then we might well be in touch with that same self-giving love which can transform human relationships in the work place as in the home.

In this sense, we might dare to speak of the Liturgy of Love within the divine mystery of the nature of God as Trinity. If that is in any way possible, then we might want to speak of that Liturgy of God as being of the very essence or super-essence of Love, whose nature is to reach out or to create the Liturgy of the World. And within that Liturgy, in the reaching out suffering and resurrection of Christ, the Holy Spirit - as always and everywhere present in the Liturgy of both the Church and the World, is made present in human experience of their existence, their potential and their purpose. And, to the extent that any of this language makes any kind of sense, there must be some kind of relationship between what we think of as the

Liturgy of, or in, the Church, as having the purpose of pointing out and supporting the work and relatedness which takes place within the Liturgy of the World and - a crucial "and" - learning from it, that which can be experienced of God in it, and through it, not least the sacramental nature of that World in its continuing relationship with God. This is precisely why the Orthodox speak of a certain spiritual liberty flowing from within the worshipping community, and standing somewhere between the legalizing tendency within Catholicism and the Puritanical controls of Protestantism, which seem to operate alongside its individualised judgment of others. But, of course, the hierarchy of the Orthodox Church are, in some places, perfectly capable of that same legalizing and controlling tendency, making judgements that limit the spiritual wellbeing and freedom of in their communities. If it is the case that there is a sacramental nature of the World waiting to be rediscovered in the Liturgy of the World, in its continuing relationship with God, then that relationship transcends, as well as works within, the framework of the Liturgy of Time[36] found in both the Church and the World. As Rowan Williams describes it, commenting again on the work of Florovsky,

> as a kind of sacramental telescoping of time, paradigmatically in the Eucharist; tradition is a victory over temporal succession, so that in the Church's worship we are contemporary with the events of Scripture and indeed with the entirely of God's saving work. For Florovsky, this is a corollary of belief in the Spirit's unchanging presence in the Church; 'Tradition is the constant abiding of the Spirit.. a charismatic not a historical principle.'[37]... Knowledge of God is thus more than a recollection of the past acts of God; it is an announcing of God's present agency in which historical recollection is itself transfigured.[38]

And liturgy speaks often of transformation, which, in its spiritual sense, can be translated within and apply equally within the Liturgy of the World and the Liturgy of the Church. Liturgy may include certain actions and programmes to bring helpful change into the reality of daily life and work, not to mention larger scale crises

---

[36] A subject discussed in Chapter Eight.

[37] Florovsky *Collected Works* vol 3 *Creation and Redemption* p 47.

[38] Rowan Williams Looking East in Winter. p 175-176

and disasters. But Liturgy is essentially a communal experience of an alternative, but lived, human reality, in ways that map out its reach to inspire and extend the work of fulfilling human potential in individuals, groups and organisations. It may be, in itself, a transforming act, or event, or intervention of love's "work", extended into human need, but it remains, in its own right, the living, present and dynamic context or framework of that work and of that experience or relatedness. As we shall see in a later chapter, the idea of "work" is, in itself, constitutive as well as descriptive of the meaning of Liturgy in both its axes of Church and World. Work is more than just the relatedness and relating that occurs within work. Liturgy is itself present in the activity and action of work itself, as expressed in the energy expended in the direction of other others, and other things.

# CHAPTER FIVE

## 5      WAYS OF SEEING OR MISSING WHAT ALREADY IS

*The liturgy is a symbolic expression of our fundamental acceptance of the absolute mystery and of the absolute mystery's free and forgiving acceptance of us. Worship is an experience of interpersonal communion with the absolute, holy mystery.* Karl Rahner [39]

## FINDING A CONTEXT IN THE THEOLOGY OF CREATION

So, perhaps these things are more than we think they are, and how we think they are; Liturgy, as well as liturgical time that is, and their relevance to our experience of living! Better to say their "presence" perhaps, rather than their "relevance", in and to the world in which we live, for it could be claimed they are already part of it, in a way that is closer and deeper within its very nature, rather than anything implied by the idea of "relevance". For if we are talking about their presence, then it is within the nature and being of all things, rather than in something separated off from things. And that statement obviously comes from a prior belief about the nature and meaning of something bigger, much bigger, as big as creation itself, creation as related to a creator or source of creation, and all that flows from that. And whatever we think or believe about "creation", our belief has to be big enough to include every thing in it, and about it, and our scientific and other kinds of knowledge of it. There are many ways of trying to understand what that might mean, let alone being able to speak of it in today's world. This is an example of what William Law, an eighteenth-century Anglican, mystical writer said about creation, as understood theologically, or rather spiritually, in relationship to a God of love.

*The goodness of God breaking forth into a desire to communicate good was the cause and the beginning of the Creation. Hence it follows that to all eternity, God can have no thought or intent towards the creature but to communicate good, because he made the creature for this sole end, to receive* <u>*good. The first motive towards*</u> *the creature is unchangeable. It takes its rise*

[39] *Theology of Worship.* Michael Skelly. SJ. The Liturgical Press, Collegeville, Minnesota. p 50

*from God's desire to communicate good, and it is an eternal impossibility that anything can ever come from God as his will and purpose towards the creature, but that same love and goodness which first created it. He must always will that to it which he willed at the creation of it. This is the amiable nature of God, he is the good, the unchangeable, overflowing fountain of good that sends forth nothing but good to all eternity. He is the love itself, the unmixed unmeasurable love, doing nothing but from love, giving nothing but gifts of love to every thing that he has made; requiring nothing of all his creatures but the spirit and fruits of that love which brought them into being[40].*

The idea of a creator is difficult to understand in a post-Copernican and post-Darwinian world. And it is surely best understood, not by rejecting the latest science in favour of biblical accounts, as so many Christians still insist on doing, but by engaging with the implications of science in order to better understand the meaning of those accounts which came out of a world concerned with the theological meaning of creation, rather than an exact science of how it happened. Otherwise, we are caught in a terrible conundrum when creationists (not just in the new church movements) insist the Bible is true and science is wrong, because if you take the two Genesis accounts literally, then they are literally wrong, and the truth can never be the enemy of God. And it is within a scientifically credible theology of creation that we can talk of liturgy and liturgical time as being part of that, or indeed having an ontological presence within it, because of its very nature. And, if that is the case, then the themes of liturgy and liturgical time will speak to the realities of creation in ways that may surprise us. They will unveil their own significance in that context, in surprising and inspiring ways. But they will do this as intrinsic to those ontological realities, rather than as something separate from them, or over and against them or occasionally imposed on them. So, already we sense the possibility that the presence of Liturgy, and Liturgical time, truly are part of the nature of things and relevant to how we perceive and understand

---

[40] From *The Spirit of Prayer*. Published in the 1750s along with his *The Spirit of Love*. These two mystical books are sometimes found published together as well as separately.

things, whoever we are, and even whether or not we have been converted to the neon light glare of "fresh" Christian discipleship.

So, Liturgy and Liturgical time might also have more to do with the ordinary business of being human than we usually think. And that might well sound like a strange thing to say, or claim, especially given what we know about the calamities and dangerous tendencies of our human nature and some of its relationships. Again, it depends on a prior belief about the meaning of "creation", which draws on certain theological assumptions about what it means to talk of a creator or source of the way the universe "makes itself". And that crude way of putting it, doesn't, in any way, discount the idea of a source and creative presence. But it does do justice to the latest cosmology and understanding of evolution within which, rather than separate from which, the processes of creation may take place, including the way humans have developed, and what may then be said about the significance of Jesus, within those processes, as the Word of God, there from the beginning, and through the beginning to the very end. The Word of God, that and who, was made flesh and dwelt among us, and whose glory can be seen in the experience of being human and therefore in the human condition, with his cross at the heart of that condition and of creation itself.

Many early, mystical theologians thought in these broad terms, although too often we think of their writings purely in terms of the Christological disputes dominating the life of the church in those centuries. In addition to that and alongside it, many spoke of what it meant to believe in God as Creator of all things. Indeed, if God wasn't and isn't the Creator, it is hard to think what else we would want to say, specifically, about God's nature and being that we can talk about with any credibility, as we then go on to talk about God in Trinity.

Ever since the Enlightenment and particularly in the last two centuries, there have been many Christian thinkers seeking to take seriously the latest science, and the latest issues of our times. Reflecting on the challenges those issues presented, those teachers and writers have had the courage to engage with some of the implications involved. Here are but three, better known examples, all from Western Church background. The Lutheran pastor, Dietrich Bonhoeffer (1906-1945) had been directly or tangentially involved in the German Officer's Plot to kill Hitler. Just a few days after it failed, and having been arrested by the Gestapo, he wrote these words in the spirit of his search for "religionless" Christianity.

*During the last year or so, I've come to know and understand more and more the profound this-worldliness of Christianity. The Christian is not a homo religiosus, but simply a man, as Jesus was a man...I'm still discovering right up to this moment, that it is only by living completely in this world that one learns to have faith. One must completely abandon any attempt to make something of oneself, whether it be a saint, or a converted sinner, or a churchman (a so-called priestly type!) a righteous man or an unrighteous one, a sick man or a healthy one. By this-worldliness, I mean living unreservedly in life's duties, problems, successes and failures, experiences and perplexities. In so doing, we throw ourselves completely into the arms of God, taking seriously, not our own sufferings, but those of God in the world—watching with Christ in Gethsemane. That, I think, is faith; that is metanoia; and that is how one becomes a man and a Christian.[41]*

If anyone has the right to talk of unreservedly throwing himself into this-worldliness, it is Bonhoeffer from within his experience of prison and the reasons for it. It is as if he was discovering something intrinsically mystical, or at least spiritual, in what we are calling the Liturgy of the World.

Teilhard de Chardin S.J. (1881-1955), Catholic priest, Professor of Geology at the Catholic Institute in Paris, Director of the National Geologic Survey of China, and Director of the National Research Center of France, was fascinated by the implications of the latest biological and cosmological science. He wrote a great deal about the nature of the Cosmos (not least in his *Hymn of the Universe*) as the arena of God's action, including quotable sentences, such as *Matter is spirit moving slowly enough to be seen...*

As a Darwinian scientist and a process theologian, he could see in evolutionary theory something profoundly important for understanding creation itself.

---

[41] *Letters and Papers from Prison.* First published in English in 1951

*The most telling and profound way of describing the evolution of the universe would undoubtedly be to trace the evolution of love.*

In his *Hymn of the Universe,* he wrote,

> *Let us ponder over this basic truth till we are steeped in it, till it becomes as familiar to us as our awareness of shapes or our reading of words: God, at the most vitally active and most incarnate, is not remote from us, wholly apart from the sphere of the tangible; on the contrary, at every moment God awaits us in the activity, the work to be done, which every moment brings. God is, in a sense, at the point of my pen, my pick, my paint-brush, my needle – and my heart and my thought. It is by carrying to its natural completion the stroke, the line, the stitch I am working on that I shall lay hold on that ultimate end towards which my will at its deepest levels tends.*

The Welsh, Anglican priest, R. S. Thomas's (1913 –2000) poetry often put the spiritual life in a cosmic context. Here is just one example in a poem called *"Night Sky"*

> *What they are saying is*
> *that there is life there, too:*
> *that the universe is the size it is*
> *to enable us to catch up.*
> *They have gone on from the human:*
> *that shining is a reflection*
> *of their intelligence. Godhead*
> *is the colonisation by mind*
> *of untenanted space. It is its own*
> *light, a statement beyond language*
> *of conceptual truth. Every night*
> *is a rinsing myself of the darkness*
> *that is in my veins. I let the stars inject me*
> *with fire, silent as it is far,*
> *but certain in its cauterising*
> *of my despair. I am a slow*
> *traveller, but there is more than time*
> *to arrive. Resting in the intervals*
> *of my breathing, I pick up the signals*
> *relayed to me from a periphery I comprehend.*
>
> **(Frequencies 1978)**

Indeed, the more one looks for these broad, inclusive,

theological themes about the human condition, in many different kinds of ideas and experience, the more they are to be found. Suffering seems to be intrinsic, rather than exceptional to the human condition, and in the nature and processes of creation itself. And those processes can not only be considered, theologically, at the level of cosmology and evolution, but, spiritually, through the ordinary daily tasks of work and living.

Rediscovered words about the meaning of Liturgy can also be offered to, and found amongst, those who have only a distant relationship with those central Christian beliefs of creation and incarnation. Yet, they may still have some indirect acquaintance with Christian worship in a local church, even if the word "liturgy" is relatively unknown, or seems somewhat alien, as it increasingly is in Western societies and many church groups. And as we have seen, many church groups have come to see worship in a fresh, but reductive way. For them, "worship" is seen as a time to be with Jesus, away from the experience of living in the world, through an experience of the Word communicated through a literal interpretation of certain Bible passages, and songs and choruses of praise that have only a few repeated words, (in contrast to the sacred hymns of the early church or even the Victorian church), a homily with a repeated message about the joys of personal salvation from sin, and prayers that are focused on a worshipper's desire to praise the name of Jesus, offering requests for healing in their personal lives and other people's.

All of that may be totally understandable in the way worship has developed in parts of the Protestant context, and perhaps even a Catholic one as well, but also in fresh, new movements which own no exclusive connection with any denomination, church, or theological tradition. And some of these movements use very little theological reflection to identify themselves, but only the label of being Christian. Some think of themselves as also being completely ecumenical, not necessarily meaning by that, inclusive of other denominations or even other faiths, but focused on a converting, evangelical mission to anyone willing to *agree* with their formal or informal doctrine[42]. The word ecumenical comes from oikumene with its root references to household management or stewardship. As we shall see, that is a very appropriate activity within the root meaning of Liturgy. Whereas the ecumenical movement, represented by the World Council of Churches, in its really active days, started with a stress on social and political engagement within the oikumene of God, as a unifying dimension amongst different denominational churches, this new kind of evangelical "ecumenism" holds out a hidden, or not so hidden, calling card which makes it clear that certain views of the Bible are a pre-condition, and that conversion is a matter of binary and often immediate choice, rather than an ongoing task of learning in order to go spiritually and intellectually deeper.

But there is another way, waiting to be rediscovered, and it is a way of understanding Liturgy that has somehow been sustained by a few in Western Christianity, and many more in the Orthodox Christian world, or at least parts of it. And we will trawl something of the significance of that to enliven a new maximal understanding of liturgy. And even amongst the Orthodox, who worship from within a tradition which speaks the language of liturgy, there is sometimes a need to enliven their understanding, as recent Orthodox writers have shown. And this is particularly the case in parts of the world where that tradition has ossified, or taken for granted that liturgical understanding in ways that have obscured its larger significance. But the truth is that ossification seems to take place in the development of any form of worship or religious ritual. People, particularly those responsible for guarding the tradition of worship, tend towards a consolidation and repetition or certain types of language or ritual choreography, even when the original reason has been forgotten or no longer needed.

In the case of the Orthodox, two examples come to mind. In hot countries, there was a need to fan away the flies that might gather over the altar where the bread and wine were placed. So, some practical fans were introduced into the liturgy, and then words added to cover the action, and then the style of those fans and words were

---

[42] See for example the University Christian Union movement's fixed and divisive doctrinal points which set it apart from other Christian denominations.

embellished over time, so that it became a more general, universal usage even in cold countries. Similarly, in countries with very cold winters, it was important to warm or heat the water used to mix into the cup of wine to prevent it from freezing. So, at some point in the past, a flask or other vessel might be used to bring warm water to the church for this purpose. In other places and perhaps time, a small heater or fire was used to warm up some water before using it to pour into the chalice. Over time, a phrase about the warmth and fervour of the Holy Spirit was added and that slipped into more general use, even in hot countries.

Now these aren't my examples, but were given to me by an Orthodox priest. I cannot vouch for their historical accuracy, but he wanted to make the point I am now making. Sometimes, actions and prayers are accrued in liturgical rituals over time and their original, perhaps practical reasons for being there are forgotten or obscured, but nevertheless they remain as part of the inherited tradition. It is important to be open about how certain movements or words in worship become "ritualized", if they run the risk of that their intent and meaning become obscured in the process. In the Anglican church, certain peripheral tasks around the edge of worship become ritualized *as if* they are part of worship. For, example, the way books are given out before a service begins can become highly ritualised, or the way an organ plays a voluntary at the beginning and after the end of a service. They too became part of the Liturgy and its culture.

Perhaps the best example is to be found in the use of rubrics. They became, in some of the first Anglican prayer books, almost a part of the ritual in itself, even though they were mostly about how to conduct the service. The words used in those rubrics have, in some cases, lasted, outlasted one might say, their original purpose. In framing how things should be done, to break with, and sustain some continuity with the past, they became symbols and habits in their own right. Now we see the same thing happening when simple, practical rubrics like "please stand", or "please sit", or even "let us pray" are repeated several times when people are already praying. They have become part of the inherited ritual itself, even when the congregation know perfectly well when to sit or stand. In many

Anglican churches, where the hymn numbers are clearly displayed on raised boards, or on service sheets, the tradition seems to require the priest to nevertheless announce them, as if the rubric of announcing has liturgical significance in itself. And in some non-conformist churches it is customary for the minister not only to announce the number but to read out the first line or even first verse in a rather prayerful way. This can be rather moving and spiritually helpful, but it easily becomes ossified as part of the ritual in ways that make it distinctive from another in a different tradition. And ossified rituals can get in the way of the spiritual flow of worship, interrupting its natural movement, giving too much emphasis and priority to the rubric, rather than the theological/liturgical meaning of that part of the service.

I've been in large cathedral churches in Orthodox countries where several hundreds are attending. There are no hymn books or service sheets given out, and yet people seem to know what is happening without a priest issuing constant, rubrical instructions about how they should move, or what is going to happen next... as in "we shall now sing hymn number..." There is no liturgical stutter to take people away from their deeper spiritual involvement in what is happening.

Over time, and from the some of the earliest liturgies, the words and movements used settle into their own rhythm as part of the tradition of how things should be done. It took a while for the first words of the Eucharist to settle into their own formulas and these varied across the main centres of early worship. As they did so, it was realised that certain important issues of liturgical meaning carried theological significance, and so the choices made in liturgical language defined what was believed doctrinally in the early debates. Over time, new prayers were added to worship, as those debates developed around particular theological themes in the liturgical calendar. The words and actions used in worship had to be of the "right" doctrine, or "ortho-doxia", (right glory as well as dogma) as it developed in reaction to developing, often conflictual ideas and praxis. Orthodoxy became the word used to carry, sustain and spread the emerging and then agreed, doctrinal formulae inhabiting the worship of the Liturgy. And worship became the defining activity of Liturgy which constituted the meaning and reference points of "church" amongst the gathered community of early Christians, in the first centuries after Jesus.

Over time, there was an obvious risk of losing touch with the significance or understanding of liturgy, which, in turn, reduced the theology of worship, present in all churches, albeit on a relative scale. And it seems that this has mostly happened in what we might loosely call Western forms of Christianity, rather than in those that developed from the earliest spread of Christian worship in the Middle East. There, although so many churches have been destroyed and their congregations and communities displaced by war or opposition, we can still find an instinctive affirmation of the significant meaning of liturgy that we might call "maximal", to contrast it with the minimal way it is understood in many Western church circles, of course with notable exceptions. It seems that the minimalist approach occurs when we allow our understanding of worship to be cut loose from any sense of its place within the whole ontology of creation – when we lose the sense that liturgy has profound significance within the very nature and being of things in themselves. That is "all things" in creation, in and of themselves. But to see it like that, requires a new sacramental understanding of the nature, and, therefore, the ontology of things in themselves. And we will come to that idea of sacrament later, to ask where it might inform the other key words used, in a more, maximal approach to the meaning of liturgy. For words such as ontology, creation, incarnation, mystery, sacrament, theosis and transformation are inter-related in that approach. But, inevitably perhaps, they have been diluted and reoriented over time in the praxis of worship, and not just in our own, post-modernist times either, where everything is reduced to the narrative experience of individuals, begging questions when conflictual narratives increase divisions and tensions, or turn differences into divisions. And such cultural undercurrents and assumptions tend to make it harder for big words and ideas to hold their inclusive meaning, or even to be believed to have the consensual capacity to do so. For the meta-narrative, behind the narratives of individual experience, has long since been challenged, although its human behavioural echoes, in the natural expression of kindness and mutual aid, empathy and altruism, still remain. They resurface from time to time with surprising traction in the Liturgy of the World, amongst the most surprising people, often in times of crisis. And when they do, we glimpse again the possibility of significance in those words, as the reference points of a maximal understanding of liturgy, way beyond its usual bounds of usage in church circles.

But meanwhile, we pause to return to the example described above (rather crudely described) of a minimalist approach to Liturgy and a certain culture which has developed around that type of worship. In wanting to create something fresh and new, the clergy have typically rejected all clerical dress and robes. The altar in the front of the church has been removed, and that place now functions more like a stage at a pop concert, well equipped with the latest lighting and audio-visual aids, including an overhead projector or TV screens. Organ and choir have been replaced by an electric piano, guitars and drums or other instruments. And the central positioning of the "band" has obliterated any last resemblance of liturgical architecture, or its reason to be there. Although there is a new tradition being established in the culture of the band and the absence or reduction of an altar. And when it comes to singing, it now seems to be *de rigeur* for the rhythms and tones to emulate the way certain American, folk singing groups might sing, with short phrases repeated hypnotically as people stand and move as they might at a concert, or in a night club, taken up by the intense emotionality of the experience, at least in the more charismatic forms of this worship. And to be clear, there is nothing wrong with being charismatic and passionate about one's beliefs in worship. The experience can be intensely spiritual. That is, so long as we remember what the New Testament says about the wider variety of gifts or charisms, and the variety of gifted people and their roles and responsibilities as teachers, administrators, physicians, comforters, guides and so on. For the Christian life is about more than not being killed by snakebites or speaking in tongues. And I suspect those early Christian descriptions of the different roles involved in organizing a healthy society, with respect for the least member who is part of the body, were an attempt to say something important about the way the Holy Spirit works in all people who contribute to the good of others.

There is nothing wrong with using any musical instrument, or indeed none in Christian worship. But these things are there to accompany worship not to be the centre stage of it. And there is nothing wrong with using a whole variety of different kinds of music in worship. But the words we use in songs, hymns, prayer and preaching do matter. What we say in worship reflects, carries and expresses what we believe. From the earliest times, great care was taken with this, because what we say and do in worship does have doctrinal significance and vice versa. It's quite possible to sing an emotionally moving tune and not really notice what words are being used, and not really inquire what they mean, or are saying about Christian belief. But, to repeat, there is nothing wrong with being creative in new forms of worship, not least the borrowing of words from a variety of sources, using poetry and prose not found in the Bible for instance. All of this and more can enhance the experience of worship[43] and extend the links between the Liturgy of the Church and the Liturgy of the World. I am not arguing for closing down any of that creativity for the sake of sticking to the tradition developed from earlier types of spiritual creativity, but I am saying that we need to be careful in what we are saying and doing, because its meaning has significance, liturgically, in how we think about the world, in the light of the most profound of central Christian beliefs.

The message from the front is usually delivered in an inspiring, emotional way, using texts to prove that the world, and everyone in it, is sinful and our only hope is in Jesus and his cross. And this is a message given with only very rare explanation of the

---

[43] For a while, in various worship services in Cathedrals and elsewhere, I used the silent, white faced Pierrot Clown from the Commedia dell'arte tradition, to represent, in mime, something of the meaning of Liturgy. I was also involved in creating installations and scripts for acts of worship at various European conferences, particularly on the Environment.

assumptions made as to why and how early, blood sacrifice theory or substitution theory for the "wrathful judgement and punishment" of God could save us from our sin. And some who rely on such a theory (like the national body running Christian Unions in Universities) rarely stop to consider the meaning of what they are saying or how they know that is the nature of God. And when such a message is delivered, it is often accompanied by attractive sounding binary choices. "Either you believe all of this is true or Jesus was lying" is sometimes how this doorstep type of salesmanship is presented. And who would want to accuse God or Jesus of lying! Therefore, *ipso facto* and QED, it is all true and by implication, goes the message, it is all true in the way we are proclaiming it to be true. And again, by implication, if not more overtly, one is next told that this conviction about the truth depends on not too many awkward questions being asked about the way in which it, and the scriptures are being used, and presented as so true that they cannot be questioned. And one is made to feel guilty by such messages, if one drifts into such questions, or allows them to sneak up quietly onto the page of truth one is now on. And come to that, woe to you if you mix too much with those who encourage such questions, for that is how the Devil gets in.

As a university chaplain, there was more than one occasion when a lecturer would ring us up saying that a member of the Christian Union, studying biology, had just handed in an essay not only dismissing the theory of evolution but implying that any academic who believed in it was doing the work of the Devil. And it is worrying that the website of the national Christian Union organisation still advocates a creationist position based on a spurious analogy with the pieces of a train set randomly coming together to illustrate what they think of biologically based evolution.

And as a chaplain in another university, where we had a good relationship with the Health Centre, a doctor rang us up to say that he had a student in tears because the Christian Union had told her she couldn't go out with her boyfriend because he wasn't a Christian. The message was clear. "We have the truth and the rest of the world doesn't, because it has not accepted Jesus Christ as its personal saviour. Therefore, it must either be converted and accepted, or shunned and avoided, with all its false teachings."

And like all commonly used, short, but big words, "sin" is only rarely explored or examined as either a moral or an ontological category of the human condition. And, of course, it has its own particular history of predetermined presence in its use by certain elements of Paul, Augustine and Calvin, based on whatever biological science or ontological and anthropological assumptions they were making, or not. And these are legitimate questions for Anglicans, committed to the pursuit of truth through intellectual questions and learning, in the balance they seek between reason and revelation. For it is only through different kinds of intellectual, spiritual and emotional reason and learning that we can seek to understand what we have apprehended from revelation, and how revelation itself has happened in historical and incarnational ways.

Of course, all of the above are only a caricature of what happens in this kind of worship tradition. It hardly does justice to its appeal, which has huge emotional and spiritual impact on those present, and is clearly commanding growing support in Western churches. It's not so much what it is, that presents us with a significant reduction of the theological riches of Christian belief, as what it misses out, not least in its understanding of God, and not least its apparent rejection of all that we mean by the word "sacrament" in Christian, liturgical tradition. Of course, there are many ways of caricaturing Christian liturgy. For example, the deep sacramental riches of the traditional Catholic service could, just as easily be reduced to the caricature of smells and bells, as it often has been. But as we shall see later, the reach of the word "sacrament" is significant if located within a theology of creation and the ontology of the nature of things, rather than just seen as referring to particular church services, rituals and "elements". And without that wider and deeper understanding, there is a risk that those services and rituals might lose their meaning, or appear to be increasingly less entwined and embedded in the nature of any kind of ontological reality outside of the activities of the church.

## AN EXAMPLE FROM A MARRIAGE SERVICE

While the sacrament of marriage makes its own obvious connections with the life of the world, I'm not sure many non-church going couples realise how profound they are. As we cut down the traditional language (which of course was once radically new) in the service, and do less and less teaching about its meaning, then it's probably inevitable that people miss the way this sacrament affects and is part of the ontology of creation itself.

Watching a marriage service in an Orthodox Church, sometimes known as the Crowning service, the couple are said to be becoming, through this sacrament, priests of creation. They are lead around the altar three times, crowned as prince and princess priests of creation, where their crowns are also a reminder of martyrs in the Kingdom of God sharing in that royal role because there is always self-sacrifice involved in the sacred mystery of marriage and love. White candles are given and held in the hands of the bride and the groom to symbolize their spiritual willingness to receive and to share with each other, and more widely, the presence of Christ as the Light of the World. The ceremony of the rings, the crowns, and the candles contribute to the symbolic idea that the couple are joining now in the very continuous fabric interwoven into the human condition since the beginning. In the ceremony of the crowns, which comes as a climax to the service, the crowns are joined by a ribbon to symbolize the unity of the couple through the presence of Christ who blesses their union and links it with Christ's union with the church and the world. They become Kings and Queens in their own home, where they will work together with humility and wisdom, justice and integrity as part of their service to creation.

They then drink from a common cup of wine in the spirit of the wedding at Cana, symbolising their transformation from the old into the new, a passage from death into life, and they each drink three times from the common cup as witness to each other and the whole world that they will, from this moment, share everything in life, bearing each other's burdens equally and the burdens of those who come to them for help. They then make that solemn and symbolic dance of joy around the altar to the singing of three hymns – one the indescribable joy that Isaiah the prophet experienced when envisioning the coming of the Messiah, the second a reminder of the martyrs of the faith who received their crown of glory from God to inspire the couple of the sacrificial love they now have for one another, so increasing that love in creation, and the final one, an exaltation to the Holy Trinity. They are moving around the altar on which are placed the cross and the Gospel book. The circular movement reminds them of the eternal presence of life into which they are now integrated in the sacrament. The cross reminds them of the suffering involved in love, and the gospel, the education of their family.

These are the first steps as a married couple and they begin with a Trinitarian dance within the church so that the sacrament can continue outside of the church building. The crowns are removed from their heads and the priest uses variations on the following words when they are back in their original places, but changed since they were last there. To the groom the priest says *Be magnified, O Bridegroom, as Abraham, and blessed as Isaac, and increased as was Jacob. Go your way in peace, performing in righteousness the commandments of God.* To the bride he says, *And you, O Bride, be magnified as was Sarah, and rejoiced as was Rebecca, and increased as Rachel, being glad in your husband, keeping the paths of the Law, for so God is well pleased.*

Hidden within these ancient words, with all their strangeness to our ears and sensibilities, and hidden within these ancient, symbolic movements and actions, there are gifts of meaning which reference much more than just a joining in marriage of two individual people in a church service. The liturgy or the liturgical dimension and context of the ceremony somehow reaches out beyond that and beyond them. The particular symbols of movement, the cross and Gospel book, crowns and candles, have wider meaning in a way that hints metaphorically to themes embedded in our understanding of the meaning of marriage within the bigger context of creation itself. And that is something that far exceeds what many in the West think of as a service in church, however special and personal it might be. And underneath this sacrament of marriage is a theology with wider reference points as part of the Liturgy of the World which may at first sound strange in our ears, particularly if we're used to locating them exclusively within the Liturgy of the Church. This is how Alexander Schmemann puts it in the *World as Sacrament,*

*The first, the basic definition of man is that he is the priest. He stands in the center of the world and unifies it in his act of blessing God, of both receiving the world from God and offering it to God—and by filling the world with this eucharist, he transforms his life, the one that he receives from the world, into life in God, into communion with Him. The world was created as the "matter," the material of one all-embracing eucharist, and man was created as the priest of this cosmic sacrament.*

There are many different ways in which people have thought about liturgy and experienced it, within, as well as between, different churches. And there are many ways of talking about the significant differences between the cultures and traditions and ways of thinking about God, within and between, those two great axes of the Western Churches, Catholicism and Protestantism. And it's not surprising, given the torturous history of tensions and wars between them, that their assumptions and beliefs diverged as well as held a sense of what really matters. And their different liturgies, or ways of doing liturgy, or the meaning they gave to them and the assumptions they drew on and projected about them, illustrate their different orientations and beliefs.

And yet, it's possibly too simple to describe the difference by referencing the dualism between Sacrament and Word as the main focus of each liturgical experience. We might proclaim, as some have from each tradition that Word and Sacrament live together, though even in Anglicanism we now see them drifting apart as the one is emphasized more than the other. And Anglicanism attempted, at the Reformation, to hold both together, not least by including Catholic and Protestant kinds of liturgy and types of clergy within the same communion. And Anglicanism added to that concoction a third figure in the triumvirate, that of reason. And reason, in its Enlightenment sense, was seen to reflect the search for truth using the human intellect as a legitimate religious activity, which would find evidence in the nature of creation by a Creator and Creative God, as well as in Word and Sacrament.

And yet, within the genius of diversity that is the Anglican, inclusive compromise, recent decades have seen a turning away from reason and a dismissal of scientific discovery, not least about cosmology and evolution. And this turning away has been inspired by a literal interpretation of the Word in scripture, and the belief that the scriptures should be trusted for holding and revealing the final truth over and above all science. And an echo of dogmatism has also been found in the Catholic tradition within Anglicanism, which emphasizes not only the authority and power of the and hierarchy of the Church, but also its liturgy where dogmas about the meaning of the Sacrament are offered to the faithful as matters of faithful obedience which require little or no discussion and debate and are rarely related to questions of truth about the nature of cosmology and evolution.

And somewhere, within the dogmatism of extremes in both traditions, individuals and movements have struggled with reasonable questions that have prompted the possibility of freeing up further theological enquiry and learning from the shackles of fundamentalism, using the wisdom or spiritual experience, and the gifts of the mind to understand and reflect on the assumptions being explored and inherited.

But there is another presence in the history of the Christian Church and its understanding of Liturgy that could breathe in a new understanding and orientation within discussion about the history of the Western Churches and their understanding of Liturgy. And, historically speaking, its claim to be closer, within its own tradition, to its antecedents in the early church is worth considering and taking seriously. More particularly, its historical context, in time and place, comes from where the earliest Christianity spread its wings in and around the Mediterranean Sea. For those Christians who have survived all the recent wars and displacements, disruptions, divisions, opposition and threats that have happened in Syria, Iran, Iraq, the Lebanon, Turkey, Gaza, Egypt,[44] and other places, see

---

[44] See *The Vanishing. The Twilight of Christianity in the Middle East* by Janine di Giovanni. Bloomsbury, 2021. A moving story of the destruction of Christian

themselves as the inheritors of the first forms of early Christianity, as it spread though those countries. For the truth is that some in Western European Christianity (if there is such a thing) with its Catholic and Protestant roots, tend to forget the significance of those early centres of Christian life and liturgy, and the way they later spread into all the countries where Orthodoxy and its beliefs, not least about liturgy, came to exist. While Kiev and later Moscow came to be the "Third Rome", after the destruction of Constantinople and before that Rome, it was the earlier adoption of Byzantine Christianity, as witnessed in Agia Sophia in that great Byzantine city, before the growing of the Great Schism between the West and Eastern churches[45], that enabled its spread in Russia and other countries. But, of course, we dare not simplistically assume that Orthodoxy, in those different countries of Greece, Turkey, Egypt, the Middle East and Eastern Europe and their autonomous Orthodox Churches, didn't have to face their own divisions and tensions. And these were sometimes serious and long lasting, although dialogical conversations continue to search for a way of steering through the reasons for those divisions.

But, it is also true to say that many recent and contemporary Orthodox writers and theologians have helped with the rediscovery of more ancient ways of doing Liturgy, and, more specifically, the meaning of its reference points wound within its own liturgical and spiritual praxis. And some would say that those jewels, tarnished though them might be, still glint with the offer of some different and sparkling insights about the meaning of liturgy which Western churches may have forgotten, or even never known.

And because of this, and because this author discovered something of this for himself in a year spent studying the Orthodox in Romania in 1967-8,[46] this reflection on Liturgy mostly draws on

---

churches and communities.

[45] Cemented in blood during the Crusades and in particular the Crusaders sacking of Constantinople and mindless destruction of Christian churches and massacre of Byzantine Christians.

[46] A hard year of learning in the Cold War context, leading up to the Soviet invasion of Czechoslovakia to subdue the "Prague Spring". It was a learning gathered more by osmosis than any formal, academic programmes, but which led to

those kinds of spiritual writers, and that kind of Liturgy[47].

And if there is, or might be, more to Liturgy than meets the eye or the senses, then it is worth knowing about, and seeking to know more about. It merits further reflection, use and discussion in the West, as we seek to interrogate the meaning of liturgy in our own traditions. And for those who attend the Liturgy of the Church, it is probably helpful to know more about what we mean by that, so that what we discover is informed by and fills the experience we have of the Liturgy of the World. And for those who have given up on the church's liturgy, or for those who have never known it, except through glimpses at baptisms, weddings, and funerals, or not even those, it might help to consider for a moment what it might, after all, be about, what it might signify in our short time on earth. I hope this book may be a pointer in that direction, at least enough to encourage further exploration. But it is offered not with a dogmatic insistence of conversion to only one way of thinking about Liturgy, and it is not meant to undervalue other kinds of experience of worship and all that they mean to so many different people.

We look back in order to move forward, reflecting on we thought we knew, in order to understand more about what we know or want to know in our present understanding. There is a mystery to the way the present experience includes the past and the future, for time itself is enough of a mystery, and liturgical time adds yet another dimension to that mystery. And liturgy might be many things, and might be badly done, or hardly even understood in the life of the church we know, but yet it might mean more than any of that, whether badly or well done, whether understood in all its potential fullness, or only partially glimpsed through the misted over memories and experiences and stories about how it has been passed on to us, which might now be at risk of being forgotten or never known.

---

a life long fascination in the Orthodox way of thinking.

[47] I've recently written a novel about that experience called "The Glow Within".

# CHAPTER SIX

## 6    HOW THEN, DID SOME OF THIS BEGIN?

*The liturgy of the Eucharist is best understood as a journey or procession. It is the journey of the Church into the dimension of the Kingdom. We use the word 'dimension' because it seems the best way to indicate the manner of our sacramental entrance into the risen life of Christ.... It is not an escape from the world, rather it is the arrival at a vantage point from which we can see more deeply into the reality of the world.* Alexander Schmemann

Before proceeding further, with what I am calling the maximal meaning of Liturgy, it might be important to remind ourselves of some historical background of the development of early Christian worship, and something of the beliefs it expressed. I stress again that I am not a scholar or expert in early Church History or Patristics, and some readers may wish to skip some of the detail that follows. There are plenty of books and online resources for pursuing this with the help of substantial scholarship and experience.

Liturgical scholars have long debated the difference between pre-Constantinian (4th century) and post-Constantinian worship. Schmemann believes there is continuity, as well as change, with the influence of synagogue patterns of daily worship on early Christianity before Constantine, which took society and time seriously through regular hours of prayer. This predates the development of a monastic pattern of daily prayer. Others[48] believe early Christian worship is world renouncing and eschatological, based primarily, if not exclusively, on the Eucharist[49]. This debate has been affected by new textual scholarship on the history of the period and the discovery of more manuscripts, as at Qumran, and by the larger question of the relationship between Hebrew and Hellenic influences (including mystery cults) on early Christian worship. To

---

[48] Notably, the respected liturgical scholar, George Dix, an Anglican Benedictine monk from Nashdom Abbey (1901 –1952), who greatly influenced Anglican liturgical theology. See also the work of Oscar Cullman, Louis Duchesne and Pierre Battifol which largely agrees with this position.

[49] See the discussion in Schmemann *Introduction to Liturgical Theology*. The Faith Press, London/The American Orthodox Press Maine. 1966. pp 41 ff.

what extent did the religious and political atmosphere of the first three centuries, with all that was happening under different Roman Empires in the West and the East, affect how early Christians thought of their lives in relationship to what they understood of their belief in the presence of the Risen Christ? Did crises, hunger, persecution, and social unrest turn them against the values of the world they lived in, believing that Christ's return was imminent and that Christ had rescued them from such a world, or was it more complicated than that? Did they somehow remain committed to making sense of the world and real time conditions in the light of their faith, or did they turn against those things in some kind of eschatological hope that everything that mattered had already changed?

*The difference between Christianity and Judaism is not in their understanding or theology of time, but in their conception of the events by which this time is spiritually measured. Judaistic time is eschatological in the sense that it is still directed toward the coming of the Messiah and the messianic Kingdom. In Christian time, the Messiah has already come, is already revealed, the Kingdom of Yahweh is at hand...... The new element in Christianity is not its conception of time or of the world living in time, but in the fact that the event which even in the old Judaistic conception constituted the "centre" of time and which defined its meaning, has already begun. And this event, in turn, is eschatological, since in it is revealed and defined the ultimate meaning of all things – creation, history, salvation[50].*

One of the earliest references, not only to the existence of Christians, but the way they worshiped, is found in a letter from Pliny, governor of Bithynia in Asia Minor from 111-113 A.D to the Emperor Trajan, and then the Emperor's reply. This is a reminder of historical context, because none of the liturgical developments took place in a political, social, or economic vacuum. That is true for us, and it must have been true for them.

Pliny to Trajan

*It is my practice, my lord, to refer to you all matters concerning which I am in doubt. For who can better give guidance to my hesitation or inform my ignorance? I have never before participated in trials of Christians, so I do not know what offenses are to be punished or investigated, or to what extent.*

---

[50] Ibid pp 56-57

*And I have been not a little hesitant as to whether there should be any distinction on account of age, or no difference recognized between the very young and the more mature. Is pardon to be granted for repentance, or if a man has once been a Christian is it irrelevant whether he has ceased to be one? Is the name itself to be punished, even without offenses, or only the offenses perpetrated in connection with the name?*

*Meanwhile, in the case of those who were denounced to me as Christians, I have followed the following procedure: I interrogated them as to whether they were Christians; those who confessed I interrogated a second and a third time, threatening them with punishment; those who persisted I ordered executed. For I had no doubt that, whatever the nature of their creed, stubbornness and inflexible obstinacy they surely deserve to be punished. There were others possessed of the same folly; but because they were Roman citizens, I signed an order for them to be transferred to Rome.*

*Soon accusations spread because of these proceedings, as usually happens, and several incidents occurred. An anonymous document was published containing the names of many persons. Those who denied that they were or had been Christians, when they invoked the gods in words dictated by me, offered prayer with incense and wine to your image, which I had ordered to be brought for this purpose together with statues of the gods, and also cursed Christ – none of which those who are really Christians can, it is said, be forced to do — these I thought should be discharged. Others named by the informer declared that they were Christians, but then denied it, asserting that they had been but had ceased to be, some three years before, others many years, some as much as twenty-five years. They all worshipped your image and the statues of the gods, and cursed Christ. They asserted, however, that the sum and substance of their fault or error had been that they were accustomed to meet on a fixed day before dawn and sing responsively a hymn to Christ as to a god, and to bind themselves by oath, not to do some crime, but not to commit fraud, theft, or adultery, not falsify their trust, nor to refuse to return a trust when called upon to do so. When this was over, it was their custom to depart and to assemble again to partake of food — but ordinary and innocent food.*

*Even this, they affirmed, they had ceased to do after my edict by which, in accordance with your instructions, I had forbidden political associations. Accordingly, I judged it all the more necessary to find out what the truth was by torturing two female slaves who were called deaconesses. But I discovered nothing else but depraved, excessive superstition. I therefore postponed the investigation and hastened to consult you. For the matter seemed to me to warrant consulting you, especially because of the number involved. For many persons of every age, every rank, and also of both sexes are and will be endangered. For the contagion of this superstition has spread not only to the cities but also to the villages and farms. But it seems possible to check and cure it. It is certainly quite clear that the temples, which had been almost deserted, have begun to be frequented, that the established religious rites, long neglected, are being resumed, and that from everywhere sacrificial animals are coming, for which until now very few purchasers could be found. Hence it is easy to imagine what a multitude of people can be reformed if an opportunity for repentance is afforded.*

## Trajan back to Pliny

*You observed proper procedure, my dear Pliny, in sifting the cases of those who had been denounced to you as Christians. For it is not possible to lay down any general rule to serve as a kind of fixed standard. They are not to be sought out; if they are denounced and proved guilty, they are to be punished, with this reservation, that whoever denies that he is a Christian and really proves it — that is, by worshiping our gods — even though he was under suspicion in the past, shall obtain pardon through repentance. But anonymously posted accusations ought to have no place in any prosecution. For this is both a dangerous kind of precedent and out of keeping with the spirit of our age.*

By the end of the third century, there had been a rapid growth of Christians groups in what was seen by the Romans as a minor cult in Judaism and Judea and elsewhere. From a small group of disciples around Jesus, this minor cult had expanded to about 10% of the population in the Roman Empire by about 300 A.D. It is true that the early Roman Governors and Emperors didn't know what to do about them, except where they were associated with trouble makers, refusing to sacrifice or to swear oaths to the Emperor. Their leader had died a criminal's death at a time when dying for a cause in a world when so many died young, had been seen as a noble idea inherited from the Greeks, and highly respected in the Roman army and Roman values. Until the beginning of the second century, as far as Rome was concerned, Christians were largely indistinguishable from Jews. The letter from Pliny to Trajan was one of the early indications that a distinction could be made. There was no special persecution of Christians per se, but they were expected to be part of everyday life and its rules. Anyone who stood out would be noticed, particularly if they objected to something like swearing an oath of loyalty to the Emperor, or their representatives. This didn't mean that the Roman Empire was the same everywhere or governed in exactly the same ways. The Governors of different provinces behaved differently in their responses to local conditions. Resources were limited, as were communications with Rome.

Most Christians were content to offer sacrifices to the Roman/Greek gods until some started refusing to do that, and anyone who met in groups and practised their own cult was seen as suspicious by the Roman authorities. The infamous Diocletian persecution began with him destroying the writings of what he saw as subversive groups, including Christians and Manichaeans, at a time of near anarchy in the Empire later in the 2nd century. The numbers of martyrs may be inflated, but many thousands were killed, tortured or imprisoned and then used as practise for the gladiators in the games – and this had started earlier under Nero (54-68) and Marcus Aurelius (161-180) and then continued under Decius (249-251) and Gallius (251-253). Persecution continued after Diocletius until Galerius (310-313) issued the Edict of Serdica. When Constantine the Great (306-337) defeated his rival Maxentius (306-312) at the Battle of Milvian Bridge, he and his co-Emperor issued the Edict of Milan in 313, permitting the toleration of all religions including Christianity. Eusebius, the Greek Bishop of Caesarea (c 260-339) [51] in the Roman Province of Syria Palaestina, wrote what some see as a flawed and somewhat fanciful history of the first Christian centuries. The story of Jesus himself is changed including events that aren't mentioned in the Gospel accounts, including a correspondence between Jesus and a local king, somewhat

---

[51] An early centre of Christian learning not least because of Origen (c186-254) and the work of Pamphilus his follower, a teacher of Eusebius. Origen left his books and with the books of Ambrosius, Pamphilius established the core of the library in Caesarea and the school of theology. Neither Eusebius nor Pamphilus knew Origen personally.

.

transforming a low or middle social status of a carpenter. Eusebius however was a powerful advocate of the Christian message and useful source of information about this early period.

In the early second century, there is nothing fixed as the "Old Testament" as yet, and no "New Testament" as know it, though the Gospels and letters, like many other letters, were circulating in places like Corinth, Ephesus, Jerusalem, Alexandria, Rome, Antioch, and Caesarea. In those places, Christian communities were finding their own way to worship and lead their communities, leaning on communications from those who wrote in the tradition of the Apostles. But communications were nothing like we know them to be in the modern world. It sometimes took weeks if not months for a letter to reach its recipients. There is, as yet, no accepted creed for the new Christian groups, scattered in their own diaspora and developing church communities. There are inherited divisions from the second half of the previous century. A structure for the appointment of Bishops, priests and deacons is only just beginning to appear. Some Christians are writing commentaries and memoires about the meaning of the person of Jesus, some of which are to prove more influential than others. There is a growing diversity of local practise and thinking. Small movements can easily become larger movements with the support of committed followers.

There are geo-political shocks and changes. The state of Judaism itself is nothing like it was before the destruction of the Temple in 70 A.D. This was clearly a long-lasting challenge to some of the foundational ideas of Judaism, although Jews had long since spread elsewhere and infused ideas from different places outside the authorities in Jerusalem. The Greco-Roman world includes towns and cities that are multi-cultured and cosmopolitan. Greek thinking is dominant when it comes to ideas, culture and religion, while Roman Law is dominant when it comes to the organising of society. And within Christianity, not yet established and formalised as it will be in the fourth century after the Council of Nicaea, gnostic and other ideas are taking shape and gathering supporters. There are subtle and not so subtle shifts of emphasis. The dangers seem to lie from within, as well as from without. Gnostics thought of themselves as Christians and found support in parts of the Gospel of John. They believed, as many Greek speaking Christians did, that we needed knowledge to be saved from our ignorance and that the Word and Wisdom of God could be the source of that salvation.

Current Hellenic ideas are already slipping into Christian thinking, as had Jewish ones from the beginning. Some of these matured into what those times called heresies. Docetism dated back to the Apostolic times and, as their name implied, (dokesis – appearance) it taught that Christ only seemed or appeared to have been a man in the fully human sense. Some denied his human nature altogether, presumably believing that nothing so material, sinful and fallible as human nature could be involved in the divine. Serapion, the Bishop of Antioch (190-203) used the word dokesis in a letter to the church at Rhossos when trouble arose because the apocryphal Gospel of Peter had been read in that church. Serapion at first allowed, but then forbade this, saying he had borrowed a copy from the sect (Docetae) who used it. He suspected a connection with Marcionism. But Docetist tendencies were referenced much earlier. Julius Cassianus[52] is thought to have been the founder, but little is now known about him. But the idea of Christ's human nature being only a semblance of reality was held by older gnostic sects. Docetism may not have started within the Church as some kind of heresy, but outside it.

Dimensions of Docetism appeared again later in Manichaeism and the great debate about the nature of reality. Was it in the hands of good or evil? Was material reality, in itself, good or evil? In order to be a good Christian, did one have to turn against material reality in order to grow closer to God? If so, what did the claims about Jesus's humanity and incarnation really imply? Many in these circles found the hardest part of the claims about Jesus in that profoundly significant sentence from John, "the Word became flesh and dwelt among us"! Their instincts were to dismiss the world of material things as bondage to an evil from which the

---

[52] Teaching in Egypt at about 170

Saviour had rescued us. Some began to talk of matter and human bodies as not really existing at all, in order to escape from this dualism. And the idea of God being born from the body, the very flesh of a woman, or Jesus suffering in a real body and dying on the cross, didn't easily fit into their worldview at all. Perhaps Christ only seemed to suffer and some other material body was substituted on the cross for his. St Irenaeus (130-202) was to write his famous book against these kinds of "heresies".

Saturninus, a Syrian Gnostic from Antioch (about 125 A.D.) made Christ the chief of the Aeons and angelic demiurges, but tried to show that the Saviour was unborn, without a body, and only apparently seen as man. Another Syrian gnostic, Cerdo, (a teacher of Marcion) arrived in Rome under Pope Hyginus (137 A.D.) teaching that Christ the Son of the Highest God appeared without birth from a woman. His supporters thought this made sense as matter could not have been the creation of the Highest God. but only of the Demiurge. And Marcion taught that Christ didn't pass through the womb of Mary but was only endowed with a "putative" body, but came down from heaven to Capernaum in the fifteenth year of Tiberius. Supporters of Marcion varied this belief, accepting Christ's human flesh but denying his birth from human flesh. Some argued that Christ had an astral body made of superior substance, something like the Superman myth today perhaps! Some distinguished between Christ and Jesus. Some admitted a human birth for Jesus, but argued it was only "passing through" a channel of Mary's body. Her body was not contributing anything, in its own right, to this divine event except hosting it! And this hinted at quite a common understanding of human biology at the time. Those who thought of a Virgin Birth and an immaculate conception could do so because they didn't understand the need for a woman's egg to be involved in the process of conception; the womb was a neutral receptacle or carrying vessel which allowed the new life planted in it by a man to develop and from which or through which birth happened.

Some, like the Gnostic teacher, Ptolemy[53] reduced Docetic views to a minimum saying that Christ's substance was spiritual and ethereal. Some writers fell over backwards to fit Christ into their ever more complicated systems of thought about the spiritual or pneumatic nature of Christ's body. Other writers like Tertullian (155-220) and Irenaeus did their best to counter these ideas, and it can't have been easy. Manichaism gave docetic, gnostic views a longer lease of life. In their (Iranian) system, Christ had to be fitted in to their assumptions about a profound separation of light and darkness and again they found parts of John's gospel helpful – *the light shines in the darkness and the darkness has never overcome it.*

It became quite common and widespread for these kinds of ideas to be picked up and adapted. Early Christians struggled to believe in the full humanity of Jesus in a world of material reality, which they saw as subject to the "bondage" of evil. In fact, it was easy to turn away from the world altogether, in order to get closer to the divine. Perhaps social/political events encouraged such a world renouncing view, but they clearly took a serious hold of early Christian thinking. And before we snigger about the way these ideas emerged, we only have to listen to contemporary Christians talking about the dualism of the sacred and the secular, using the former to reject the latter, or indeed non-Christians taking sides in favour of the secular over and against anything to do with the sacred or the religious.

We can't, of course, know all the individuals concerned, or what it was like, even for some of the main players in this part of Church history. But to the degree that we still live in times when many people take astral and other types of non-corporal spirits, star signs, fate, and heavenly bodies seriously, and where it is

---

[53] dates uncertain but still alive in about 180, a disciple of Valentinius (100-180), active in Alexandria and then Rome; probably the most influential of Gnostic teachers in early Christianity. Only fragments of his teaching survive. He believed only humans of a spiritual rather than a psychical or material nature received the gnosis that enabled them to return to the divine Pleroma. The others would reach a lesser form of salvation, except the material ones who would perish.

sometimes easier to think in religious terms about the heavenly realm than it is about material realities, we can surely empathise with the struggles of those times. I think of those early theologians desperately trying to steer a path through a plethora of new ideas and myths about the world, and we might even say superstitions, in order to hold on to what must have seemed like a ridiculous claim that God, the creator of all that was material, could have this incarnate relationship with creation in the person of Jesus, living in the specific times of a certain Roman Emperor and Governor in the turbulence of first century Palestine. And how was anyone supposed to talk about a Son of God or Messiah who could be crucified?

There are manuscript records of early liturgies, but many of these are dated quite late. The principal locations for the early appearance of Christian worship and the theological reflection, sermons, and commentaries on its meaning include those in the following list below. They are all places where real people lived and struggled, as all humans struggle with daily realities, as well as larger, geo-political changes. And there were turbulent changes and crises enough taking place all the time. We only have to think of the social and political tensions in Rome and the Empire during the first century B.C.[54] to the eruption of Vesuvius in 79 A.D., the greatest natural disaster of its times. Rome had already nearly collapsed in the 3rd century A.D. with various assassinations, rebellious movements and reforms. Large scale internal and external forces brought about its collapse by the fifth century A.D. and all of these events took their toll on quite distant parts of the Empire. And of course by then the momentum of the Empire had shifted further East to Constantinople and its different culture and atmosphere.

Worship developed in that context of internal tension and change, and it evolved from within the human story of what was happening at the time, and from within the human condition. And

---

[54] And before that, the Second, Third and Fourth Macedonian Wars as well as the Second and third Punic Wars of the second century B.C. which put their stresses and strains on the Romans.

that human story included the actions taken by the individuals involved, the development of their theological worldviews, and their personal biographies. The Holy Spirit's wisdom worked its inspiration and guidance through these things, as the individuals and groups concerned met to remember their Lord and share their understanding of His presence and its meaning. We have some early manuscripts of different, Eucharistic prayers and acts of worship. What we cannot know for sure is what these words and acts meant, or felt like personally, to individuals in the particular communities gathering in different places and situations within the political, social and religious context of their times. What follows is a list of some key moments. Like all lists, it can only be an inadequate and superficial reflection of what was really happening on the ground within the experience of particular individuals and movements. It is an abstraction from years of complex cultural and religious developments. My own ignorance will be shown by the way I've tried to summarise and comment. But by reducing the complexity and length of such a list, I hope I have at least protected the reader from a much longer and more involved account.

Scholars have of course been working on the detail for at least the last two or three centuries. Before that, there were early, notable historians of the early church like the polymath Eusebius of Caesarea (c 260-339) and Bible translators like Jerome (345-420)[55] as well as the countless theologians and Bishops, known and unknown, in both the Eastern and Western traditions, seeking to understand what they had inherited, and to navigate through all the disputes of the past in order to deal with the challenges of the present. And there was much to understand, and only a few people had the access or the knowledge of languages to do it. This may be hard for us to appreciate, given our

---

[55] educated in Rome, an ascetic and traveller, he knew Greek and Hebrew, spent 23 years translating the Bible into everyday Latin (The Vulgate) when there were many Latin versions of the Greek text, many badly translated or copied. In 1546, the Council of Trent declared his translation as authentic but a corrupt form of it circulated throughout the Middle Ages. His text added impetus to the use of Latin in Western worship leading later to a liturgy and Bible lay people couldn't understand.

ubiquitous access to knowledge at the touch of a button through the internet. We can even access libraries from our screen that, until a few decades ago, were restricted to registered members, and then only accessible by physically visiting them. For most of human history the records of human history have been inaccessible to all but a minority of people. And, of course, the knowledge that minority accessed, gave them particular authority and power over others as well as significant responsibility for the way they passed it on and shared it. Here is a list of some of the key places of early liturgical development.

JERUSALEM; In Semitic languages and Greek in the 4th/5th centuries. The earliest Eucharistic Liturgy being that of St James, from a 9th century manuscript but possibly referring to a 4th century Liturgy. It's no surprise that many of the most ancient rites and ceremonies of the Liturgy of the Church, the ones that have survived in both the East and the West, are to be found in the services of Holy Week. Their roots go back to the foundation of the Holy Sepulchre Church in Jerusalem from the 4th century onwards and perhaps even before. Many Western, Catholic and Anglican Churches have retained strong resonances with those ceremonies, particularly the Liturgy of the Last Supper, Good Friday, the Service of the Holy Fire[56] on Holy Saturday, which has remained in the Orthodox world as the service of Resurrection. And then of course the Easter Sunday celebration of the Resurrection and the themes of the Sundays which followed. Over time the ceremonies involved have become shortened and much has been omitted or forgotten in the West. In many new Christian movements, they have disappeared altogether.

SYRIA; The earliest liturgical instruction books, the late 1st century *Didache and Didascalia* c 230, *The Apostolic Constitutions* c 380, *The Epitome* 5th century, *the Acts of John* c 200 and *the Acts of Thomas* 3rd century. The 5th century Armenian Ordo based on East Syrian models shows patterns of baptism and Eucharist. The poetry and hymns of St Ephrem c 306-74. The 3rd century Anaphora of Addai and Mari. The 4th century *Liber Graduum* and 5th century *Liturgical homilies of Narsai* on the meaning of baptism and Eucharist. The 4th

---

[56] Which I tried to describe in my novel *The Glow Within* set in Romania.

century *Sogitha on the Temple of Edessa.*

ANTIOCH in West Syria; Including extensive liturgical descriptions e.g. John Chrysostom 4th century, Theodore of Mosuestia c 350-428 on baptism, Eucharist and catechumenate. Severus of Antioch 6th century, the liturgical year, Lent and the cult of martyrs. The Anaphora of the Twelve Apostles and several liturgical calendars and commentaries. The Liturgy of Saint Basil of Caesarea (330-379), in Cappadocia, powerful advocate of Nicene doctrines, supporter of the poor and establishment of community monastic life in Eastern Christianity, (brother of Gregory of Nyssa and his friend Gregory of Nazianzus.

Rome; Justin Martyr's *First Apology* c 150. The edited *Apostolic Tradition* includes comments on how to perform liturgy from 2nd century. Sermons of Leo the Great (590-604), the 6th and 7th century sacramentaries.

CONSTANTINOPLE; Post-Constantine significant church buildings, including Hagia Sophia c 360, with processions between them, and decoration related to the needs of liturgical choreography continued with Justinian (527-65). Bishops Gregory of Nazianzus (379-81), John Chrysostom (398-403) left extensive theological commentary on liturgy as did 5th century historians Socrates and Sozomen, the 6th century Theodore, the 7th century *Chronicon Paschale* commentary on early liturgies and processions. The Byzantine chronicler Theophanes the Confessor 752-818 and 10th and 11th century commentators on "stationary liturgy" including the Trisagion chant. The city developed a wide pattern of church liturgies.

NORTH AFRICA; Tertullian (c 195-230) early descriptions of Baptism and Easter services, Eucharist, Agape and daily offices. Cyprian Bishop of Carthage (248-258), roles of presbyters and bishops, baptism and Eucharist as sacrifice and memorial, public penance, readmission of apostates. Augustine Bishop of Hippo (396-430) sermons on different rites and liturgies, liturgical calendar, funerals, movement towards standardization to counter heretical texts. Clement of Alexandria (c 150-215) and Origin (c 185-254) developed the symbolic meaning and theology of liturgy. As early

Trinitarian and Christological controversies divided parts of the church, they and others like Athanasius, Bishop of Alexandria (c 15-215) were highly influential, drawing out the theological significance of early Liturgy, particularly during Lent and Easter.     Epiphanius, bishop of Salamis in Cyprus (367-403) commented on the origins of festivals like Epiphany and Christmas in 4th century Egypt. Monastic writers and mystics like Pachomius (c 290-346) and Cassian (c 360-435) left commentary on the development of monastic non-Eucharistic prayer. Other liturgical texts include the *Canons of Hippolytus* c mid 4th century, which resonated with the *Apostolic Tradition* of Rome. Sarapion, Bishop of Thmuis in the 4th century in Lower Egypt left us the *Sacramentary* Prayer Book which included Eucharistic prayers and blessings. There are liturgical fragments in the *Strasbourg Papyrus* and, the *Anaphora of Saint Mark* from the 5th century. Coptic liturgy in Egypt was influential in the development of the liturgy of Ethiopia, down to the present times.

NORTHERN ITALY; Ambrose Bishop Milan (373-397) prolific writer on hymns and antiphons, baptism and Eucharist, *De sacramentis*, c 391 links with both Roman and Eastern rites. Gaundentius, Bishop of Brescia (c 397). Zeno, Bishop of Verona (c 362-375). Maximus Bishop of Turin 5th century. Peter Chrysologus Bishop of Ravenna (c 400-50). The *Rotulus* of Ravenna 5th - 7th centuries, lectionaries, gospel books.

SPAIN; Some later texts including Mozarabic rite. Prudentius (348 – 410).

GAUL; St Irenaeus, Bishop Lyons (c 130-200) extensive commentary on baptism, Eucharist and Death. *Statuta Ecclesia Antiqua*, late 5th century. Various Councils and synods 4th-7th centuries. Bishop Caesarius of Arles (c 470-542) and Bishop Gregory of Tour (573-94) on liturgical texts. Bishop Germanus of Paris (555-76) on Syrian influence on Gallican liturgy. Various writings on the saints of Gaul, daily prayer, healing and anointing, Eucharist, baptism, funerals and the rise of monastic influence on parish worship by Gregory of Tour.

So, Christianity spread around the Mediterranean and in the Middle East where it so quickly took hold, often in Greek speaking parts of the Roman Empire. Much of this process is unclear because in the beginning we are talking about a scattered diaspora of house churches, small family and kinship groups in an environment of suspicion from Jews, Romans and Greeks alike. And in that scattered diaspora, the early Christians showed both a continuity with Judaism and a discontinuity. The earliest letters we have in what became the New Testament, or those circulating around it, show us how divisions arose very early on in matters like circumcision and the place of the gentile converts. This took place in communities where Jewish refugees had also settled, particularly after the destruction of much of Jerusalem, and the Temple itself, when the Romans had reached the end of their tether with troublesome Jewish leaders, or zealot like, rebellious groups.

Diaspora, and all it meant in terms of displacement, uprooting and adjustments to new religious and political environments, was as prevalent then as now. It meant learning new languages and customs, as well as fighting to maintain the old. This was hard and divisions travelled with them as they were forced to rethink old assumptions and adjust to new cultures. So, although the law and prophets of Judaism and the scriptures and commentaries of the Rabbis were the fertile ground out of which Jesus the Jew had appeared as something radically new, his followers had to learn how to cope with the inevitable tensions and splits which followed. It's not surprising that early Christian worship borrowed habits acquired from the use of the scriptures in the teaching of the synagogues. Already by the second century, if not earlier, we see that the early theologians were teaching that the same ancient scriptures were good for learning about the Christ, if not taken literally. They could be seen as prefiguring the meaning of salvation in that which was radically new, if they were understood allegorically, spiritually, symbolically, and metaphorically. Their earthy meaning pointed to something divine, but that spiritual significance could be lost when taken at face value. So, it became an early habit for those second century Christians to take a reading from those Hebrew texts (what we call the Old Testament), adding to them the new texts they called Gospels and some of the carefully chosen letters of the apostles, teaching and preaching from them to demonstrate their deeper and wider reference points and meaning, believing that the first Gospels had been written to draw out examples of the significance of the life, words, signs and deeds of Jesus, as well as the meaning of those horrific days of suffering from which resurrection happened as a complete surprise.

It would have been natural, following the synagogue model, for questions to be asked and discussion to be inspired amongst those listening, as Jesus had once listened to the rabbis in the Temple courts, and as Jesus had once preached on the reading from the scroll of Isaiah. And his radical words had gone straight to the profound meaning (as opposed to a literal meaning) of the words read out, confronting them with the challenge that their true significance had become present and real in their hearing because of his presence. And this was the Jesus who had taught in parables and stories that still must have thrilled and perplexed his new followers.

## MOVING OUTSIDE TO BE IN OTHER CULTURES

Taking part in those early acts of worship drew people together around those stories and their meaning for their new situations in a non-Jewish cultural milieu in the wider Gentile world. And being part of that world challenged those early Christians to broaden their message, to enculture it, as God had encultured the nature of God's being in the incarnation itself. And if God had so acted, far be it for them to do anything less. We can only guess at the tensions they experienced in wanting to reach out, inside-out, to their friends and neighbours, and at the same time be careful and cautious in the way they did it, not least because of the risk involved in certain parts of the Empire. And we know how they had to wrestle amongst themselves with questions of balance and adjustment. Some wanted to keep Christian worship and practice anchored in Jewish Law as a way of holding them together. Others, including Peter and Paul and their followers knew they had to break free from its restrictions because the Law had brought only the condemnation of sin, while Jesus had brought a new freedom from the restrictive limits of the law, from sin and death. So, they struggled with those tensions and others that kept arising from this or that movement of new thinking, seeking a new understanding of what really mattered and what was really at stake in their belief about God and God in Christ. As they moved beyond the limits of the inherited Judaic milieu of teaching and worship, then then had to face the challenge of non-Jewish and non-Christian ideas in the Greek speaking world and the ever present and often daily challenges of surviving against the grain of changing Roman politics and religious cults. in order to be incarnated into the reality of the gentile world in which, over time they absorbed the Greek understanding of the meaning of Liturgy as public works. The examples from Jesus' life seemed ever more relevant as a frame of reference for their own. They found meaning in Jesus as the revelation of the creator God in whose presence the Samaritan woman at the well, the Roman centurion and his daughter, the Jewish tax collector, and the Prodigal son were as welcome as anyone else. If that was how God in Jesus had shown them how to relate to men and women from other backgrounds in difficult situations, then who were they to reduce that vision or to harm that message. And as they remembered the stories of Pentecost, so they found themselves moved with the inspiration of the gifts of the Spirit to people of all kinds of languages and cultural assumptions. And so, following in the memory of those early apostles, the early leaders and teachers found new ways of explaining those gifts and the meaning of Jesus in relation to God and that same Holy Spirit.

Behind this variety of liturgical development and serious theological controversies, certain forms and ways of worship emerged. Monasticism in Egypt and Europe was to develop later patterns, particularly of non-Eucharistic daily prayer. Some, like the Benedictines (St Benedict of Nursia 480-547), saw worship as part of their daily offering of work and evolved a theology of work and worship in a dynamic relationship with each other.

Different parts of the early church passed on the traditions of worship they'd inherited, often labelled in relation to well know mystics and saints. Some of them came from Bishops involved in the early synods and councils of the church where many of the disputes arose. From an early time, some of those disputes became ossified in different Western and Eastern Church practices. And while the Great

Schism didn't take place until the 11<sup>th</sup> century, the tensions had already surfaced in those early Councils, often reflecting the difference between Latin and Greek ways of thought and the misunderstandings that could arise because of that, not least in the Christological disputes from the 4<sup>th</sup> to the 9<sup>th</sup> or 10<sup>th</sup> centuries.

The Eastern Church somehow sustained the three great liturgies still known as those of the saints James, John Chrysostom and Basil. They are still used today though much later material from other mystical writers has been added over time, which partly explains why those liturgies are so long and sometimes repetitive. It could be argued that their length is another expression of how "maximal" they are. Many of those accumulated prayers seem like mini theological sermons or reflections. They are profoundly symbolic and analogical in their theology which means that they have become in themselves a significant source of Orthodox theology. They bring Old Testament architypes into their language showing how the truth of Christ has been pre-figured from of old. If you want to know what the Orthodox believe about the central beliefs and festivals of the church, go to their liturgical books. They provide a rich variety of liturgical commentary on, for example, the themes of Christmas, Lent and Easter, and they do it using mystical theological reflection in a way that surprises many Western Christians.

*There the Virgin has borne a Babe and made the thirst of Adam and David to cease straightway. Therefore let us hasten to this place where now is born a young Child, the pre-eternal God.*

In the West, we have lost much of this approach to a multi-dimensional, theological understanding, where connections are made between Old Testament, prophetic images and the events of Jesus' life. If you want to talk about the death and resurrection of Jesus, then reflect on the images of Jonah and the whale. If you want to understand more about the Incarnation, then consider for example the relationship between Bethlehem and Eden, as in the following,

*Bethlehem has opened Eden; come and let us see. We have found joy in the secret; come and let us take possession of the paradise that is within the*

*cave. There the unwatered Root has appeared from which forgiveness flows forth; there is found the undug Well whence David long to drink of old.*

Or consider the story in Daniel 3 about Shadrach, Meshach and Abednego being thrown into the fiery furnace by Nebuchadnezzar but not consumed, as the Burning Bush is not consumed in Exodus 3. These images are often repeated in Mattins, the Liturgy, and the Great Vespers of *The Nativity according to the Flesh*. Layer upon layer of theological meaning is offered. Images from the Old Testament re-present or pre-figure something else, symbolically applied to these major Christian events, reinterpreting their meaning in repeated proclamations and prayers unveiling those layers of interpretation through poetically, rich phrases to explore and rehearse the drama of that meaning in canticles and canons. Add to that an extensive use of the psalms, prayers to cover the meaning of movement in the liturgy, and the development of icons and frescoes which illustrate the central themes of the church's year, as part of the environment and context of liturgy, and we can see how it has been expanded to become a holistic experience with sensory appeal to the imagination and the intellect, but, above all, communicating a sense of profound mystery.

A non-Orthodox visitor only has to enter an Orthodox church for the first time to notice the obvious differences. And those differences might, over time, and with some explanation, begin to attract rather than repel, as their meaning becomes more apparent. For all is not quite as it seems. The candles, sounds, incense, singing, movements and length of the liturgy can be inspiring as well as alien, and certainly somewhat demanding for Western Christians. It is obvious that these liturgies are different from the first acts of Christian worship, but they sustain many of the theological ideas and words from the early liturgical sources mentioned above. Although the Byzantine world of later centuries introduced its own additions and changes, we seem to be in touch with something particularly early that has lasted. And as it lasted, so some early theological worldviews were passed on and developed, not least through the celebration of the Eucharist. Let's forget, for a moment, questions about its words and actions which imply that somehow the priest makes the "change" in the bread and wine by reciting or performing them. That would certainly be a common assumption in the Catholic Church and parts of the Anglican Church, while in the Eastern church the emphasis would be on the Holy Spirit as the source and inspiration of their transformation. And let's also forget, for a moment, the detailed arguments in history about the how or when, it might take place. Instead, let's go back to something significant in the liturgy of St Basil, Bishop of Caesarea in the 4th century, and look at the words we have from his usage and times. We do this because there is a certain surprise waiting for us there, which also throws some light on the theme of this book. There are many who have written scholarly articles on the Eucharistic theology of those early centuries. Michael Zheltov, in his article *The Moment of Eucharistic Consecration* in Byzantine thought,[57] examines the words used or not used, in early texts, in the Eucharistic Prayer (or Anaphora), the words of Institution, other relevant parts of the liturgy including the *Prothesis* (preparation of the bread and wine and the act of bringing them to the altar in the Great Procession) and *Ephonesis* (the elevation and the calling to participation in the communion) as well as particular actions and movements. Here is the relevant passage.

*In some anaphora God is asked to manifest or to show, rather than to convert or to make, the offered gifts the Body and Blood of Christ. If the Name is Christ himself then the application of the Name to the gifts should result in a manifestation of Christ in them.* This is referencing the possibility that by simply using divine names we are already invoking something of their meaning and presence in an act of worship. This may have been the assumption in the earliest of liturgies. He then quotes the epiclesis in the anaphora of St Basil, admitting it is known in various *versions, where the epiclesis includes the verb "to show".*

*Therefore Master all-holy we also, your sinful and unworthy servants, who have been held worthy to minister at your holy altar, not for our righteousness, for we have done nothing good upon earth, but for your mercies*

---

[57] Maxwell E. Johnson (ed.) Issues in Eucharistic Praying (Collegeville (MN), 2010) accessed via academia edu

*and compassions which you have poured out richly upon us, with confidence approach your holy altar. And having set forth the representations of the holy Body and Blood of Your Christ we pray and beseech You, O holy of holies, in the good pleasure of Your bounty, that Your all-holy Spirit may come upon us and upon these gifts set forth and bless them and sanctify and show this bread the precious Body of our Lord and God Jesus Christ and this cup the precious Blood of our Lord and God and Saviour Jesus Christ which was shed for the life of the world. And unite with one another all of us who partake of the one bread and the cup into communion with the one Holy spirit, and make none of us to partake of the holy Body and Blood of Your Christ for judgement or for condemnation, but that we may find mercy and grace with all the saints who have been well-pleasing to You*[58].

We note the tone of humility and unworthiness at the beginning and end of this prayer as applied to both priest and people. We note the crucial idea that the invocation to the Holy Spirit (epiclesis) is to come down on *"us"* as well as the *gifts*. So, we may take it that the Liturgy of the Eucharist involves everyone present. This is different from the development in the Catholic church that a priest could celebrate the mass on their own. Most importantly, we note the use of the word *re-presentations* (antitypes) and *"show"*. The idea of re-presentation, in this case, the bread and wine standing *as* an antitype of the body and blood presence of Christ will be important for what I discuss in the section on art in the Liturgy of the World. To show is used in the Greek word meaning to reveal what is already there, i.e. if only we knew how to look, we who are involved in this Liturgy, as partakers of its meaning. In other words, the prayer to the Holy Spirit is that the gifts may represent to us, who are involved, a showing and making real the meaning of the words we are using in the whole Liturgy but particularly in the anaphora, including the Words of Institution and the epiclesis and the showing forth, or calling to communion in the elevation of the ephonesis. Show us what this already means, make it real to us in that showing, teach us the truth of it, reveal its meaning and significance in our understanding of its reality. In the asking of this re-presentative truth to be revealed to us by the Holy Spirit, it's as if we are opening up

---

[58] P 269

ourselves, hearts and minds and bodies, to the perception and knowledge of the possibility that what is shown to be the case, then appears to be the case in our partaking of it through our belief in it.

There are many ways to understand the meaning of "showing" in this context but then to apply it to the Liturgy of the World as well as the Liturgy of the Church. There is much that needs be shown, made real, in the representative meaning of things in the world. What this early liturgy seems to be doing, in its focus on the words of this epiclesis, is not so much to put the emphasis on a moment of priestly change in the transubstantial of the bread and wine, but a moment of new understanding of what is already latently true in the meaning of what is re-presented to us, in and through the bread and wine.

Later, the use of *antitypes* (representation) for this purpose (which appears in Basil, the *Apostolic Tradition*, the Syrian *Didascalia*, Irenaeus of Lyon, Cyril of Jerusalem and Gregory Nazianzen and others) disappears or is reduced and questioned, possibly because of the Nestorian conflict of the 5th century and beyond[59], and later in the Iconoclasm disputes. It was later defended however for use in relation to the un-consecrated bread and wine of the prothesis. Over time, the words of institution themselves were considered insufficient on their own to encompass the "consecration". Michael Zheltov also references the Barcelona papyrus[60], one of the earliest surviving manuscripts of a Eucharistic prayer when the Greek word for "to show" means to make more solid, to depict, to represent (as in art).[61]

In the seventeenth century (in the Ukraine), the elevation was added to the Byzantine rite to accommodate Catholic practise,

---

[59] where Nestorius, Patriarch of Constantinople (in 428) asserted that the human and divine persons of Christ were somehow distinct from each other. Cyril of Alexandria condemned his teaching as heretical and issued a series of anathemas against him. This was confirmed at the Council of Ephesus in 431 and the Council of Chalcedon in 451.

[60] A 4th-century papyrus codex in Greek, (containing also a few Latin texts), from Egypt said to be the oldest liturgical manuscript containing a complete anaphora, now conserved in the Abbey of Montserrat.

[61] P 267

accompanied by the words, "offering you your own". The elevation was seen as controversial in some versions of the rite, but eventually it largely remained. If pressed about "the" moment of consecration, many Orthodox would have said that the *Ephonesis* (calling to communion) including the elevation is also crucial. "Holy things to the holy". Gradually, although only in late Byzantine practise, this became the climax to the *Anaphora* and the consecration, and the beginning of the communion itself. The fact that this is the moment of the "breaking of the bread" might be significant. It became its own climax going back to apostolic description of "the breaking of bread" as the significant moment of recognition or what was represented, particularly in the Emmaus Rd account. Michael Zheltov also refers[62] to the *Prothesis* - preparation of the bread and wine and the Great Entrance - in which people recognised, as it were, that the bread and wine already had a new significance prior to the words of Institution, the Epiclesis and the Elevation. In fact, the word antitype from St Basil is again introduced by some commentators. The fact that all of this happens after the iconoclastic movement in the eighth century shows how much eucharistic theology developed in the East as well as the West.

Meanwhile, out of the great variety of worship experiments and cultural traditions in those early centres of Christianity, some "family" of regional rites emerged in the 5th to 7th centuries and beyond. Hybrid forms of the Roman rite dominated in Europe along with the Mozarabic rite of Spain, the Ambrosian rite of Milan, the Celtic rites, the Coptic and Ethiopian rites, the various Syrian and Middle Eastern rights, the Armenian rites and the Byzantine in Constantinople and Asia Minor, Bulgaria, Romania, Greece, and Russia, the earliest Indian (Syrian and Mar Thoma) rites in Karala, and then the developments in the Far East and Colonial countries not touched by Christianity before the arrival of different European Empires.

And across all these historical shifts and movements, over those centuries of change and growth, agreement and disagreement

---

[62] Pp 303-305

hovered around the pivot points of the baptismal initiation of new Christians, the Eucharist and their interpretation. Around these focal points other things accrued in the trend from early simplicity to more complexity. But we know from the evidence of the four Gospels, written in different places, by different people, at different distance from the events described, how natural it was for different interpretations to emerge as the vehicles of communication and understanding. And we know from the evidence we have in the *Acts of the Apostles,* and the different early letters that ended up as different books in the New Testament that there were tensions from the beginning about how this faith was to be understood and applied in different circumstances. It is noteworthy that these tensions and disagreements, for example about what difference being a Gentile or a Jewish convert made (the circumcision issue) were not edited out of the content of the New Testament collection. Incredibly, those early followers of the Jerusalem church and then Paul or Peter found a way of coming together, however briefly, in what is known as the First Council of the Church to discuss their differences.

But differences there were and that seems to have set a pattern for everything that followed. On all sides of those differences, individuals, and groups of supporters, believed they were acting with integrity and sincerity as they held on to their experience of what was important and true to and for them. As the context around them changed, there were times when persecution drove them closer together or when it drove them further apart. There were times when the cost of different expressions of belief was high within the Christian world let alone outside it. Where the Christian initiation of baptism had required huge courage in the face of possible martyrdom, it became a rite that could lead to status and position in the running of the State. It could also lead through its different practices, to internal Christian opposition. And there were other changes like the shift from adult to infant or whole family baptism with associated changes to the place of the catechumenate. The shift from private home space to public space for the Eucharist brought its own changes in the way Eucharist was experienced, and to arguments about the changing status of those who lead it and those who participated in it.

As the prayers in worship became more fixed, so there was potential for more disagreement about their content and meaning. The public building setting took the Eucharist away from the intimacy of small groups of people, who knew each other well and often provided mutual aid to each other, and away from the meal setting and atmosphere it could occupy in a private home. In the 4th century the legalization of Christianity introduced the enculturation of the ritual into the Imperial Cult and the role of the Emperor in convening, chairing, and influencing theological disputes, as we can see from the far reaching Council of Nicaea, with all its large scale agendas and disagreements, affecting centres of Christian life across the Empire. Slowly, the Liturgy of the Eucharist would take on some of the style and glories of the court itself through the pomp and ritual that were possible in larger buildings. This relied more on the role of clergy and that role meant a level of separation and specialization needed to organise and maintain the public services, and inevitably the public understanding of their meaning.

This must have been a significant shift of power and control from what had happened in the house group celebrations. The Eucharist becomes less of a shared meal to remember their Lord and more of an awe filled mystery where participation was distanced in visual and physical terms, and less equally shared by all present. Over time, the frequent and regular receiving of communion became less common, as it still is today in most Orthodox countries (for a variety of reasons). An increase in size and the larger number of participants, and the increasing role of the clergy in running the service through a formalized ritual of words and actions reduced the possibility of active participation or at least changed its meaning. The focal point was no longer what happened on the common table in the centre of a small group, but what happened over "there" (and slowly over time behind a screen), at a physical and visual distance from participants within the words and (secret) actions of the clergy. This may have been inherited from a memory of Jewish practise in the

Temple, where the Holy of Holies was separated off from ordinary people.

In the Western Church, meanwhile, there were even more pronounced changes. There was more controlled order under the authority of the Bishop of Rome and the early Holy Roman Emperors after 800. Latin had become the language and cultural vehicle for worship and doctrine, and the latter tended to become more dogmatic in tone than the Greek language and culture in the East. The use of Latin in Christian worship continued well into the twentieth century. Some monastic orders retained a measure of independence under the authority of their abbots and passed on the learning of the church and the education of the wealthy. The monasteries were responsible for the production and study of manuscripts. On the fringes of the Empire, those Christians speaking other languages had to manage with the Latin for worship. New rites of initiation, penance, marriage, anointing the sick, ordination appeared. The 7th century, *Ordo Romanus Primus* gives an account of the choreography rather than the text of the Papal Mass at Easter in Santa Maria Maggiore.

The Catholic Church in Spain unilaterally introduced its own significant changes, such as adding the Filioque Clause (the Holy Spirit proceeding from the Father *and* the Son) to the creed, which was interpreted by the Eastern Church as affecting Trinitarian theology. Priesthood accrued to itself the doctrine of celibacy in the West, and there were disputes about leavened or unleavened bread in the Eucharist well before the formal East-West split in the Great Schism of the 11th century.

The Vatican was not only seen as a centralizing power in church matters, but also politically. The Pope had certain powers over political appointments in the divided Italian States and elsewhere, including the Holy Roman Emperor, while in the East, the Emperor was seen to hold a quasi- priestly and theological power over the church. Shifts that seemed minor were to become more significant, as tensions increased, particularly from the 7th century onwards. But they were somehow manageable to a degree, right up to the point when the Vatican delegates laid a Bull of excommunication on the altar in Constantinople in 1054, and the Western Crusaders then massacred Orthodox Christians there in 1204, weakening that city and the Byzantine Empire, so that it more easily fell to the Muslims under Mehmed 11 of the Ottoman Empire in 1254. Although long, the content of this Bull is worth quoting in full for the insights it gives into the reality of division, and the language of heresy used that had built up over the previous few centuries. It was to have far reaching implications for the way East and West developed in the future.

*Humbert, cardinal bishop of the holy Roman Church by the grace of God; Peter, Archbishop of Amalfi; and Frederick, Deacon and chancellor, to all the children of the Catholic Church. The holy, primary, and Apostolic See of Rome, to which the care of all the churches most especially pertains as if to a head, deigned to make us its ambassadors to this royal city for the sake of the peace and utility of the Church so that, in accordance with what has been written, we might descend and see whether the complaint which rises to its ears without ceasing from this great city, is realized in fact or to know if it is not like this. Let the glorious emperors, clergy, senate, and people of this city of Constantinople as well as the entire Catholic Church therefore know that we have sensed here both a great good, whence we greatly rejoice in the Lord, and the greatest evil, whence we lament in misery. For as far as the columns of the imperial power and its honored and wise citizens go, this city is most Christian and orthodox.*

*But as far as Michael, who is called patriarch through an abuse of the term, and the backers of his foolishness are concerned, innumerable tares of heresies are daily sown in its midst. Because like Simoniacs, they sell the gift of God; Like Valesians, they castrate their guests and promote them not only to the clergy but to the episcopacy; Like Arians, they rebaptize those already baptized in the name of the Holy Trinity, and especially Latins; Like Donatists, they claim that with the exception of the Greek Church, the Church of Christ and baptism has perished from the world; Like Nicolaitists, they allow and defend the carnal marriages of the ministers of the sacred altar; Like Severians, they say that the law of Moses is accursed; Like Pneumatomachoi or Theomachoi, they cut off the procession of the Holy Spirit from the Son; Like the Manichaeans among others, they state that leave is ensouled (animatum); Like the Nazarenes, they preserve the carnal cleanness of the Jews to such an extent that they refuse to baptize dying babies before eight days after birth and, in refusing to communicate with pregnant or menstruating women, they forbid them to be baptized if they are pagan; And because they grow the hair on their head and beards, they will not receive in communion those who tonsure their hair and shave their beards following the decreed practice of the Roman Church. For these errors and many others committed by them, Michael himself, although admonished by the letters of our lord Pope Leo, contemptuously refused to repent. Furthermore, when we, the Pope's ambassadors, wanted to eliminate the causes of such great evils in a reasonable way, he denied us his presence and conversation, forbid churches to celebrate Mass, just as he had earlier closed the churches of the Latins and, calling them "Azymites," had persecuted the Latins everywhere in word and deed. Indeed, so much [did he persecute them] that among his own children, he had anathematized the Apostolic See and against it he still writes that he is the "Eumenical Patriarch". Therefore, because we did not tolerate this unheard of outrage and injury of the first, holy, and Apostolic See and were concerned that the Catholic faith would be undermined in many ways, by the authority of the holy and individuated Trinity and the Apostolic See, whose embassy we are performing, and of all the orthodox fathers from the Seven Councils and of the entire Catholic Church, we thus subscribe to the following anathema which the most reverend Pope has proclaimed upon Michael and his followers unless they should repent. Michael, neophyte patriarch through abuse of office, who took on the monastic habit out of fear of men alone and is now accused by many of the worst of crimes; and with him Leo called bishop of Achrida; Constantine, chaplain of this Michael, who trampled the sacrifice of the Latins with profane feet; and all their followers in the aforementioned errors and acts of presumption: Let them be anathema Maranatha with the Simoniacs, Valesians, Arians, Donatists, Nicolaitists, Severians, Pneumatomachoi, Manichaeans, Nazarenes, and all the heretics — nay, with the devil himself and his angels, unless they should repent. AMEN, AMEN, AMEN.*

The Bull began with diplomatic niceties and then proceeded to condemn Patriarch Michael with little regard for how the "other" side had experienced the behaviour and beliefs of the Western Church. "We are right and you are wrong" seems to be the pattern it established or reflected. And this pattern seems to be firmly entrenched in geo-political relationships as well as church ones.[63] The tendency is for one side to distort the truth of the other in order

---

[63] as it still is in some recent events, noticeably the Cold War years and the surrogate wars fought during that time, and now in the statements made by the President of Russia about the invasion of the Ukraine.

to prove "them" wrong and it right. "We are right and you are wrong" so easily becomes "we will do violence to you to make you see what is right and wrong". Torture, burning and execution was used to "convert" people back to the truth of the Catholic Church from their "heresy", a religious word for those who disagreed with centrally controlled, doctrinal positions, and heretics could be found within Christianity and not just in other religions.

In 1184, Pope Lucius 111 sent bishops to the South of France to deal with the Catharists and then the Waldensians in Germany and Northern Italy. There were horrific massacres and thousands were tortured and executed. By 1231, Pope Gregory had charged the Dominican Order to take over the job of the Inquisition, the active seeking out and persecution of those charged with heresy. It was easy to make mistakes, and to use the charge of heresy to get rid of whomsoever you disliked. Count Raymond VII of Toulouse was known for burning heretics at the stake even though they had confessed. His successor, Count Alphonese, confiscated the lands of the accused to increase his riches. The accused received no counsel to defend them, and local people could take advantage of the Inquisition to falsely accuse others of heresy. Its worst severity was in Spain with thousands of executions including Jews and Muslims. In 1478, a priest called Tomas de Torguemada created the Tribunal of Castile to investigate the credibility of the *Conversos.* Jews were forced into ghettos, separated off from Christians, and the Inquisition expanded to Seville. In 1481, about twenty thousand Conversos confessed to heresy and hundreds were burned at the stake. Pope Sextus heard of the severity of the Inquisition, but Torquemada was still made Inquisitor General. Torture became more systemized and Pope Alexander V1 tried to temper his excesses by appointing four other Inquisitors General.

Under Ferdinand and Isabella, from 1492, the year Columbus set out for the Americas, Jews and Muslims who had refused to convert were expelled or tortured, and their property confiscated, so ending a long period of comparative peace between Christians, Jews, and Muslims under Muslim rule in Andalusia. After Isabella's death in 1504, Ferdinand promoted Cardinal Ximenes de Cisneros the head of the Catholic Church as Inquisitor General. He even pursued Muslims into North Africa and encouraged Ferdinand to take military action. Thousands were expelled and it wasn't until Spain revoked the Alhambra decree in 1968 that Spain granted Sephardic Jews the right to citizenship. In 1307, about fifteen thousand Knights Templar were tortured in France resulting in many executions. And it was in France that Joan of Arc was burned at the stake for heresy by the English in 1431.

In 1542, Pope Paul 111 created the *Supreme Sacred Congregation of the Roman and Universal Inquisition* to combat Protestant heresy. It put Galileo on trial in 1633. In 1545, a list of European books considered heretical and forbidden in Spain, was published based on Rome's Index *Librorum Prohibitorum*. In 1556, Phillip II took the Spanish throne having taken the Roman Inquisition to the Netherlands to persecute Lutherans. In the sixteenth century the Inquisition expanded into the Americas burning Lutherans and Protestants and the indigenous population. In 1580, Spain and Portugal were both under the Spanish crown; Jews that had fled Spain for Portugal were now rounded up and executed. Phillip renewed the persecution of the Moors and many were sold into slavery. Under Philip III, Muslim uprisings were severely dealt with and Muslims who had converted to Catholicism were banished. *We are right and you are wrong. Not only that, but our way of dealing with your wrongness is to torture and burn you.*

Of course, we are horrified by the thought of such an illiberal society, until we pause to reflect on the new puritanism of a *woke,* cancel and counter cultural generation. There is violence and exclusion in some of our universities, but of course nothing like the times of the Inquisition. Jobs, careers and invitees to speak might be at stake, but we can be grateful that no physical violence or torture is involved. But where conversion or adherence to strong causes morphs into ideologies built on a dogmatic certainty which judges others to be wrong, then we have a serious moral problem.

In 1808, Napoleon ordered the Inquisition to be abolished, but after his defeat in 1815, there were attempts at reinstating it. The last person to be executed by it was a Spanish schoolmaster charged with heresy in 1826. The *Sacred Congregation of the Roman and Universal Inquisition* still exists under the name *Congregation for the Doctrine of the Faith*. And I have known at least two Catholic priests who have suffered at its hands by their books being condemned and banned and their ministry declared illegal.

# CHAPTER SEVEN

## 7  SACRAMENT OF THE LEAVEN AND THE WHOLE LUMP

*The Purpose of the Eucharist lies not in the change of the bread and wine, but in the partaking of Christ, who has become our food, our life, the manifestation of the Church as the body of Christ. This is why the gifts themselves never became, in the Orthodox East, an object of special reverence, contemplation, and adoration, and likewise an object of special theological 'problematics': how, when, in what manner their change is accomplished.* Alexander Schmemann[64]

Many Christians in Britain today seem to think Christianity began just a few centuries ago, and probably in England with the Church of England! Of course, they don't think that, when they stop to think about it, but that is the way they often seem to accept what they have been given or know as normative, even if it is a kind of worship that no one would have recognized a few centuries ago, let alone in the early era of the Christian churches. I remember several conversations with strong minded church goers who said they hated the new service (this was back in the 1970s and 80s) and would rather have the "old". When I said I entirely agreed with them and courteously asked whether they would prefer the liturgies of Saint John Chrysostom, James or Basil, or even something earlier, I received the looks I deserved.

When I explained that the 1662 Book of Common Prayer, the one they thought of as being the "old one" had followed various, previous versions and, in its time, was controversially new and different, not least because it was translated into English (beautiful English to our ears), they began to see what I meant. When I pointed out various words and asked them what they meant, e.g. "whose property is always to have mercy" they thought they knew, until they paused to think about it. This was a good example of how easy it is to internalize beautiful worship language without always knowing or needing to know what it meant. When I hinted that the "old" service had come from a complicated combination of Catholic and new

---

[64] *The Eucharist; Sacrament of the Kingdom*

Protestant teaching and was meant to be a helpful, new compromise, they began to see my point. What was once radically new, easily becomes the next generation's "tradition" that they will defend against anything new! And when I said, that the Bible hadn't first of all been written in English or even Latin, and that there were now hundreds of translations, and that, over the centuries, there were different versions copied and…. I think they began to see more of what I meant. But this of course left me feeling like a pedant, who had used his little knowledge for the wrong reasons!

Behind the early, formal developments in different parts of the Christian world, we can glimpse and surmise something of the liturgy of the first churches that appeared before special buildings were built or adapted, and before the form of worship was standardized and codified. We know that before Christianity, Judaism and Greek/Roman religion included the sacrifice of animals to the gods. There were also certain festival meals that had religious significance. Christian worship replaced animal sacrifice with a belief in Christ as victim and priest, according to the book of Hebrews. But this was only one, albeit dominant strand, in the way beliefs about Christ were incarnated in Christian worship. Later Judaism, after the destruction of the Temple, has been left with ambivalent feelings about whether animal sacrifice should ever be introduced again, if the Temple should ever be built again. It's clear that the idea of "sacrifice", whether inherited from Judaism and/or Greek and Roman practise (and before that earlier religious beliefs), was a dominant theme in how humans believed they needed to placate the gods. The early Christians were clear that something new had happened in Christ which made the old covenant of blood sacrifice redundant. 1 Corinthians 5 includes these verses,

*Your boasting is not good. Do you not know that a little leaven leavens the whole lump? [7] Cleanse out the old leaven that you may be a new lump, as you really are unleavened. For Christ, our paschal lamb, has been sacrificed. [8] Let us, therefore, celebrate the festival, not with the old leaven, the leaven of malice and evil, but with the unleavened bread of sincerity and truth.*

The idea of Christ as the Paschal lamb certainly comes from

the Passover tradition that was so important for Judaism at that time. These words (and to some extent the assumptions behind them) still resonate in twenty first worship today where, at Easter time, we can hear the phrase "Christ has been sacrificed for us therefore let us keep the feast". The Eucharist, with its likely reference points in the Passover meal (though some scholars dispute whether the Last Supper was that) became the centre of Christian worship from the earliest times, certainly by the time Paul wrote

*The Lord Jesus, on the night he was betrayed, took bread, and when he had given thanks, he broke it and said, 'This is my body, which is for you; do this in remembrance of me.' In the same way, after supper he took the cup, saying, 'This cup is the new covenant in my blood; do this, whenever you drink it, in remembrance of me. 1 Corinthians 11:24–26.*

We find similar words recorded in Mathew 26. 26-28, Mark 14. 22–24.

Luke 22. 19–20. There were also Agape friendship meals, as if between Christian friends, sometimes associated with the Eucharist, although according to Jude 1:12, this was confusing enough to cause some divisions, leading to the clearer separation of the two. In 1 Corinthians 11, we find Paul describing the tradition of the words used at the Last Supper, but in the following context and after this passage.

[17] *In the following directives I have no praise for you, for your meetings do more harm than good.* [18] *In the first place, I hear that when you come together as a church, there are divisions among you, and to some extent I believe it.* [19] *No doubt there have to be differences among you to show which of you have God's approval.* [20] *So then, when you come together, it is not the Lord's Supper you eat,* [21] *for when you are eating, some of you go ahead with your own private suppers. As a result, one person remains hungry and another gets drunk.* [22] *Don't you have homes to eat and drink in? Or do you despise the church of God by humiliating those who have nothing? What shall I say to you? Shall I praise you? Certainly not in this matter!*

Acts 2 gives a vivid description of the "breaking of bread" sharing that happened in the Temple courts soon after Pentecost. At first sight that might seem an unexpected choice of location for their meetings, although it's fairly clear that the Eucharist only happened in their homes.

*42 They devoted themselves to the apostles' teaching and to fellowship, to the breaking of bread and to prayer. 43 Everyone was filled with awe at the many wonders and signs performed by the apostles. 44 All the believers were together and had everything in common.45 They sold property and possessions to give to anyone who had need. 46 Every day they continued to meet together in the temple courts. They broke bread in their homes and ate together with glad and sincere hearts,47 praising God and enjoying the favour of all the people. And the Lord added to their number daily those who were being saved.*

It is hard to know what this inspiring description of an early Christian Eucharistic experience must have felt like for those present, or, later, those hearing or reading about it. Perhaps this quality of sharing was inspired by some crisis or general need of mutual aid. Perhaps, it was inspired from without, as well as within their Christian faith. Perhaps, it was its own form of Liturgy as used in the more maximal sense which we will explore later. Perhaps, its true meaning was Liturgy in action. As I write this, I'm thinking about a radio 4 programme on food related issues in the Ukraine, and for those hundreds of thousands, now more than a million displaced people, refuges on the road away from their homes and bombed out cities, moving for safety into adjacent countries or indeed already having arrived there. Apparently, there is a bakery in one of the main cities of the Ukraine which has either been destroyed or is just closed because of danger and curfews. The baker now bakes from his own kitchen. People bring him what yeast or flour they might have left, and he turns this into bread which is then distributed by volunteers. What better example could there be of the meaning of that Acts passage. What's more, it is focused in that wonderful but simple food, "Bread"! We are told "they broke bread in their homes", and we know the early church distributed that bread amongst those gathered, and that it was also taken by deacons to those in need. This bread this baker in the Ukraine makes is taken down by volunteers into the basements, where there is little or no food and, somehow, to those homes which haven't as yet been destroyed, but where vulnerable people, particularly the disabled and elderly, are trapped without water, without food, without heat or electricity. Some are even breaking into their radiators to try and get some water for their daily needs.

And in the refugee camps and centres close to the border in Poland, Romania, Slovakia, Hungary, volunteers in their thousands are joining the agencies trying to help those who have arrived after days of hard and frustrating travel in cold weather, day and night, often without shelter or easy transport and without food. And somehow, because of the humanity of their human nature, volunteers, willing to reach out across borders when help is needed, are rushing to donate clothing, food, medicines and the basics of life even shelter in their own homes to these hundreds of thousands of precious individuals and their children. And, like all refugees, they are only bringing with them what they can carry or transport in small suitcases and bundles, which have probably been packed in a hurry. And what would any of us choose to take if we were faced with that crisis situation? And some have walked for many miles and for days on end. Families have been separated. The wife or mother or sister or daughter has had to say goodbye to husbands, sons, brothers and fathers because the men are required to return back to their cities and homes to fight. And which of us can bear the thought of that separation, for that reason, the implication being that no one knows whether they will ever see each other again, let alone whether they will ever return to their homes. We aren't given the details but we know there were times of hunger and war and crisis in the Roman Empire when those Christians gathered together. *All the believers were together and had everything in common. They sold property and possessions to give to anyone who had need.*

They did it then, and they are doing it now, in the most appalling and inhumane of situations, and all because the Russian President wants to expand his power, his territory, or, as he puts it, to reach out to his people, his cousins and neighbours, by shelling their cities, even though he says he isn't, and is telling the Russian people that these are just military exercises not a war, and even though he has put his battlefield nuclear weapons on alert on the basis of a possible threat from NATO countries which would never have been a threat if he hadn't invaded Ukraine in the first place. But this is the

Ukraine, the BREAD basket of the world[65]. Already, because of the destruction and sieges, ship loads and lorry loads of grain are not getting to their destinations in Africa and even in China. And because of that lack of supply, prices are going up, and because of that, more people will be going hungry, and because of that, who knows what will follow in terms of protest or even riots, and certainly greater global instability.

And meanwhile, in Poland, despite historic tensions with the Ukraine, people are *sacrificially sharing their bread*, that most basic of foods as a sacrament of their generosity and concern. And that generosity is springing from a place which seems to be natural to human beings when faced with a crisis, natural at least to many, human beings. And all around the world, or most of it, people are giving of their time and money and energy, bringing material things which express the care, concern, anxieties and empathy they feel for the people of the Ukraine. Suddenly, those material things take on an extra dimension – which hints at, or even reveals the sacramental meaning of the Liturgy of the World in praxis – for they carry something profoundly spiritual with theological significance. They carry an expression of love moving in the direction of the other, which surely reflects what we believe about the nature of God's love shown in the incarnation. God's love may be, transcendent of our human expressions of love, but as we reach out to other others, we are surely expressing something of the nature of that *image and likeness* embedded within us. We are bringing it to the surface of its nature and meaning, as it moves in the direction of the need of other others.

*Bread, the breaking of bread, and then the sharing of bread and the holding of every thing in common.* This is at the heart of the foundational sacrament for the sake of others in the Liturgy of the Church, and surely in the Liturgy of the World, albeit in a different way, but still carrying a special meaning. We find it in the Acts of the Apostles, and

---

[65] And the Nazis, knowing this, had a plan to starve the Ukraine. Now it seems the Russians are following in their footsteps while Putin calls those who are fighting to defend the Ukraine, including their Jewish President, neo-nazi nationalists and terrorists.

we find examples of it in unexpected places in the human heart and behaviour everywhere. We found it at the height of the Covid pandemic, as people discovered and responded to their neighbour's need in new ways. And now we find it in the worst of humanitarian disasters in Europe since Bosnia and WW2.

We are lucky to have this cameo picture of the early Church, given to us by Luke in Acts. It may only be a cameo, and the context which made this possible was soon to change, but the spirit of this sharing has lasted through time in the Liturgy of time, as through the ages, people, some people, perhaps even most people, have spontaneously given of the little they have for the needs of those who have even less. And it is usually the poor who are the most generous, as Jesus pointed out when the widow who had little, gave much to the Temple treasury (Luke 21. 1-4). And there, in the midst of all those who give generously, is the Christ presence reflected and represented in acts of generosity responding to the needs of other others. Inner feelings and beliefs manifest themselves in outer action as examples of the meaning of sacrament and Liturgy inside-out. And with less media coverage, and on a smaller street and community level, this is happening every day in our Food Banks and other projects and programmes of humanitarian aid in response to other's survival and development needs. This morning, over coffee after Sunday worship, I was talking to a couple who had done extra shifts all week in the local, Food Bank, because several volunteers had been off sick. There wasn't a hint of complaint about the personal cost of giving up a week to do this. And then on Monday, the first day of that week, I went to a local warehouse where twenty or more volunteers were helping to pack up palette loads of goods, enough to fill two large trucks to be driven to Poland to help the needs of the hundreds of thousands of Ukrainian refugees. I knew this was happening up and down the country. The strange thing is that in giving we receive, and in giving to and for others, there is a certain joy and liberation and fulfilment. And sometimes, despite the work involved in giving, we are less tired than we thought we would be. Perhaps love fills itself up as it gives itself away! A lesson from both the Liturgy of the Church and the Liturgy of the World.

In the *Acts* passage, gone are the references to sacrifice in the traditional sense of animals having their throats cut being thrown onto the fire. These are replaced by the idea of self-giving inspired by the sacrifice of Christ. The Eucharist is a non-bloody, non-burnt, offering/anamnesis of Christ's sacrifice on the cross, where indeed blood was shed. Sacramental theology of the Eucharist has struggled ever since to find ways of talking about that sacrifice, without using the framework of Temple sacrifice, or the efficacy of physical blood shedding as a religious act which changes the covenant relationship with God or vice versa. There have been many attempts through history to interpret the idea of blood being shed as the outpouring of life itself. For many non-Christians, and some Christians, now as then, a crude use of the words of institution could indeed look like a religious rite of sacrificial cannibalism, through its language of eating flesh and drinking blood. In the *Acts* passage, our attention is focused elsewhere. The breaking of bread is associated with a time and situation where material possessions were held and shared in common. It's as if something central in the worship overspills into something that affects daily life in the most basic of ways. Is this a hint already about the meaning of "Liturgy" that was later to be brought into Christian worship?

But very soon the Temple would be destroyed along with much of the city. In the terror and horror of that event, many Rabbis and priests were scattered to the area around Galilee and further beyond, particularly after the siege of Masada in 73-74 A.D.[66] The time of active persecution of Christians was to follow quite soon in the next century, and we have records of those days of horror in the Roman world. In that context, it was natural that the early Christians,

---

[66] where, according to Flavius Josephus at least, a group of Jews committed suicide rather than be conquered by the Roman legions camped at the bottom of that mountain where they built a huge ramp to get to the top. Every Israeli schoolboy and soldier is taught that story, but the archaeological evidence is challengingly uncertain, though the atmosphere at the top and the views are stunning. The evidence for the Roman ramp and the camps at the bottom of the mountain is still there.

certainly in Rome, met for worship and support in the catacombs or other secret places.

The Eucharistic meal was a simple and frugal meal and that was surely part of its genius. We can imagine it celebrated around a simple table in private houses to escape from it being seen as a public act, challenging the laws on public religion. Anyone who has taken part in a house communion will know how moving and intimate an experience that can be, with an atmosphere quite different to that in a large church building. And it was from within that domestic atmosphere that the first Eucharistic experiences took place from the time of the Emmaus Rd "breaking of bread" recognition of the risen Christ onwards. Perhaps that scene was written out of such experiences. As Eucharistic worship developed, and particularly in the fourth century as it moved more into public places and larger buildings, an inevitable change took place in the style as well as the content of the Liturgy.

A wise and experienced priest friend of mine, who has studied many ancient documents said the following about worship in that early period, as far as I can remember the words he used. They were something like this.

- *Originally, religious ceremonies included, or were centred on, rituals of offering to the gods. It took two or more centuries for the Eucharist to close in on itself. Prior to that, it had external reference points, and fitted into a culture of offering the collectivity of the action which creates the presence of Christ. So perhaps it was a natural move from public works into Eucharist, because that which was on the table came from outside. The bringing in and eating together, is given a form of anamnesis to commemorate outwardly a sense of being incorporated into Christ, the giver of the feast. This was based on the Jewish notion that the presiding figure of a celebratory meal is the giver of the meal; in him, from him, the bounty flows. The closing in, is to reference that which is outside. The deacons take the substance of the meal outside of the gathered group. The substance brought in is inhabited as gift and then taken out to those in bodily and spiritual need. So the gathering is a focusing in, in order to go out in dispersal to take the body of Christ. The codification of this takes a while, and, then, eventually the content of the liturgies are closed back down in on themselves, except for what remains of the reference at the end to going out. How can we see what is consecrated in what is not? The true sacrament is in everything here, all the food and all the people.*

During those first three or four centuries, there was only slowly appearing a fixed form of Liturgical worship. In the process of evolving, it was clear that the words used were an expression of what was happening to doctrinal beliefs at the same time. In fact, the one became an articulation of the other. Now, in our times, we are using what we have inherited and disputed about the meaning of those beliefs as they appear in the different kinds of worship service we use. The basic structure of the Eucharist (for those who use a structure) has stayed basically the same in all denominations, however much the language in parts has changed and its meaning been debated. But it is possible that, over time, the reference points of that language have changed or even lost their immediacy.

There are aspects of early Eucharistic theology which made assumptions we might find difficult to understand in our times. For example, it was possible for the Catholic Church to develop its doctrine of transubstantiation of the "elements" because it was drawing on an Aristotelian view of the relationships between substance and accidents. That would have been viewed as a natural reference point in order to express the theological significance of what happened to the bread and the wine in the Eucharist. Today, some Anglo-Catholic churches still use the phrase, *may the Lord accept this sacrifice at your hands.* That clearly references back an ancient idea of sacrifice achieved by the "hands" and actions of the priest. It is sometimes defended as really being about the final sacrifice of our Lord on the cross not a reference back to animal sacrifice. Yet the phrase "at your hands" has survived and clearly refers to what the priest is doing, not what Christ did on the cross. Surely, the priest cannot "sacrifice" in the way Christ did, nor by the use of those words pretend any sacrifice offered *at his hands or by his hands* can in any way equate with or even represent the sacrifice made by Christ once for all. It is easy for the symbolism of word and action in the Eucharist to slip away from the anchor of original usage or reference points, in ways that no longer carry the same meaning. So, symbols and the way they are understood are clearly significant in the way we understand the Liturgy of the Church and the Liturgy of the World.

SYMBOLS

One of the insights to be found in the arts world, over at least the last few centuries, is a rediscovery of the place and meaning of symbols, that used to be more commonplace in the classical world. We know, from the Renaissance and in some classical art from Greek and Roman times, (if not before, right back to cave paintings), that symbolic objects appear in their artistic work on the assumption that onlookers would understand their significance and reference points. Thus, certain flowers, like lilies, could stand for virginity, a skull for mortality and so on. One could say that portraits are symbolic of a real person in their own right, however they are painted. Even by the best and most realistic of portrait painters, what they paint is only a symbolic representation of the sitter. When we look at a painting it isn't the person or object painted. There are many ways through which the same person or object can be painted and then seen. But there is a connection, a symbolic one, between what is painted and what it represents to us, the onlookers, the recipients of its impact and message.

The great historical paintings of the Renaissance weren't just examples of technical achievement. They were storytelling, symbolic lessons from the past about how to understand, and then live this difficult, demanding life in the present. They were meant to inspire new thoughts and new ways of living in this world, to increase our understanding of its dilemmas and tragedies. They carried their own liturgy of life's tragedies and ideas, spiritual and moral ideals on which civilisation could be built and developed. They brought to the surface hints carried by ancient myths in stories of great events and the lives of historic figures, representing archItypes of emotional and psychological experience in narratives of the human condition. And it was from out of the dark days of the Reformation and religious tensions in Britain and Europe that the Enlightenment artists and the well-off did their Great Tours, amazed by the classical art of Italy. They borrowed its reference points, the way light was used for symbolic effect, the carefully observed and copied detail not just to decorate their art and architecture, but to add a new dimension to their vision of how to live the good life.

There are so many ways in which the themes and imprints of the Liturgy of the World embraced and informed themselves by the learning and discoveries of public culture, as a vehicle and expression of public values. And although, as ordinary people, we live out our limited perception of wider horizons without always appreciating their historical significance, as we look back, we see more clearly evolving and changing themes on a larger canvas of intellectual experience; themes which changed outlooks and assumptions of our ordinary lives. Public art was always a mirror into public culture providing subtle or overt hints as to what really matters in public values. The mirror seemed capable of refocusing ordinary and extraordinary things hidden within the great tales of old or the apparently ephemeral details of daily, domestic life. Great portraiture taught us to look again at the appearance of human faces to catch something deeper about the life lived. With or without added physical symbols of that life to represent something memorable and significant, the very portrayal and representation of the person could be a symbolic reminder of the shifting relationships between appearance and reality, essence and character and likeness.

With Liturgy, we are delving into the territory of symbolism through our contemporary understanding, or not, of what that might mean, both in symbolic words and symbolic actions. Both words and actions in themselves could be said to have symbolic meaning in the sense that a painting does. The word and the action re-enact and re-present meaning and reflect something of the reality in the process. In ancient usage, they became the meaning. They didn't just stand for it, on its behalf, like hieroglyphs or road signs might. For example, a sign for a person crossing a road with a stick stands for an old peoples' home in the vicinity. It communicates straight away the reason for the sign to be there, but it is nothing like the reality. We are used to such symbols as signs to represent something else. They trigger the communication of the meaning without having, or partaking in, the nature of the thing being symbolized. They only stand for it, re-present it, depict or describe its presence, as if they were neutral outsiders serving only to provide information about it, or point us in the direction of the real thing. Such symbols don't even need to look like it in any literal sense. They are separate from it, but serve the purpose of symbolizing it, as, for example, in chemical formulae and musical notes. An object can also, with popular usage, becomes a symbol for an abstract idea. For example, the shape of a heart can stand for love. Although looking nothing like the thing depicted, a symbol can take on an association with an abstract idea, or another material thing. Sometimes it's enough for a symbol to depict a part of a thing, a recognizable aspect of a thing, for it to conjure or represent the thing in its totality.

Then there are certain kinds of symbols which take on, as far as is possible, the shape or look of a thing. They try to reproduce more of its presence as their way of bringing it to mind. And then, even further along this continuum, we come to another form of symbolic presence. This is when something looks as much like the thing depicted as possible, whether in sculpture or paint, without actually being it. The point is that it can never actually be "it" even when it reproduces it, or rather its appearance almost exactly.

We might also say that all words used, in any language, are symbols of the thing itself. The word "finger" is not an actual finger, but it serves its purpose well, that of communicating through sound what we are talking about and what we mean by a "finger". In fact, our brains have developed so that they hear words almost as if they are the thing in itself, because they translate the impact of that word in ways that seem to conjure its reality. As soon as we hear the word finger, our relationship to its meaning is perhaps more "direct" than a visual symbol of a finger might be. Early languages developed as proto-literate symbols by attempting to draw or depict the shape of a thing, in hieroglyphs ("holy writing' in the Greek translation of the Egyptian word) and pictograms for example. As language developed[67], the symbols or characters being used replaced pictures. They represented sounds which made up many different words, and in

---

[67] Possibly under the influence of Sumerian useage.

certain words came to be associated with the thing described. A finger no longer had to be a symbolic drawing of an actual finger, but a word made up of sounds which, joined together, became a language symbol for the finger. We have become so used to the way this happens, in our own language, that it is a surprise to have to learn different sounds making up different words for the same thing in another language. We are so used to our own language that we associate the sound symbol for the word finger as almost being the same thing as the finger itself and this is true in most if not all languages.

And then there is Liturgy, where we believe, at least in its maximal sense, that the words and actions and objects used, take us into the reality of the thing itself. They represent it in the sense of re-presenting the thing in its ontological self. What happened once is happening again in our re-presenting of it, our making memorial of it, our receiving of its meaning into our hearts and minds and lives. It lives again through us and in us. The words and the action take us into the meaning of the words and the actions, in so far as we choose to enter into that meaning. And this is an important point. The words and actions have a kind of ontological meaning that exists in their own way, because they are part of Liturgy, but they are still dependent on our epistemological and psychological perception of that meaning, which will vary from human to human, in different times and places. Perceptions are, after all, changing according to changing assumptions or worldviews, in the beliefs and ideas which influence them. They also change because of certain experiences and how we've perceived and understood them.

Ontologically speaking, the words and actions of Liturgy become again, take on the meaning again, of what they represent, as if this is what they are, what they stand for and re-present to us, and for us, and in us. But our level and type of experience of them depends on what we bring to the encounter, and to what extent we are willing for it to be a dynamic and living encounter which gives the ontology of a thing the chance of being what it is, in our perception and experience of it. And our perception is influenced by our cognitive knowledge of a thing, and how we understand its meaning in relation to other things. Perception precedes experience, but is influenced and changed by experience. We need a certain level of conscious, active cognition to analyse and understand experience. But, unless we block it, new experiences can change our perception, as we seek to understand their implications for our understanding of the world.

We know a good deal now about the processes involved, both of perception and the way our brains order experiences both passively and actively. There is mystery still in the relationship between the two, and the way in which memory remembers an experience in order to make later sense of it, as part of the changing continuum of perception. Sometimes, it is not the experience we are remembering, but subsequent memories of its affects and associations, particularly in the way we perceive new experiences.

And when we come to talk about formative experiences, we may well resort to images, or metaphors, and analogies, to capture what is hard to articulate or describe. Prophets like Isaiah and the writers of the psalms did this all the time. Some of the experiences they attempted to describe needed such metaphorical language in order to do justice to the nature of the experience, or the nature of what it symbolized for them in their perception of it, and its affects or implications. And we still use their language, their attempts to remind us of the nature of religious experience often hidden in plain sight within the ordinary things of life, which then take on extra layers of meaning. We think that all this and more is involved in how Liturgy "works".

And some artists are used to working in this way, using physical material to symbolize something that they perceive to be embedded within it or something that is totally different from it. And some of this is true of the mystery of daily life, as we handle and experience ordinary things in nature, or the transformation of nature into something else. In the history of art, we have been reminded that ordinary everyday things have their own intrinsic value; a value that would be easier to take seriously if we showed them in an art gallery setting, rather than when they are seen or used in a bathroom or kitchen! This was particularly true in Flemish art. As demand increased for pictures in the home, the fashion turned from great historical and narrative art to depictions of everyday objects and scenes. For there, in the manufacture of anything, a moment when the useful is also perceived to be beautiful or appealing. We want to pick it up and touch and handle it, not just because of its utility for this or that function, but because there is an aesthetic pleasure in doing so. But there, somewhere between aesthetics and utility, are all the ethical questions which are also spiritual questions. And there, in the nature of things and their ordering and use, we sometimes discover a spiritual experience in the relationship between who we are, what the object being used is like, what the purpose of the use entails, and how this affects our surroundings or others in creation. As in art, so in Inside-Out Liturgy, a symbol can bring this to mind and bring the presence of the thing symbolized into our horizon of perception and understanding. In so doing, it can enlarge our horizon of interest and concern to the point that no things are perceived any more as having no value or significance.

So, we confront the issue of meaning in the territory of symbolism and the arts. And this is nuanced and difficult territory in our contemporary culture, which differs from more ancient times. But we are used to the idea that one thing can symbolically represent another, in advertising as well as in the arts. As we have seen, sometimes it does this by looking or being like the reality symbolised. A dynamic connection is made which involves us and immerses us in its significance. At other times, it needn't look anything like the thing symbolized, but be used only as a representative symbol for it, as with characters in words and in language itself, in all its different ways of representing a thing[68]. And

---

[68] Putin has proved, time and time again, how seriously they take the power of language. Recent laws, rushed through their system, criminalised the use of the word "war" to describe the war in the Ukraine. However, it seems they do not believe that language can have objective meaning in its use and application. When it comes to the penal codes, they use them to their own purposes, unrelated to any objective meaning of the language used. Putin himself is something of a master of misrepresentation and obfuscation. He commonly uses the word "certain" as in certain circumstances, certain persons, certain forces, to imply that he knows the

this can be as obvious in quite a literal of direct way, or it is conjured by poetic and other imagery which require us to understand the oblique references or metaphors.

With Liturgy all that can be true, but more might be involved. So, a cross can symbolise the suffering and salvation of Jesus. A Gospel book may represent the Word of Life as recorded in the words and actions of those involved. And a Liturgical movement or action can deliver a meaning based on the idea that its themes are entwined within the realities represented, just as liturgical time entwines itself through the meaning of ordinary time. So, for example, the festival of Christmas brings the meaning of the incarnation into the days it covers. The calendar says for example, December 24 and 25th, but the Liturgical time of Christmas brings the hope of the incarnation into the reality of that ordinary time, to make it special time, based on the belief that mirrors the image of God as a reality becoming Emmanuel. The belief remains a belief, but it claims its meaning, as expressed in the theme of its liturgical time, can be accessed through ordinary time for those willing to share in that belief.

So, for example, when the couple move three times around the altar wearing their crowns in the Orthodox marriage service, this is not just religious theatre. It is believed they are participating symbolically in something that has ontological significance for them and for those present. The symbolic meaning of the movement and the crowns becomes real meaning, because its nature enters and expresses something intrinsic to and about the nature of reality, as transformed by and symbolized in the liturgical event.

To those who don't share this belief in the incarnation any such symbolic links will sound tenuous at best, but at worse incredulous and irrelevant. That of course limits the claim made for the ontological nature and significance of what is symbolised. This is clearly complicated and perhaps even confusing theology. It comes from ideas and worldviews that themselves depend on the radical nature of a belief in the incarnation. This creates a view of the <u>ontology of the nature of things in themselves as being shot through</u>

details but doesn't want to reveal anything of their detail or meaning.

with this meaning, however opaquely, and to the presence of its implications for real life, real time and place, though not confined by that, even as it expresses implications for all time and all place and all people. But, because of the nature of the incarnation as an emanation of the nature of God in human form, then none of this is imposed on the nature of reality, because its purpose, its ways and its nature is love. There is no imposition, but that doesn't mean there is no presence and therefore no symbols of that presence, as worked out in different parts of Liturgy of the Church as it has meaning for the Liturgy of the World and vice versa.

# CHAPTER EIGHT

## 8    HOW THEN SHALL WE PUT IT, TO DESCRIBE IT?

*In the radiance of His light the world is not commonplace. The very floor we stand on is a miracle of atoms whizzing about in space. The darkness of sin is clarified, and its burden shouldered. Death is robbed of its finality, trampled down by Christ's death. In a world where everything that seems to be present is immediately past, everything in Christ is able to participate in the eternal present of God.* Alexander Schmemann,

These words hint at some of the ways contemporary physics might want to talk about the world in a way that past science couldn't. They remind us that, although we still lean on the mechanics of earlier physics – for example Isaac Newton's equations for gravity[69] - contemporary science is discovering how much more complicated the nature of reality really is. In speaking about the Liturgy of the World, we have to be talking about the world as we now understand it, rather than as it was understood in the past. Contemporary physics has reminded us that time isn't as easy to understand as we thought, as is also the case with gravity. At one level, these things are, or appear to be, straightforward and within the bounds of common sense. Time is a measure of the movement going forward. But through what and into what? Why does it change according to the position of the measurement taken, and our perception of it? Does it even exist in its own right, separate from context and perception or ideas about it? Of course it does, doesn't it? That's why I wear a watch, and when it is set correctly according to my time zone, it tells me what time time now is.

Gravity is surely a force acting on the weight of things which brings them down to earth. The closer the two objects the greater the force. The further away the less strong the force. Despite being a weak force, gravity could be a cosmologically significant, attractive force, but it could also rip things apart. The pull of the earth was enough to deform the moon's surface. And all this was eventually

---

[69] Not least in NASA's calculations about using the mass of the earth of the moon or the planets to generate sling shot energy in space flight.

well known, calculated, and set down in equations which told us everything we needed to know about the forces involved. At another level, it is much more complex and counter common sense. Einstein's great discovery was that according to his theory of relativity, all matter bends, including space. And matter bends space. Planets and galaxies bend and curve the very fabric of the universe. Curved space-time is created by the huge mass of a star. So, does time move along straight-lined paths within the curved paths of space time? According to Relativity, everything is "falling" through space-time created by matter.

Even Einstein himself struggled with the implications of his theory of General Relativity. It seemed to suggest that the universe is stretching out or shrinking down, over time, rather than standing still. If the Universe is expanding from what it used to be, it might have logically had some kind of a beginning, so the Big Bang theory made more sense than eternal, steady state[70]. But this was a shocking possibility – that the Universe had a beginning and origin somewhere or somewhen[71]. The other shock was that gravity could squash something so small that even light couldn't escape from it. So, a black hole can be small but massively dense, and exist for example at the centre of our Milky Way galaxy. They can be tiny or massive, particularly a stellar mass type black hole, producing an extreme example of warped space-time. The more mass is compacted into a small space, the more it can curve space. They can curve space-time so much that not even light can escape. Other scientists found this to be an absurd claim to make, but then a photo was taken of a black hole, at the centre of M87[72]. It was about six billion times the mass of the sun. It was predicted by Einstein's theory to exist, but only recently seen.

---

[70] And so was eventually proved not least by the Hubble measurements of the speed at which the space of the universe was expanding, in all directions.

[71] Certainly, too shocking in its philosophical implications for scientists like the astronomer, Sir Fred Hoyle (1915-2001).

[72] A galaxy 53 million light years from earth discovered in 1781 by the astronomer Charles Messier

But what does it mean when we say space and time are linked together, or that together they can be curved, and that this, in some way, not only affects gravity, but is gravity? And if it doesn't look or sound like common sense, how can it be true, if that truth seems to deny common sense observation or experience? And if those things still seem to work in human experience, doesn't that mean they can be true at the same time as the most recent science can be true, even though it's based on different, sometimes contradictory ideas and observation. To talk then of "normal" experiences of "normal" life might be misleading and unwise. Perhaps normal life and our experiences within it, are much more complicated. In which case, any understanding of Liturgy in the "normal" experience of the world has to be much more complicated, if it is do justice to the truth of things as we understand them now, not least scientifically. And, so, we dare not assume any experience of life is simply normal, in any simplistic sense, even while, at the same time, we talk about it in that way, and even experience it in that way. Both might be true at the same time. In which case, liturgy has to weave in and out of contradictory ways of experiencing things. It has to be capacious enough for it to "work" in contradictory or complementary experiences of the world. It can be experienced through our common-sense observations and our scientific calculations even when they conflict with each other.

What then does it mean to say - in *a world where everything that seems to be present is immediately past, everything in Christ is able to participate in the eternal present of God?* What kind of underlying view of time is involved in this kind of belief statement? How does it affect our understanding of time, particularly if we are to talk of participating in eternity, as well as a world where everything that seems to be present is immediately past? Past, but not lost, because the memory capacity of our brains is able to bend time in the way of its own operation, to make it appear that the things remembered are brought into the present by the way we experience our memories of them. And if this is true, do our speculations about the near or distant future make any difference, if by thinking about them our brain brings them into the present?

What then is the spiritual dimension of what we are learning about time and gravity from the latest wonderful and quite beautiful, if disturbing and confusing, science? At the very least, doesn't it demonstrate that the world we take for granted, in its "normality", is both normal and works quite normally on the one hand, and, on the other, something totally surprising and highly complex. For it seems at the quantum level that there is still much we don't understand, just cosmology involves so much more than we ever thought. And if we are to talk about the Liturgy of the World meaningfully, then our understanding of how Liturgy "works" within the cosmos and the nature of this planet, has to be just as surprisingly subtle and nuanced, just as unexpected, as well as, just as taken for granted. It has to "work" within what we know from experience about normal daily life, and what we don't know from experience, or, what, from experience, we know that we can't know. And although equations may be brilliant at revealing and predicting the range of what happens within normal, cosmological reality, on a daily, normal basis, and, although they may be experienced by those who understand them as beautiful and elegant in the way they collect our knowledge of those things, they also have to be capacious enough to reveal what we don't know, and indeed what cannot be known. And they have to be able to contain contradictory things at the same time as both being true, or part of the same truth. And ideally, if that is an appropriate word to use here, they have to be able to do justice to our experience based on common sense, and our experience based on counter-intuitive, unlikely and contradictory facts about our common-sense experience, all at the same time.

The early mystical writers of the church interpreted much in the Bible, and in Liturgy, allegorically, certainly much more than we do today. They would not have understood a literalist interpretation, and certainly not employed it in the way many new Christian movements do today. They would probably have been more able at understanding, and reflecting on the richer, deeper levels of meaning in Bible passages and their implications, and also in parts of the Liturgy and its implications than we manage today. It would have come more naturally to them, because of the way their beliefs about it, influenced their perception of it. It was their starting assumption that the meaning of heavenly or divine things had been enfleshed in ordinary, earthy things in the writings of scripture and in the ways of the Spirit. And so, in their writings about those meanings, they saw it as their task to unpack, unveil, explore, discover and rediscover the divine meaning hidden within the words and stories found in those texts and in the world around them. They assumed that the language used had mostly been given allegorically and metaphorically to convey something deeper and more significant than what appeared on the surface of things.

This happened in the Old Testament a lot, particularly in the prophetic literature and the Psalms. For example, in Psalm 104, we find this kind of language used about creation.

*The Lord wraps himself in light, as with a garment; he stretches out the heavens like a tent and lays the beams of his upper chambers on their waters.*

*He makes the clouds his chariot and rides on the wings of the wind. He makes winds his messengers, flames of fire his servants. He set the earth on its foundations; it can never be moved.*

It is full of wonderful imagery that poetically sets out its own creation theology to explain or rather describe the way nature works. It could not help but include its own assumptions and references to explanations in this description, as we would today. Back then, it was natural to think of this world in terms of its three tiers with water above and below the flat earth. There is no reason why we shouldn't use it as a psalm, without taking the "science" of its explanations literally, let alone as something to be defended against our present understanding of cosmology and nature.

There are many different genres of writing in different books of the Bible and sometimes even within the same Book. Some fit into what we might call wisdom literature, prophetic material, the commandments of the codes of the Law, psalms of praise, chronicled history, and so on. They come from different eras in the history of a people who constantly look back from their present experience, pre-Exile, or post-Exile, to understand more and to interpret and reinterpret what has happened to them. Certain parts of that history dominate their thinking, as for example the experience of being in exile, captivity, slavery and liberation, or the different Covenants made between them and their God with implications for righteous behaviour in following the agreements or "treaties"[73] made with God. Bible passages were, in their own way, metaphoric symbols of something more, something else, something deeper, something heavenly. Beneath their human language they spoke a divine language, at least as far as it could possibly be understood, apprehended, or revealed in human terms. Mostly, that was never fully possible, and they knew that any meaning glimpsed could only be partial, representational, approximate. It helped to approximate ourselves in a closer position of understanding, belief, acceptance and love of God, but this could never be the same as the "thing" in itself, because the nature of this thing involved the nature of the being of God. At the centre of all of this, was the person of Jesus and the words and actions of Jesus, as the human visibility of the divine invisibility. Visible, or more visible, not because of our understanding, but because of God's pre-emptive love for us as evidenced in creation and in the incarnation.

And they knew Jesus himself had spoken in symbols, allegories, metaphors, stories, parables to convey something deeper, or something not as yet understood, or to challenge and surprise, or heal and reconcile us. A story about a thing, a new way of looking at things, left space for more to happen in the interaction between the content of the story and what was not said, or its indirect implications in how that transformed the listener's experience of life at a deeper level. That is why discipleship really was a matter of continual following and learning through layers of misunderstanding and not understanding. Time and time again, the disciples of Jesus, those closest to him that is, those should know most about his meaning, find themselves still being left behind or far away from a real understanding of who he was, and what he really meant. And the

---

[73] Many based on Hittite Treaty models, often sealed with a sacrifice cut in two to symbolize the responsibility of either side to the agreement, the stronger one usually taking most responsibility.

amazing thing is that the writers of the Gospels didn't edit out this rather embarrassing fact about those closest to him. Perhaps they realised this was the path, the journey of discipleship. It was about learning and then a process of removing the prejudicial blocks that prevented a fuller understanding in that learning. Perhaps the misunderstandings of the disciples were not edited out to enhance our understanding of what was really involved, and what was being asked of us, as disciples in every age.

One of the first to realise there was a "mystical" reality to our knowledge of God, a mystical theology in their terms, (because "theology" meant knowledge of God in a relational sense) was a Greek author known as Pseudo-Dionysius. Although he was sometimes associated with Dionysius the Areopagite mentioned by Paul (Acts 17.34) in Athens, he actually lived in the late 5th to early 6th centuries and was thought to come from somewhere in Syria. His writings became more extensively known and translated both in the East and the West. He came to have extensive influence on later mystical theology. He wrote a book (now sadly lost) called *Symbolic Theology* as well as one called *Mystical Theology.* As we look back across time to those early mystics of the church, we find many who taught that we can go deeper into the mystery of God through a kind of prayer that came to be known as the prayer of the heart. Origin, Maximus the Confessor, the Cappadocian theologians, Palamas, St John of the Cross, Julian of Norwich, the author of the *Cloud of Unknowing* are some of the better-known exponents of this. We can read many of the early prayers and advice and commentaries on prayer in a book called *The Philokalia*[74] .The Byzantine church and its inheritors in Orthodox theology have absorbed much in this tradition and made it their own. In Russia, in the nineteenth century *The Way*

---

[74] The Russian text (following an earlier 18th century Greek text) – a translation by Bishop Theophan the Recluse in the 19th century – is a collection of writings from the 4th-14th centuries. First published in English in 1951 Faber and Faber. The Slavonic and Russian versions helped to encourage the rebirth of monasticism in Russia and the use of the Jesus prayer with the recognition of the prayer of the heart as something the "Fathers" called the science of sciences and the art of arts.

*of the Pilgrim* related stories about the *Jesus Prayer* and its way of taking awareness of God down from the mind in to the heart. In the eighteenth century in England, William Law was to write about this in his own way. Two examples will illustrate his approach. The first shorter and the second longer.

*Seek for God in thy heart, and thou wilt never seek in vain, for there he dwells, there is the seat of his light and Holy Spirit. For this turning to the light and Spirit of God within thee is thy only true turning unto God, there is no other easy of finding him, but in that place where he dwelleth in thee. For though God be everywhere present, yet he is only present to thee in the deepest and most central part of thy soul.* From The Spirit of Prayer

The longer passage indicates his belief that a relationship with God is possible in what I am calling the Liturgy of the World, or "the common business of life", as well as the Liturgy of the Church. He thought this sense of God's presence was intrinsically present and accessible through creation and in every human heart through the spirit and in truth.

*The pearl of eternity is the church, or Temple of God within thee, the consecrated place of divine worship where alone thou canst worship God in spirit and in truth. In spirit because thy spirit is that alone in thee which can unite and cleave unto God and receive the workings of his divine Spirit upon thee. In truth because this adoration in spirit is that truth and reality of which all outward forms and rites, though instituted by God are only the figure for a time, but this worship is eternal. Accustom thyself to the holy service of this inward temple. In the midst of it is the fountain of living water, of which thou mayest drink and live for ever. All is done and known in real experience, in a living sensibility of the world of God in the soul. There the birth, the life, the sufferings, the death, the resurrection and ascension of Christ are not merely remembered but inwardly found and enjoyed as the real states of thy soul... When once thou art well grounded in this inward worship, thou wilt have learnt to live unto God above time and place. For every day will be Sunday to thee, and wherever thou goest, thou wilt have a priest, a church, and an altar along with thee. For when God has all that he should have of thy heart, when renouncing the will, judgement, tempers and inclinations of the Old Man, thou art wholly given up to the obedience of the light and spirit of God within thee, to do his holy will, to love only in his love, to be wise only in his wisdom, then it is that every thing thou doest is as a song of praise, and the common business of thy life is a conforming to God's*

*will on earth as Angels do in heaven.*
From *The Spirit of Prayer*

Every day *will be a Sunday to thee* and *every thing thou doest is as a song of praise*! In what Rahner called daily mysticism, William Law reminds us, as did the Benedictine movement that *The common business of thy life is a conforming to God's will!* But with these and other obvious exceptions, it was from Orthodox spirituality that this understanding survived, developed, and was integrated into an understanding of Liturgy and its orientation back into the life of the world.

Vladimir Lossky (1903-58)[75], Alexander Schmemann (1921 – 1983), Nikolai Berdyaev (1874 –1948), Nicolai Bulgakov, Georges Florovsky (1893-1979), and, latterly, Metropolitan Anthony Bloom (1914-2003)[76] and many other notable Orthodox thinkers and their families were emigrees from the changes in Russia after the Revolution who came to Berlin, Prague or Paris (St. Sergius Institute and seminary co-founded by Bulgakov or St. Dionysius Theological Institute) and some (especially Schmemann and Florovsky) then went on to New York (St Vladimir's theological seminary) to teach and write about these things. They had different careers and came from different backgrounds in different parts of Russia, (some from the Crimea and the Ukraine) but shared a commitment to writing and teaching the distinctive contribution of Orthodoxy in the face of new science, political and social change, and the challenge of the Marxism-Leninism embedded in the excesses of the Soviet Union which followed. Many had experienced persecution, exile or

---

[75] *The Mystical Theology of the Eastern Church* 1944

[76] Founder of the Diocese of Sourozh, (referencing the historic episcopal see in Sudak in the Crimea) the Patriarchate of Moscow's diocese for Great Britain and Ireland. I had the great privilege of speaking with him on several occasions and learning from his teaching on prayer and spirituality. He graciously agreed to give a public lecture on "Death" at Newcastle University when I was the chaplain there. His influence went well beyond the Russian speaking congregation of the church in Ennismore Gardens London, which was in the midst of several stages of juridical tensions with the Patriarch of Moscow, not least over certain reforms in the Liturgy, his work with the Anglican church and his openness to non-Orthodox.

imprisonment. It seemed natural for them and most Orthodox theologians, philosophers and some scientists, to assume the context of an all-embracing creation theology, within which the Liturgy of the Church and spirituality could be positioned and expressed, using the apophatic approach to knowledge of God. And, like most, if not all Christian writers and mystics, they spoke of the Love of God in relation to Creation and not just to Jesus. Some insisted on the need to understand the Incarnation within the context of creation and the Word present there from the beginning. Indeed, the opening words of St John's Gospel picks up and references the words about the beginning found in the opening of the book of Genesis.

*In the beginning was the Word, and the Word was with God, and the Word was God. He was with God in the beginning. Through him all things were made; without him nothing was made that has been made. In him was life, and that life was the light of all mankind. The light shines in the darkness, and the darkness has not overcome it.* (King James authorized Bible version)

I end this chapter with another quotation from Skelly's book about Rahner on this subject. *Our superficial experience of the world does perhaps correspond more to the first model of nature and grace. Most often God's absence is much more painfully obvious than God's presence. The world frequently appears to be much more deeply permeated by sin and evil and suffering than by gracious love of God. But Christians claim that the world is not as it may appear to be. ... The world as "nature" is not a self-sufficient independent reality to which grace is subsequently added by God. God lovingly sustains the natural world precisely as the potential recipient of the divine self-communication... ... Consequently, nature as it actually exists is never purely and simply secular; it is always oriented towards and endowed with God...[77]*

There are many ways of describing the relationship between the world as nature and as creation. There are many ways of representing the idea that creation is in relationship to the loving and creative act and presence of God as love. We might speak of intrinsic presence, of potentiality, latency and propensity in the pattern paradoxes of creation, that is, in both the science and the theology[78].

[77] Skelly, p 59/60

The point is that the way we choose to describe how God is present as Creator in creation cannot undermine the way Love itself creates and works. Love does not impose itself, does not act in ways that take away the freedom of the other, does not manipulate creation for its own benefit. Love is endlessly and unconditionally present without taking away human freedom to deny, reject, or ignore that presence.

---

[78] For a development of this idea of "pattern paradoxes" see my trilogy on "Love's Energy" on cosmology, quantum and evolution.

# CHAPTER NINE

## 9    WHAT'S THE TIME AND WHERE ARE YOU?

*We cannot explain how it is possible for God without ceasing to be God to freely enter into the kind of interpersonal communion with us that we suggest takes place in worship. ... Christians believe that through God's gracious self-communication we are invited to participate in God and so to be transformed and become like God. The question is what do we mean by this? What does it mean to say that the horizon of our transcendence comes near to us?*[79]

## LITURGICAL TIME

*Christians were tempted to reject time altogether and replace it with mysticism and "spiritual" pursuits, to live as Christians out of time and thereby escape its frustrations; to insist that time has no real meaning from the point of view of the Kingdom which is "beyond time." And they finally succeeded. They left time meaningless indeed, although full of Christian "symbols." And today they themselves do not know what to do with these symbols. For it is impossible to "put Christ back into Christmas" if He has not redeemed—that is, made meaningful—time itself.      Alexander Schmemann;*

"What is the time" is a significant and revealing question as we learnt from Einstein. Supposing, for example, we said that the ancients thought liturgical time was entwined around and within ordinary time - the hours, days and weeks of the year in ordinary time, by which we measure the movement of the mystery of time. Suppose we stuck to that idea of "entwining" and even insisted on it to counter the proposal that liturgical time was separate from ordinary time, as the sacred is supposed to be separate from the secular in the views of some. And that might have been true in religious thinking until something happened to change it. And that something was the coming of Christianity in the person of the coming of Jesus, as the revelation in human form of the nature of the divine. And after that new and radical change, early Christians fought to avoid any kind of dualism between the sacred and the

---

[79] Michael Skelly p 44.

secular which had been the way of many religions at the time, including what were called the mystery religions.

And if we pause to consider those words about the incarnation, even for a moment, we know how ridiculous they might sound and how preposterous a claim they represent. If it's hard enough to understand the scientific and philosophical meaning of time itself, then it is even harder to understand how the themes of Liturgical time might weave themselves within it, or rather within space-time. Then, even harder than that is the Christian belief about how the divine enters the limits of time and all that might mean. For surely the nature of the being of the divine can never be known and will always be so transcendent of our knowledge and experience that it is further away, not so much in space, distance and time, but because of its nature and being. And yet, the ancients talked of a metaphysical reality that was just that – beyond anything physical, however measured in distance and time, and then they talked of the incarnation, as the moment of intersection when the metaphysical became physical. And this wasn't about some happy clappy friendship in Jesus our personal Saviour. This was about the being of God who is somehow the creator and source of everything that exists in the space-time of the cosmos, being known in and through the being of the humanity of Jesus of Nazareth.

Not surprisingly, it took centuries for those early Christians to work out how they might say such a thing, or rather how to try framing it in different kinds of words. How can any words show that the human could contain the nature of the being of the divine and still be in any real sense human, and how could any words express the belief that that which is the revelation of the divine could remain just that, in the suffering experience and death of that which is human, in ways that led to the resurrection of that which is human. Somehow, they found, through their long and painful struggles, words that insisted on the possibility of two impossible things entwining themselves together in one and the same thing, like strands of string becoming one single bowstring. And for them, anything which took away the significance of each strand, the divine and the human, was a reduction and contradiction of what they meant by the incarnation.

And, yes, of course, in trying to assert that two such contradictory things could be true at the same time, their words strained within their own limits, and spiritual imaginations struggled to expand their capacity to make such a claim and as the central belief of everything else in their faith. And many attempts were made at different ways of doing this. And many ended up reducing the nature of the incarnation, either by making the divine too dominant in the human, or the human too human to contain the divine. And that kind of slippage, understandable now with the hindsight of history, occurred in both directions, so the single bowstring became unwound and weaker at certain points, and in some cases stopped being the same bowstring altogether. And, yes, even the image of a bowstring hardly does justice to the nature of this entwining of the divine into the nature of the human that was, and is, the mystery of the incarnation.

And if we are to take that seriously in the way we apply it theologically to the different dimensions of what we call "reality", then it must remain true to its incarnational nature, and do nothing to undermine that in anything we say or think about religion. And that applies to the mystery of time and the mystery of liturgical time and how they are related. For if they are not related or only related as opposites in a dualistic way, then already something is present that risks undermining the nature of the incarnation, and the claims made about it in the different gospels of the New Testament. For He came and lived among us, within the time and space limits of those days, in order to incarnate some greater truth and the promise of a new creation that transcends our old understanding of that and everything else. He rooted all he said and did within those limits of earthly reality in order to unveil something of that which is a reflection of the nature of the divine.

So, this starting point is already a given. Whenever and however we speak of liturgy or liturgical time, then it must be embedded within that incarnational movement of the emanation of the nature of the divine within human form, in order for it to be something more that fulfils or expresses its real nature. The strand of time that carries the themes of liturgical live can be known within the science of its own nature. We live in and through our calendar type measures of the movement of time and its cycles of months and years, based on well-known physical and astrophysical laws about the nature of how our solar system works in one galaxy amongst so many. And at the same "time", we live within the liturgical seasons and cycles which attempt to incarnate the themes and meaning of Christ's life within time, through the movement of time as we measure it in our usual ways according to time zones and relative positions according to the rotation of the earth on its axis in relationship to the sun. So those of us who believe in the incarnation believe that something of God has been glimpsed in the time of that incarnation as it moves through its pivotal pillars of meaning from Christmas through to Holy Week, Resurection, Ascension and Pentecost and so on. And that Liturgical time has entered the very nature of the strand and stream of space-time so that it is present, even when we don't acknowledge or attempt to understand it. It is there, say we Christians, even if we don't enter its meaning through the Liturgy of the Church, but that through the Liturgy of the Church we can discern and touch the movement of the Liturgy of Time through our ordinary times.

And these are earthed in the bigger picture of the creation of the otherness of the universe, which came from the Otherness of the mystery of God in ways that speak of the self-giving emanation of the energy of God, making possible the propensity of time and space to exist, and all the forces which make possible the existence of matter as the universe created itself in evolutionary ways. And we remember that the cosmos evolved just as different species evolved on this planet but that it happened over aeons of time that are as hard to picture as are the number of stars in any one galaxy and the number of known galaxies within the observable universe. And as we live our mortal lives through and with the passing of time, and the movement of space in a material world, so we live within its laws and ways, knowing its science as part of what we also know as and about creation.

Skelly,[80] writing on Rahner's understanding of how ordinary time and activity is infused with the potential to experience the presence of the mystery of God, comments in the following way,

But the experience of God is so completely and constantly available in daily life that it is frequently ignored, misinterpreted or suppressed. "In everyday life this transcendental experience of God in the Holy Spirit remains anonymous, implicit, unthematic, like the widely and diffusely spread light of a sun which we do not directly see, while we turn only to the individual objects visible in this light in our sense-experience."[81]...For those who are confused or frustrated by the quality of our liturgical life.... they must be shown that worship is the explicit celebration of the divine depth of their ordinary life, that what clearly appears in it and consequently can be. More decisively accepted in freedom is what occurs always and everywhere in the ordinary course of life...We need to be guided towards that absolute mystery which is, "the underlying substrate which is presupposed to and sustains the reality we know".[82] Our preapprehension of this mystery is the condition of possibility for the acts of knowledge and freedom that fulfil our existence. As Rahner says,

We exist, think and act in freedom only in virtue of the fact that we have already all along transcended that which is specific and particular, that which we can comprehend, in a movement which knows no boundaries. The moment we become aware of ourselves precisely as the limited being which in so many and such radical ways we are, we have already overstepped these boundaries... We have experienced ourselves as beings which constantly reach out beyond themselves towards that which cannot be comprehended or circumscribed, that which precisely as having this radical status must be called infinite, that which is sheer mystery.... It is present as the abiding mystery.[83]

This is a crucial and realistic appraisal of the human condition and its limits and boundaries within space-time. Rahner's genius is to use that appraisal as the launchpad for recognising how those same limits can be overstepped in a constant reaching out for that which is present as the abiding mystery of God in ordinary life. Skelly then warns us to be careful not to presume that our positive experiences

---

[80] In *The Liturgy of the World; Karl Rahner's Theology of Worshi*p.

[81] Karl Rahner. *Experience of the Holy Spirit.* p 199

[82] ibid. p 155

[83] Ibid, p 155-6

are the ones that will best, or most often, provide us with an explicit experience of God.[84] This takes us straight into his understanding of Rahner's approach to the problem of theodicy. According to Skelly, Rahner takes very seriously the negative experiences of human life as potentially explicit experiences of the mystery of God. The important and neutral sounding word here seems to be that of "limits" which seems to stand for that which has traditionally been called "sin", in the finitude of the human condition.

> *Where the definable limits of our everyday realties break down and are dissolved, where the decline of these realities is perceived, when lights shining over the tiny island of our ordinary lives are extinguished and the question becomes inescapable whether the night that surrounds us is the void of absurdity and death that engulfs us or the blessed holy night already shining within us is the promise of eternal day.[85]*

Skelly comments,

> *To know that we have limits but to perceive that there is something beyond those limits is to experience transcendence…. To perceive that there is something beyond our limits and to affirm the good we may glimpse only dimly there, is to experience God. And to do this again and again is to gradually discover that God is present in every experience no matter how negative…*

*There is no event in which we cannot experience God. This does not mean that suffering and evil are actually good things, they are not. The plight of the world's poor for example is an intolerable injustice. The fact that we might glimpse the presence of God in their suffering does not give us license to be complacent but should only rekindle our desire to do everything in our power to alleviate their injustices. If God is present with them in their pain, we should be as well…. We continue to experience God in these moments precisely because they continue to be painful reminders of our limitations, And the painful parts of these events are much more likely to dominate our attention that the presence of God is…. The liturgy is not a refuge from a harsh and merciless world. We should never treat it as an escape from the emptiness and meaninglessness of our lives. We do not have to ignore or deny the intractable suffering of the world in order to preserve some semblance of*

---

[84] Michael Skelly, *The Liturgy of the World; Karl Rahner's Theology of Worship* p 78-80

[85] Karl Rahner, *Experience of the Holy Spirit.* p 199-200

*faith in God. We can find God in all the moments of our day, even the ones that seem furthest from God...*

*Every event, no matter how profane or mundane it might seem, is a potential experience of God. The basic material of our experience of God, the, need not be anything that is overtly religious. We do not have to conceptualise or articulate our experiences in religious categories for them to be experiences of God.... The explicitly religious moments of our lives, experiences of the Church's liturgy for example are necessary and important symbolic manifestations of the presence of God in all our moments....*

*We will only be able to recognise the presence of the absolute mystery in the liturgy if we recognise its abiding presence throughout our lives and our world. The mysticism of daily life will not guarantee that our liturgical assemblies will become transparent experiences of the kingdom of God. Worship will always seem somewhat awkward, archaic and confusing, Communion and communication with the living God are perplexing even for mystics. God is so radically different from us that it will always be difficult to achieve a personal relationship with God. Nonetheless, Rahner thinks that if we were to become mystics we would develop a much deeper appreciation of worship.[86]*

**But in this mysticism of daily life, Skelly broadens our understanding of Liturgical time in relationship to the movement of historical time.**

*And at some level of our free acts, we are always accepting or resisting God. Every moment of every day has the potential to become an explicit, mutual experience of God in which God chooses to become present to us and we choose to become present to God. .... Every moment in human history, no matter how inconsequential or profane it might seem, has the potential to manifest God. Every people in every age somehow experiences the presence of the absolute mystery, even if this happens only in very obscure ways...When this interaction with God in history becomes explicit, it is not necessarily grasped in specifically religious ways, Ordinary and ostensibly secular events in the world's history become explicit manifestations of our relationship with God... Ordinary and ostensibly secular events in the world's history become explicit manifestations of our relationship with God. Our individual experiences of the absolute mystery, then, are small parts of a much bigger process, a process that includes all of human history from beginning to end.*

---

[86] Skelly. Rahner's *Theology of Worship* p 82-84

*Participation is an inescapable, secret ingredient of human history. In other words, the history of the world is a liturgy. By saying this we are not presuming that we already know what we mean by liturgy. Our goal is not to explain history in terms of liturgy but liturgy in terms of history. For Rahner, the history of the world is the original liturgy; it gives the primary content and meaning to our concept of liturgy... Whenever he addresses a particular question about liturgy, worship, sacraments or prayer, Rahner ultimately refers the topic back to the fundamental experience of the liturgy of the world.... For Rahner all theology of worship is primarily theology of the liturgy of the world.*[87]

With this in mind, how can we understand the theological significance of time itself, in relationship to what we are calling Liturgical time?

## AN EXAMPLE – THE EIGTH DAY

So how might this approach to Liturgical time be understood or illustrated? To do this we have to go back to the very early days after the resurrection and the creation of Sunday as the Day of Resurrection in the early church. The Jewish Sabbath was remembered on the seventh day, the Saturday, as the end of the cycle of the seven-day week which Genesis tells us was a holy day on which God rested after the creation of all things during the other days of that week. Of course, this understanding of "days" in the divine act of creation has always been contentious. Some have said that every day was like a thousand days. Other scholars have looked to the provenance of this passage from the Jewish writers in exile in Babylon, reflecting on their experience of the Temple worship of that city, and in particular the inheritance from the Persian world of a liturgical week representing the creation. Others that the seven-day cycle emanates from a very human understanding of a working week and the need for a day of rest from "work". But there is more.

The resurrection happened on the day after the seventh day. The early Christians felt it inaugurated something radically new, so it was seven plus one in the pivot point between the old week and the new week. This was the initiation of something new to replace the

---

[87] Ibid p 85-86

old. And it was around that pivot point that the meaning of resurrection was understood to have changed everything in time itself. But, the seven plus one didn't exist in the rhythm of time passing through a calendar of a seven-day week. And so it became an eschatological day that didn't exist within the calendar of ordinary time, and yet, it did function as the turning point between everything that was old and now everything that was new. And it happened on the day after the Sabbath, which was the day Christ was in the tomb, as it were ending the old weekly cycle with his entombment. So, the new Sabbath was the first day of the beginning of a new cycle that ended in the silent death of the tomb. The resurrection day was an eschatological day. It existed within time but it transcended time. It had to become the new Sabbath that was a Sabbath plus one, to become the pivot point of that new covenant.

But what had the old Sabbath meant in the creation story, which had to be referenced by something that represents a new creation event in the resurrection of Christ? The Sabbath was a holy day. Of course, the number seven already had huge symbolic significance in parts of the Old Scriptures. The seventh day Sabbath was the day when God rested from the work of creation. We are used to various Protestant traditions which, as in Judaism, banned all work on the Sabbath. We see, in the Gospels, how the Pharisees tried to trap and condemn Jesus and his disciples for doing even one good work for someone on that day. However, the holiness of the Sabbath was not so much about moral behaviours, as it later became in some religious circles, who became fanatical about defining the boundaries and meaning of Sabbath rest, but about a resting from creation in order to stand back and see the goodness in it. It was as if the painter put down his brushes, stood back from the easel to gain a proper perspective on it for the first time. The divine perception was that everything created had goodness within it.

So, the Sabbath is our chance, as Christians, to hold onto this original meaning. The Sabbath isn't a day for arguing about don't do this, and don't do that. Should the shops be open or closed? Should I go to work or not? Should I run in an Olympic race or not, (a pivotal issue for the Christian, Eric Liddell, as displayed in *The Chariots of* *fir*e). It's far more basic than that, important though those things might be in some places. The Sabbath, seventh day plus one, is about seeing the goodness in creation if we are to follow the pattern set in Genesis to be touched by resurrection as the new creation. It is about our joyful acceptance of the goodness of creation as an ontological truth, and our participation in that belief if we choose to perceive it that way. Never mind if the science of the order of creation in both Genesis narratives is a bit wonky to say the least. This ontological truth is to be understood theologically, not scientifically, though the two needn't and shouldn't be exclusive of each other in our times.

So, the idea of rest on the Sabbath was not about absence from work so that we could add more and more regulations about how to spend it, but to join with that rest from the work of God from which its goodness can be perceived and affirmed as being truly good. The Sabbath delight in creation is a chance to sit within the sacredness and fullness of everything being seen as good, of goodness existing within everything, which is the crowning of the rhythms and meaning of all space-time. Therefore, it has cosmic and eschatological implications. It is not a shifting of the cycles of time so that the week ends on a different day. It is the entrance into the world and time itself of a new aeon of creation time, as recapitulated and restored by the presence of resurrection life within time. And resurrection life is Eucharistic life as seen through the filter of the new pivotal, Sabbath eight day. At least, that is how we might understand something of its "maximal" meaning. This is how Schmemann puts it,

*The liturgy of time… was therefore preserved in a way by necessity – as the completion of the Eucharist, without which the application of the Eucharist to time or any real sanctification of the life of this world would be incomplete… It (the Eucharist) cannot abolish the liturgy of time because then time would be really emptied and deprived of meaning, would be nothing but intervals between celebrations of the Eucharist. Thus the new cult (of Christianity), an eschatological cult in the deepest sense of the word, required for its real fulfilment inclusion in the rhythm of time, and its combination within this rhythm with the liturgy of time as the affirmation of the reality of the world which Christ came to save*[88].

But the Sabbath cycle in the liturgy of time is also a reminder, if not a remembering of our exile and alienation from God, the turning away from the goodness within creation because of the way we see it and use it. For the cross is always there at the heart of the suffering of the world and of creation to remind us of this. And so the Sabbath day had to look forward to the day of redemption, and, for that, a new day of creation was needed. But that hardly fits into the rhythm of the seven days, that is, unless it is both the end of something and the beginning of something new at the same time. So there emerges the idea of a new liturgical day or a new beginning with liturgical significance for the rhythm of time itself. And this liturgical day can only be initiated by the coming of a new kind of time. That is the eschatological time contained within the Kingdom of God because of the action of God in Jesus and his suffering and death and resurrection.

So, the liturgical theme of resurrection, because of what happened in Jesus, enters into our time and entwines itself within it, for all time. The new Sabbath, plus one, added onto the Jewish Sabbath on a Saturday, becomes the beginning of the new creation initiated in him by the resurrection. The Sunday becomes the symbolic end of the old week and the symbolic beginning of the new week, all contained in that one day of Resurrection and the resurrected goodness which enters into creation and into time itself.

And to incarnate this in Christian worship, early church architecture often used octagon shapes with eight sides to do something more that stress the holiness of the number seven, so often found in the Bible. The Eighth day (7 plus One) was the eschatological day within time, just as the eight sides of a church dome held eight different frescoes and contained the meaning of the eighth day liturgy, which happened within its structure. But what they called the "incarnation" changed their understanding of everything else, including time and space, which we know from Einsteinian physics are closely related.

The following is how Paul M Blower talked about the Eighth

---

Day[89] when thinking about the contribution of the three great Cappadocian theologians of the fourth century[90].

*At last the cosmic significance of the resurrection of Christ, its meaning within the larger oikonomia, was for the Cappadocians already framed in the thoroughly contemplative medium of the church's liturgy, as evidenced especially in the bishops' Paschal homilies. Gregory Nazianzen emphasizes that the resurrection as the inauguration of a new creation not only resounds in Pascha-Sunday itself but in the following 'New' (Octave) Sunday after Easter. The liturgical sequence between the two Sundays, he suggests, ties together the continuity between the original Hexaemeral creation and the new, eschatological creation:*

*"Last Sunday was the day of salvation, but today is salvation's anniversary. Last Sunday revealed the boundary between the grave and the resurrection, but today reveals, in all its clarity, our second beginning. So just as the first creation had its beginning on a Sunday (and that is clear: for the seventh day after it is the Sabbath, which brings cessation from work), so the new creation must begin again on the same day: the first of the days that come after it, the eighth of those that come before, more exalted than what has been exalted before, more wonderful than previous wonders".*

*This carried forward a tradition much older than the Cappadocians of connecting the resurrection with the 'Eighth Day', the new eschatological Lord's Day that fulfills the old creation while also transcending it, so that in some sense every Sunday, as a miniature Pascha, celebrates this new beginning. Gregory of Nyssa, in his signature way, also sought to describe the inner mystery whereby Christ's resurrection specifically unfolded a 'new creation' of human nature, deferring again to the richness of the notion of the New Adam who brings to fruition the 'fullness' of humanity: [91]*

Paul Blower believes this tradition predates the fourth century, but clearly surfaces then in the liturgical thinking of some of the most influential theologians. It is interesting that he sees this *new*

---

[89] in his *In Beauty Tragedy and a New Creation, Theology and Contemplation in Cappadocian Cosmology*

[90] **Basil the Great (330-379), Bishop of Caesarea; Basil's younger brother Gregory of Nyssa (c. 335 – c. 395), Bishop of Nyssa; and a close friend, Gregory of Nazianzus (329–389), who became Patriarch of Constantinople.**

[91] **pp 27. 28 International Journal of Systematic Theology, Volume 18 Number 1 January 2016**

*beginning* as having importance for the fullness of humanity. Repeatedly in this book, I am attempting to illustrate and point out this Inside-Out orientation of Liturgy when understood in this way. It is what Rowan Williams has called *Liturgical humanism*[92] and therefore of significant interest and relevance way beyond the normal bounds of liturgical focus.

## SACRED SPACE INSIDE AND OUT

From the earliest times, humans have had spiritual experiences in particular places, or in places that were then remembered as being special or holy. This was notably true of mountains, desert places, deep caves, groves, particular trees or rocks, streams or wells, and even a view onto wider vistas of the sea, or sunsets. Perhaps, looking up at the stars in the night sky was at least as much of an awesome sight, if not more so, than it is now. Some of these scenes have stimulated questions about the nature of these things and places. How did they get there? Why are they so magnetically attracting, or frightening, or awesome? Why are they so compellingly beautiful, or "sublime" as the Romantics used to say? Whether or not the Romantics were doing more than just reacting against a mechanical, rational and scientific view of the world, they gave us ample illustration of the meaning of the sublime in natural things and hinted of the mystery of the transcendent in the process.

Sometimes, in more "ordinary" places, unexpected "epiphanies" happened, which people then interpreted as being in some way holy or on holy ground. These were places where visions had been seen and voices heard. The Old Testament made much of the Pillar of Fire by night and the Cloud by day. These were Burning Bush type places. Places associated with some kind of vision or sacrifice. Sometimes, as recorded in the Old Testament, people would then erect a memorial or shrine to honour the experience[93]. And a tradition would then be passed down through

---

[92] In *Looking East in Winter* p 141 ff

[93] The great tree of Moreh when Abram entertained 3 strangers. The High Places,

generations of that particular place being special, sacred, holy and it was often named accordingly.

Let's pause for a moment and look at some of the detail in the beginning of Exodus chapter Three. I've wondered for some time about the voice which warns Moses to take off his shoes because the place on which he treads is holy ground. Was it Holy because of something that had happened before? Or was it holy because the voice of God was associated with that particular experience? If the latter, then one implication might be that wherever there is some kind of religious experience, or ephiphany, or revelation, or spiritual experience, then we might argue that ground is holy wherever it is.

Or, we might go further and argue that all ground is potentially holy, because of its ontological relationship with a creator who is Holy. And that, of course, has ethical implications for how we tread on it, use it, develop it, or misuse it, and take it for granted. And if we were a society which still held onto this sense of "creation", as do for example the Aboriginal people in Australia and New Zealand, then it might be that its ethical treatment would come more naturally to us. The belief system would overflow into ethics. Arguably spiritual belief about the ontology of things comes before any ethics of how we should treat those things. Ethics can of course function within a metaphysical or ontological vacuum and be constructed out of various kind of human value system. The experience of behaving ethically can in turn influence or create a sense of underlying ontology as well as nourished by it. Also, an ontology of spirituality

Green Oaks, Shechem, Bethel, Jacob's well, Moab, the pillars and altars of Baal and the Asherim, the Burning Bush, Mount Sinai, Horeb. A classic reference is 2 Kings 17:29–32. "But every nation still made gods of its own and put them in the shrines of the high places that the Samaritans had made, every nation in the cities in which they lived. The men of Babylon made Succoth-benoth, the men of Cuth made Nergal, the men of Hamath made Ashima, and the Avvites made Nibhaz and Tartak; and the Sepharvites burned their children in the fire to Adrammelech and Anammelech, the gods of Sepharvaim. They also feared the Lord and appointed from among themselves all sorts of people as priests of the high places, who sacrificed for them in the shrines of the high places." At one stage, according to 2 Chronicles there were high places for burning incense to other gods in every city of Judah. References to the "high places" are numerous.

overflows into ethics at some point, in order to be what it is, to express and fulfill the nature of what it is. And therefore, moral behaviour is a spiritual matter. And the spiritual points us to the nature of matter as well as beyond it.

Is holiness then something to do with our experience and perception of ordinary things, the things we can, and do, take for granted? Is it, therefore, part of the givenness of our human relationship with land, the ground, earth, and its use? The Garden of Eden story has accrued many meanings over time. Could we view it as a paradigm of the potential, sacramental significance of the land and all that is in it, dependent on such a belief system and therefore our perception of it, and therefore our use of it? It makes sense that the myth was a reminder of a vision of our relationship with God in the garden of the whole earth, and our responsibility for how we act within it as the place where God can be known as creator in the holiness of ordinary things. And isn't this a mark of significance in the Liturgy of the World which then becomes remembered and expressed in the Liturgy of the Church?

Is Eden a reminder of our human role and responsibility as gardeners, not just of the earth and agricultural land, and our pretty gardens - if we are lucky enough to have them or access to them - but as the bearer of the fruits of a diversity beyond our imagining, however many gardening programmes we watch? And is nature a gift for the healing of mind and body, not just because of specific things like herbs we might grow in it, but the indefinable reward of being in it and looking at things within it? And, because of that looking, are there subliminal things we've learnt from the structure and appearance of nature and its vistas, that we've unconsciously transferred into our sense of shape and design, and the way we try to reproduce what feels and looks right in our buildings, and the objects we use and make? And is that one significant reason, maybe a sacramental reason, why painting and sculpture and the reproduction of our perception of nature in those forms, is so compelling and interesting. And in that work of re-producing and re-presenting, are we not agents of creativity in the ordering and re-ordering of the things of nature? And does that agency put us in touch, or back in touch, with the possibility of a sensory spirituality of matter, as well as its aesthetics and utility? And is the spirituality of matter part of the ontology of creation, and our relationship with nature within it? And, if any of this is true, or even helpful, then we might indeed acknowledge that the ground on which we tread is holy ground, or might again be seen as such, whatever language we choose to use about it? And isn't this a mark of significance in the Liturgy of the World which then becomes remembered and expressed in the Liturgy of the Church?

And when we are at work, as Moses was with his father in law's sheep, and when we look and notice that the bush of nature is, as if it were, on fire but not burning up, wouldn't we think about taking another look? Wouldn't we think, as Moses did, that this is a strange sight, and that it raises all sorts of questions in our minds, not least scientific ones, such as why doesn't the bush burn up? And supposing when we "go over to look" as Moses did, that we are motivated by those questions, intrigued by them in our minds and imagination and therefore more ready, spiritually, to hear the voice, the sense of a voice, or a meaning coming to us from within the nature of the bush? And wouldn't we recognise this voice as if it were speaking to us, revealing something new to us in our exploration, our "experiment" of what it all might mean for us? And isn't this a mark of significance in the Liturgy of the World which then becomes remembered and expressed in the Liturgy of the Church?

And in such a case, wouldn't we recognise something in ourselves, our nature that is connected to this nature of new meaning inside the nature of the bush – "Here I am". And wouldn't we then be surprised to recognize something new about the situation that we'd never thought of before, however accustomed we might be to the nature of that place or that thing, particularly a thing that was part of the normal environment of our workplace or in our scientific study? And wouldn't we feel a sense of awe, that might lead to us taking extra care. *Do not come any closer.* Stop, pause, reflect, consider where you are and what you are doing, for this, whatever it is, must be something special, compelling us to treat it with the utmost respect. *"Take off your sandals, for the place where you are standing is holy* ground." And isn't this a mark of significance in the Liturgy of the World which then becomes remembered and expressed in the Liturgy of the Church?

And supposing we suddenly realised that, and knew that for the first time, seeing and recognizing where we are, and what we are doing, as if for the first time, wouldn't our spiritual sight and perception be opened in a new way to understand the significance, the holy significance of that situation? If we change the language and the assumptions it carries, then it is surely a common experience in science and the arts for humans to situate themselves and know they have been situated within the mystery of time and place which is larger, or deeper, or more profound than they've realised before. And then, wouldn't it be a natural thing to feel humbled beyond expectations in the awe-filled face of this ordinary thing, that appears so transformed by an energy within, one that you might have missed, one you have missed before; an energy of the very nature of holiness, of that which is beyond expectations and understanding but there, just there in front of you, inside this extraordinary ordinary thing, and inside you at the same time? *And Moses hid his face because he was afraid to look at God.* And isn't this a mark of significance in the Liturgy of the World which then becomes remembered and expressed in the Liturgy of the Church?

And then, after such an experience, wouldn't you be more receptive to the possibility that you are called to do something or be something different. And wouldn't you feel liberated to be more aware of the need for liberation in others? *I have seen the misery of my people in Egypt.. and I am concerned about their suffering.* Because of this experience, wouldn't you want to follow this calling and responsibility, and yes, like Moses wouldn't you feel unworthy and anxious? *Who am I that I should go to Pharoah and bring the Israelites out of Egypt?* And isn't this a mark of significance in the Liturgy of the World which then becomes remembered and expressed in the Liturgy of the Church?

And how then would you react, when this thought came to you? *I will be with you. And this will be the sign to you that it is I who have sent you: When you have brought the people out of Egypt, you will worship*

*God on this mountain.* And isn't this a mark of significance in the Liturgy of the World which then becomes remembered and expressed in the Liturgy of the Church?

Fine, you might think. All very well, you might think, but suppose.. and suppose… and suppose.. And isn't this a mark of significance in the Liturgy of the World which then becomes remembered and expressed in the Liturgy of the Church?

"O.K. Look, suppose I do actually do it, and then they suddenly ask me something really hard like, 'what is his name?' What shall I tell them? And suppose I gave them the answer *"I am who I am"* sent me. And suppose that was a real surprise, because they knew there were lots of names for different Gods, (especially in a place like Egypt and especially if you'd been brought up in the household of the God like Pharoah), but nothing like this – a God with no name, something beyond a name in the transcendent holiness of his nature being revealed in something ordinary, a natural thing from creation itself." And isn't this a mark of significance in the Liturgy of the World which then becomes remembered and expressed in the Liturgy of the Church?

You could understand, if you'd been in any way successful, that worship could take place back in the same place, back on the same high place, away from all the trouble, but to go in the name of the "I am who I am" is something else. It tells me nothing and it tells me everything about the nature of this holiness, this divine voice and calling, this God. It tells me that nothing can be known except that which is revealed in the place and time of ordinary things, and on ordinary ground, that no longer feels the same as it did before. It tells me that this *"I am"* is a source of divine care for the suffering of people and that this *"I am"* inspires particular unworthy humans to help other others in the human condition. It tells me that the bush of spiritual experience burns but doesn't burn up or destroy itself, or others. It tells me that an experience of holiness leads to a sense of complete unworthiness and yet, at the same time, a task of responsibility for the liberation of others. It tells me that my agency is dependent on the presence of the *"I am who I am"* holiness of God and that when, and if, I follow the call of that agency, it will take me, or bring me back to this place, this place of vision on the mountain, where I stood aside and looked at something extraordinary happening in the ordinary bush of nature. And isn't this a mark of significance in the Liturgy of the World which then becomes remembered and expressed in the Liturgy of the Church?

In every religion, there are stories of sacred places, and often small businesses developed next to them, selling figurines and mementos, as they still do today, in all the well-known Christian shrines or places of miracles, healing, and pilgrimage. This is not just an ancient or medieval custom. It is not just Christian. People seem to value taking a material thing as a symbolic reminder of something special and spiritual that is happened, taking it home to keep the memory of their visit or experience alive. In Jerusalem and many other "holy places", the streets are crowded with visitors and pilgrims going into shops to purchase such a symbolic reminder for themselves or as a gift for others.

In England, there are still places remembered for their holy wells. People still find climbing mountains a compelling attraction and they often erect little stone cairns at the top. It may be just the physical challenge of the climb. It may be the view from the top, or just a sense of exhausted achievement. On the other hand, it might be any of these things and something else as well, including a sense of one's own significance, or insignificance, or God's transcendence as Creator of these things in ways that can open up unexpectedly as something sublime. And that sense can apply to those working with the very small as well, through microscopes for example. The microcosmic and the macrocosmic experience of the wonders of creation can give us pause as we reflect on the nature of nature as "creation". And isn't this a mark of significance in the Liturgy of the World which then becomes remembered and expressed in the Liturgy of the Church?

There is no point in saying this, without acknowledging that nature can be hard and unpredictably dangerous. There can be volcanoes as well as wonderful views from mountain tops. There can be earthquakes and floods that destroy homes and crops and human life. There can be diseases and disasters, and in case we become too romantic about nature, there is entropy all around us and within us. And yet, we can stand back and see all of this as still part of a "wonderful world", as Louis Armstrong used to sing in a song that is more popular than any other on Radio 4's Desert Island Discs. It seems we are programmed to have heightened senses when it comes to the things of nature in the small or larger landscapes of our existence and perception. And you can say it is wondrous, or awesome, or you can say it is holy, in that it partakes of a creation truth about a divine creator, although the way we speak of that is another and challenging question, especially in a cosmos where evolution makes its own journey through time.[94]

## HOLY PLACES

Early monks from Ireland who came to places like Iona brought with them the spiritual echoes of the 3rd and 4th century movement into the desert that had happened partly in reaction to the Emperor Constantine's espousing of Christianity. There's was a Celtic form of Christianity, different from the Roman kind that entered Britain via Canterbury. We have evidence, from artefacts found, of trading links between Constantinople in the East and Ireland in the West, despite the great distances involved. What is now known as Celtic culture was well known across different parts of Europe. Monks like St. Cuthbert, in the 7th century,[95] brought a new austerity in the search for creating holy and sacred places where they could engage with the Kingdom of Heaven on Earth, away from, and separated from the way the rest of the world seemed to be moving.

---

[94] See my trilogy "Love's Energy" on cosmology quantum and evolution, available on Amazon.

[95] Probably born at Melrose and very drawn to the monastery there. His influence in many places in Northumbria has lasted through place names and traditions. In death, his body was carried away from Lindisfarne and around the whole area for seven years as his monks fled from Lindisfarne to escape from the Viking invasions. It ended up back in the new Cathedral of Durham.

The famous Gospel book of Lindisfarne, produced where Cuthbert had become a Bishop, shows, in its famous illuminated illustrations, how symbols of nature were included as part of their understanding of creation. On Iona, away from the Benedictine monastery buildings of later centuries, the archaeology reveals evidence of how the early monks lived in their wooden church, their meeting place, and the small huts surrounding them. All of this was contained with a sacred space separated off from the outside land by the vallum. To enter that space was to enter the sacredness of that part of creation, and the sanctuary it provided to those who needed it. Spirituality and sanctuary informing each other. It feels as if the separation of ground, dedicated to their holy task, was intended, but perhaps it was more to focus that holiness already present in creation itself. We can't be sure. The worship and prayer of the monks was as austere as the environment on Iona and on Lindisfarne. Prayer five times a day and three times in the night helped to fit them for the toughness of their holy enterprise.

On Lindisfarne and the Inner Farne island, Cuthbert pushed himself ever more into that austerity as the way to sanctity, allegedly sleeping on stone and standing in prayer in the cold waters for hours on end. This was nothing like a later touristic, or Romantic interest, in getting away from it all, to be in the countryside or the wilderness away from the bustle of life, especially in towns and cities.[96] To go there, to enter into those tough, holy places was to accept the austerity of a life far distance from the later medieval monasteries, their buildings, estates, farms and growing influence and wealth. It was a chosen austerity at a time when poverty and austerity were common things, particularly in isolated areas of these islands. It was a life the desert fathers had chosen before them.

It became a tradition for sacred space to be designated as separate from holy space. This began in their understanding of the

---

[96] Although many find this spiritually helpful. Retreats and time away for mediation and silence are still popular. As a university chaplain at Newcastle, I used to take groups of students to retreats on Lindisfarne.

land dedicated for, and by, the monks in, and of, itself. The division spread to include parts of the later, larger church buildings especially those included in monastic foundations. It later included burial grounds, building on pre-Christian ideas of that ground being especially hallowed for that purpose. Some argued that the presence of buried people made the ground sacred wherever it occurred. Others that special ground had to be set aside and hallowed, in order for it to be used as a burial ground. Clearly there were practical reasons why burial grounds had to be designated as special, from the earliest times. And such places were often understood as holy places in many cultures and religions well before Christianity. The Egyptians offer famous examples of this, and how the dead were buried in order to facilitate their entrance into, and needs in, the afterlife. In some traditions, cults of the dead and the ancestors would develop, increasing that sense of sacredness at burial sites.

The tension, in the idea of the sacred and the secular, continued as between, on the one hand, the focused and separated sacred place as something radically different from the rest of the land around it, and on the other hand, the focused sacred place serving as a reminder and representation of the sacredness of all life and all places in creation. At times, both ideas were held together, and, at other times, they distanced themselves from each other. This may date back to the beginnings of monasticism, at least in its gathered, community forms. It probably began in practical ways, as the early monastic communities needed to protect their space and way of life from other places and ways of life, as well as to order their affairs and worship within it, or even to protect their communities from invaders. But running throughout early and later monasticism was an affirmation of withdrawal as a positive thing to discover and reaffirm the presence of God everywhere. Within this latter view, the monastic vocation wasn't a rejection of the world, but a withdrawal (sometimes an extreme withdrawal into silence itself) into a dedicated life of service offered to God as part of that world. The tension continued through the centuries, and different views were espoused by different monastic communities themselves, as well as having different assumptions foisted on them by outside observers. What does it mean when religious people, Christians and others, talk about being in the world, and not of the world? How is this tension to be understood and what is its starting point? And, we might add, what is added to this conundrum by the latest science which insists on a relationship between time and space within a General Theory of Relativity. And how different this orientation is from the assumptions and values of a Newtonian world, which, for centuries before Isaac Newton and after, thought that every thing and every place (including the solar system itself) was fixed in an immutable position by a divine creator. And so changing scientific understanding affects our perception of the processes in the Liturgy of the World which then, hopefully, become included in the way we understand the Liturgy of the Church. And that dynamic interrelationship between and within our understanding of Liturgy is a remind of its implicit significance and meaning.

# CHAPTER TEN

## 10    LESS OR MORE THAN THE TOTALITY OF THINGS

*We must discover the unchanging yet always contemporary sacramental vision of life. But what is a sacrament? It is always a passage, a transformation. Yet it is not a passage into "supernature" but into the Kingdom of God, the world to come, but which is in the very reality of this world and its life as redeemed and restored by Christ. It is the transformation not of "nature' into "supernature" but of the old into the new. A sacrament thus is not a "miracle" by which God breaks the "laws of nature" but the manifestation of the ultimate Truth about the world and life, and personhood and nature, the Truth which is Christ. In Christ, life in all its totality is returned to our humanity to be again sacrament and communion, to be again Eucharist. It is this life and not some other that is given to be a sacrament of the divine presence.* Alexander Schmemann

We may well meet different attitudes towards the "world" when in at worship in church. This surfaces in the prayers, or the sermon, or in discussion with other church goers, or in what people might say to us casually from time to time. We may not even pause to think about it, or perhaps we sometimes stop and wonder what these differences might mean or imply. Do they, for example, represent substantially different, underlying views of God? Broadly speaking (and rather stereotypically or simplistically) we might describe them flowing from two main approaches.

The first is easier to spot and probably more attractive to many Christians because it doesn't beat about the bush. It suits a temperament that wants to find simple answers, especially if they divide things up into what we call "binaries" of the "yes" or "no" type. It also suits a view of Christianity which goes with that temperament and needs to get things clear. According to this view, things have to be one thing or the other. It helps, of course, if you can find echoes of this approach in the way you choose to interpret certain Bible passages. It also helps if your experience of the world is that it's going to hell in a handcart. Everything is wrong because everything is sinful. Sort the sin out and everything will be right again. And who wouldn't want that! So yes, it involves a radical view of sin that writers like Paul, Augustine and Calvin have propagated.

The Fall produced the down-fall of human kind from semi or complete perfection to its exact opposite, and a complete mess ensued. Without the salvation offered in Christ, who comes in as the divine "repair man", if I may put it like that, nothing would or could change. The movement is from being, on the one hand, completely subject to a kind of ontological sin, passed on in the spiritual DNA of the human condition through the generations, to, on the other hand, an opposite state of redeemed salvation where our sin has been taken away and we are created anew back into a state that reflects how we should be in our created human condition.

What are the implications of this for our understanding of Liturgy? God intervenes in the "normal" state of this fallen, "secular" world at special moments in history, (the revelation of the Law and the prophets, the coming of Jesus and the Holy Spirit….) to change it and redeem it. The word "intervenes" implies, of course, a certain absence or distance at other times. The world, in itself, and all those within it who aren't disciples of Jesus, are seen as essentially secular, if not the source of evil. The sacraments of the church (where these are present and affirmed) could be seen as the way through which God intervenes through the ministry of the Church. Even more likely, the preaching of the Word of God is seen as the more crucial intervening, witness moment, emanating from the worship of the Church, or, even more powerfully, the mission of individual Spirit filled Christians to evangelize and make new disciples in a direct, person to person way. Indeed, the disciple-makers often make little of the idea of sacraments or even priests, as those things appear secondary to the task of evangelism. And many are called to this ministry not least through new Christian movements.

The second way, broadly speaking, is to stand back from the idea of God intervening in an evil world to change it, and move more towards the idea of God's presence within the reality of the world, however that is understood. It is the presence of a Love that fully respects human agency. It is a presence that doesn't remove human responsibility, but works within it and transcends it. Within this sense of presence, God affirms what is already true within the nature of creation and the human condition. This is a God who, as we are told in Genesis One, saw everything as being "good". This is a goodness that has not been radically destroyed, even though it might be distorted by the theological meaning of the Fall. Here, the world is no longer seen as dominated by the Fall, and Sin is interpreted differently.

This approach can be found in St Irenaeus of Lyon for example. He seemed to understand sin not as a radical reversal of the goodness of human nature from all good to all bad, but as a realistic description of our need to develop and mature, just as small children need to learn and grow up. Yes, humans are still capable not only of frailty and failure, but of devastatingly destructive behaviours. But their finite capacity and their wicked ways are mixed up with the nature of the human condition and always have been. The Fall wasn't some single, historical event with metaphysical or ontological consequences, and there was no such thing as a pre-fall condition of perfection. This fits with what we know from the historical evidence of evolution for example. There were no semi-gods walking the earth in a state of bliss and grace. Adam and Eve, were not two historical figures at the beginning of time, but stand for all humanity as subject to a mixture of motives and intentions which could go either way, and are largely interconnected within the complexity of the human condition. They are also part of the nature of nature as creation. And creation, in itself and of itself, can be viewed as an ontological sacrament of God's presence. God does not need to intervene from outside, but is waiting to be discovered and affirmed as part of the givenness of Creation in his transcendent and immanent being. This creator God creates in ways that guarantee the continuing autonomy and freedom of humans as they have evolved within the way nature evolves. And the possibility of self-aware relationship exists and is restored by the presence of Christ. He is the dynamic model for our new humanity, within which we can respond to God in a new way and from within a new sense of relationship within creation. And we have full responsibility for what we make of that, within our autonomy and freedom. This freedom is seen as itself a gift and grace in the human condition, and one that flows from the nature of the creator as love. And, as theologians like Karl Rahner have claimed, there is grace in that outflowing; grace which infuses the whole of creation, and all humans in their latent capacity to relate to each other and to God.

It is of course all too easy and natural for Christians to speak of creation or even "the whole of creation". One difference between the Liturgy of the World and the Liturgy of the Church was that, in the former, people stereotypically viewed nature as "nature", and not as "creation". In fact, many of those in the Liturgy of the Church, (at significant times from the early period on, and then from the eighteenth century in a new way) who perceived nature as created nature, also recognised nature as having its own internal, natural processes, not least from a scientific, as well as a theological point of view. So, in one sense, despite their obvious differences and contradictions, these points of view had, and have, something in common. They both take nature seriously. And that means they have to take it seriously in its entirety, including all its unpredictable, destructive forces which are, from a different perspective, part of the bigger story of its creativity. And that also means taking the entombed dormancy of winter's death and dearth seriously, as the source of spring resurrection fecundity. Clearly those looking at nature from within the Liturgy of the Church would want to keep that kind of language, whereas many in the Liturgy of the World would not find it appropriate, except perhaps in a poetic sense. And taking nature seriously also means committing to a serious investigation into nature's ways, with an open mind exploring assumptions and new discoveries. And it also means appreciating the overwhelming beauty of combinations of shapes, scale and colours which create different reactions and moods in the human gaze and perception. And while that is happening, taking it seriously would entail finding ways to incorporate, into that human gaze, the reality of nature's contradictions, conflicts and competitive ways, just as the human perceiving these things, through their human gaze, have to accept those ways and processes within their own nature and the nature of their perception.

For this and other reasons, the idea of the "whole of creation" is important, and was important from the very beginning of

Christianity. It was the reality into which the meaning of the Word being made flesh was accommodated and interpreted. It was a reminder that the God of creation was, as Creator or Source, in relationship with the very nature of all nature, including humans on this planet, who remain within that relationship whether or not they acknowledge or accept it. According to this view, our main task isn't to convert people, but to discover and affirm that which is of God in everyone. This is underwired by our commitment to do what we can through social support and community development programmes; engagement in all sectors, to address the causes of disadvantage, criminality, need, alienation, loss of purpose, structural inequality, poverty, lost agency, or anything which blocks personal and spiritual development and integrity, joy and thanksgiving. And the latter are all part of the Eucharistic experience of the Liturgy of the Church as it overflows into the Liturgy of the World, and has its significance there; a significance that perhaps it was always meant to have. This is how Schmemann talks about it in ways that link the Liturgy of the World with the Liturgy of the Church.

*The world as man's food is not something "material" and limited to material functions, thus different from, and opposed to, the specifically "spiritual" functions by which man is related to God. All that exists is God's gift to man, and it all exists to make God known to man, to make man's life communion with God. It is divine love made food, made life for man. God blesses everything He creates, and, in biblical language, this means that He makes all creation the sign and means of His presence and wisdom, love and revelation: "O taste and see that the Lord is good".*

*Centuries of secularism have failed to transform eating into something strictly utilitarian. Food is still treated with reverence. A meal is still a rite— the last "natural sacrament" of family and friendship, of life that is more than "eating" and "drinking." To eat is still something more than to maintain bodily functions. People may not understand what that "something more" is, but they nonetheless desire to celebrate it. They are still hungry and thirsty for sacramental life[97].*

There, at the heart of his thesis, is the idea that hunger for a sacramental life is a "natural" part of our human experience,

---

[97] The World as Sacrament.

Meanwhile, those two, crudely depicted approaches or broad categorisations I've made above, are too simplistic a depiction of the variety of positions adopted by different churches and different parts of churches through time. Both have important points to make. Of course, we must take seriously the presence of sin and our need for forgiveness. Of course, we believe that the incarnation was a divine intervention in our direction to move from within the human condition to restore our capacity for spiritual development and not to be dominated by our worst instincts and behaviours in our relationship with others and with God. We dare not say Christ did not come to save sinners in particular, or in general. But we dare not ignore the theological and spiritual significance of creation, nor the naturally indwelling skills and goodness of so many people. Dare we reduce the territory of sacraments to what happens in the Liturgy of the Church alone, and ignore the sacramental significance of creation itself, as being in an ontological relationship with God? Dare we ignore our place in the wider context of creation and its use and misuse, or the wider and deeper context which influences our personal development and decision making and their spiritual significance?

It is all too easy for those Christians who primarily see themselves as evangelical "disciple makers" to ignore those crucial contexts or dismiss them as being irrelevant to our eternal salvation. I suppose neither approach I've categorised should be considered in isolation from the background influences which have inspired and nurtured them. We could say they need each other and, where a mutual learning and influence has taken place, it can be but a healthy and edifying opportunity. But this is rare. I suspect the distance between them is as great as it ever was in the history of the church. Each orientation has produced its own fundamentalist, if not extremist advocates. I, for one, believe we can be helped by a new orientation that takes us back to something which developed quite early on, that may now have been largely forgotten, or rejected, or was never even known in some circles. Several Orthodox theologians of the last century have been working on it. Writers like Olivier Clement, Vladimir Lossky, Christos Yannaris, and Alexander

Schmemann, not to mention notable others from different church backgrounds who have been touched by this early theology, people like Rowan Williams for example. This approach is well summed up by these short, powerful sentences in the Schmemann's book,

*In Christ, life in all its totality is returned to our humanity to be again sacrament and communion, to be again Eucharist. It is this life and not some other that is given to be a sacrament of the divine presence[98].*

There is a generosity of inclusion here that I suggest we dare not unthinkingly reject or take lightly. It puts the Eucharist centre stage but then positions it within the *totality* of all life as a sacrament of the divine presence. This goes to the heart of what I'm calling Inside-Out Liturgy. In a Western context, this is a very rare and precious way of understanding the world and one rarely found in sermons and teaching within Catholic, Protestant and Anglican church circles. In a devastating critique, Schmemann makes that well quoted statement,

*Whether we "spiritualize" our life or "secularize" our religion, whether we invite men to a spiritual banquet or simply join them at the secular one, the real life of the world, for which we are told God gave his only begotten Son, remains hopelessly beyond our religious grasp[99].*

With these compelling and challenging words, we are invited to look again at what we assume we and others mean by our Christian beliefs, and the attitudes which flow from them. We sense a completely different orientation, somewhere between, or rather beyond, the way we normally use the juxtaposition of the sacred and the secular in religious talk. We sense we are being taken back to basics in the "real life of the world", and the metaphor used for that, in this short quotation, is that of a meal. In other words, a daily and normal human activity, whatever the quantity or quality of the food provided, and that of course can't be taken for granted. The need to eat is part of the biology of all living things. It is crucial for life itself. The human species has developed various social and cultural rituals associated with eating and drinking. We have evolved skills of

---

[98] The World as Sacrament.
[99] Ibid

presentation as well as the production and distribution of food. We have studied the genetics of food products and through science made their production more efficient and safer. We have passed on the skills of cooking and invested hugely in the training and status of cooks. It is hard to imagine now any special occasion from births, marriages and funerals through to birthdays, anniversaries and passing exams without any food or drink associated with it. We may no longer include domestic science or cookery in our school curricula, but advice or books on cooking and diet are ubiquitous in the shops, online, and in media commercials.

And throughout the world and in most religions, a meal is a place where hospitality is shown, where hurts are healed, where reconciliation happens, where good news is announced, stores and jokes shared, where friendships are celebrated or renewed, where people fall in love, where generosity to strangers helps them to finally relax and feel welcome as strangers no more. And all of this and more happens because the table is laid and a meal is shared, a meal that has been prepared with great care and often at great cost. Everyone on this planet knows what it is to spend time producing and preparing and then sharing and consuming food, at whatever level and whatever cost. Meals may come in all kinds of different ways and forms, but there is something basically true about all of them, that is so normal we may miss its significance. We eat every day, those of us who are lucky enough not to be malnourished or starving. Whatever it is we eat, and however it is done, it is a basic biological need that can also have the dimension of a social need and relational occasion. Some are forced of necessity to eat on their own and they know it is a different experience. Many families in the West eat without sharing the same table at the same time, or even the same food. Many hardly stop what they are already doing to quickly eat and drink as if it is an unfortunate necessity they have to give into occasionally. A meal then is something basic to the Liturgy of the World. This is what Schmemann said about it. *The natural dependence of man upon the world was intended to be transformed constantly into communion with God in whom is all life*[100].

Many, probably most people in the world, don't stop to think of a meal in this way. Indeed, many Christians don't. The virtue of saying a prayer before a meal was that it made us pause to at least consider its deeper significance. Yes, sometimes the prayer implied that human hands had nothing to do with its provision as if it came straight from God. Yes, sometimes, the prayer was just a formulaic ritual. But it was a pause, a moment to consider what we are really doing when we eat together. And, yes, it provided a framework to eat together around the same table. I know, from personal experience, how easy it is for that habit to slip. Working lives often mean we rush breakfast and have it separately because of different schedules. We rush a sandwich at work while we are still doing something else, for proper lunch breaks are now rare, except in certain work places or where people can afford to entertain others in restaurants. In my working life, I can't remember ever stopping to eat a sandwich on a proper break away from my computer unless it was a business lunch of some kind. We grab something to eat on the way home or send out for a take-away, while we turn to our small or larger screens. It's so easy not to even notice what we are eating, what it really tastes like, where the food comes from, and who prepared it.

While all this is part of contemporary life, there is more attention than ever to media programmes about the value of nutritional balance in a healthy diet. Most food advertising companies promote their wares on the basis of some ethical or aesthetic appeal, while many choose fast food and low-price which seduce large numbers of people living busy family or working lives where money is short. And then, occasionally, there is a special occasion; a child's birthday, an anniversary, a celebration for this, that, or the other, for which we book or cook a special meal, dress up, take our time, lay the table, light a candle, invite friends round.

And it's the meaning of those occasions or the conversation, or the simple pleasure of it, that makes the meal so special, as well as the wonder of the quality or type of the food. And underneath all that, lies hidden in plain sight the basic truth that the meal makes the

[100] For the Life of the Word

occasion of heightened relational communion possible, which makes the pleasure, the being together possible, and expresses the generosity and love involved in what is being done and offered. For love is the divine gift within the heart of human nature, often suppressed, hurt, or taken for granted, but there, in the countless and unrecorded gifts of charity for and to others. And that love, in all its "ordinary" expressions in the Life of the World, touches the very heart of the Liturgy of the World, as a mirror image of the Liturgy of the Church. Alexander Schmemann has this to say about it.

*The Church, if it is to be the Church, must be the revelation of that divine Love which God "poured out into our hearts." Without this love nothing is "valid" in the Church because nothing is possible. The content of Christ's Eucharist is Love, and only through love can we enter into it and be made its partakers.*

So often, as a student in Romania, I was invited into people's homes where they brought out the best they had, the best they could afford which was often more than they had for themselves. Their hospitality and generosity felt genuine and heart-felt. I count it as a privilege in my memories of those days. At Easter, after the Holy Saturday evening Liturgy of the Resurrection light, I had been invited back to their house for the Easter meal by a priest and his wife in Bucharest. We carefully walked back from the Cathedral, along with hundreds of others, protecting our still lit candles from the wind. We arrived at their house at about one in the morning. We lit the candles on the table from our Easter candles. We sat as a family. Somehow or other a meal appeared, and I could see how much trouble they had gone to, imagining how much it must have cost them. And that meal, combined with the sense of joy engendered by the Easter event, went on until the first light of dawn. They somehow managed to make simple food stretch into several courses, interlaced with good conversation. There was, at least in my perception, a light shining in their eyes with the sheer pleasure of hosting that meal, of giving of themselves in that way and somehow it overflowed its presence into my experience of that special occasion.

Most Sikh Gurdwaras will demonstrate wonderful generosity as they practice open hospitality. There are meals in church halls where ecumenical partners are invited, Jewish Synagogues where Arabs and Palestinians are invited. Meals attract their own rituals. On special occasions, the rituals of a meal become their own form of Liturgy. Liturgy incorporates the cultural traditions and habits of different places and situations. And the simplest of foods can make up a banquet where generous love transforms a variety of tensions and difficulties.

In England, the offer of a cup of tea and a biscuit can be the beginning of a new friendship, or help offered in bereavement, reassurance given in sorrow and failure, or just the reaffirmation of an easy acceptance during normal times. In some places and situations, a cup of water lovingly brought to someone in need is enough to express something deeper to those who thirst. And underneath all these ways of expressing love in the rituals of meals, we find meaning for our understanding of the Liturgy of the World and the foundational words of Christian thinking. Words like Incarnation and Sacrament for example. These continue to be central pillars for the theme and ideas of this book on Liturgy.

# CHAPTER ELEVEN

## 11    SACRAMENTS OUTSIDE-IN AND INSIDE-OUT

*Rahner assumes therefore that the "secular" world is, from the outset, always encompassed and permeated with the grace of God's self-communication. God's self-communication is present in our world and our history in two forms; as an offer made to our freedom, and as the acceptance or rejection by our freedom of this offer... The offer of God's self-communication is never withdrawn, no matter how hardened or resistant we might be to this invitation. And the self-communication of God is offered not only to the human community but to the entire universe as well. God invites every part of the cosmos to enter into communion with the absolute mystery according to its own capacity. The material world cannot enter into an interpersonal relationship with God, but it can be united with God as something loved by God[101].*

*In the Orthodox ecclesial experience and tradition, a sacrament is understood primarily as a revelation of the genuine nature of creation, of the world, which, however much it has fallen as "this world," will remain God's world, awaiting salvation, redemption, healing and transfiguration in a new earth and a new heaven. In other words, in the Orthodox experience a sacrament is primarily a revelation of the sacramentality of creation itself, for the world was created and given to man for conversion of creaturely life into participation in divine life. If in baptism water can become a "laver of regeneration," if our earthy food - bread and wine - can be transformed into partaking of the body and blood of Christ, if with oil we are granted the anointment of the Holy Spirit, if, to put it briefly, everything in the world can be identified, manifested and understood as a gift of God and participation in the new life, it is because all of creation was originally summoned and destined for the fulfillment of the divine economy - "then God will be all in all[102].*

## LITURGY AS PIVOT POINT BETWEEN DUALISMS

The intersection or conjunction of the divine and the human, in the incarnation, has to be the pivot point around which sacramental theology develops. It is the door through which we

---

[101] Skelly Karl Rahner's Theology of Worship. p 58

[102] Alexander Schmemann; *The Eucharist; Sacrament of the Kingdom*

glimpse the sacramental significance of all creation, restored to us by the act of God in the incarnation. It radically changes our understanding of what we mean by the holy or the sacred, for now that is embedded in what we understand about the world into which God is en-fleshed. Although it sounds foolish and scandalous to some religious people, and ridiculous and irrelevant to those who choose to ignore or reject religion, the holy and the sacred are now revealed to be hiding in plain sight, intrinsically, within the landscape of what is often described as the secular, or even profane (from a word meaning before or outside the temple and therefore un-consecrated, and defiled).

In this sense, the incarnation challenges any simplistic dualism between the sacred and the secular, or the religious and the profane. The writer of Mathew's Gospel thought this was so important that he gave us the image of the veil in the Temple, (separating the sanctity of the holy of holies from the main and other courts, not to mention those that were pro-fanum), being rent in two at the time of the crucifixion[103]. This part of the gospel is sometimes overlooked when all the other salvation implications of Christ's suffering and death are discussed by contemporary writers. It is a moment of huge, symbolic importance. It points to an effect of the crucifixion that changes everything in creation, or rather the way Christians perceive creation. The abolition of the old way of doing religion, and its dualisms, is now transformed, as part of the new covenant in Christ with obvious implications for any Liturgy of the World. Through the human life of Christ, humanity is hallowed and creation becomes again holy ground on which to tread joyfully, but carefully. Put even more symbolically, we might say that the garden of Eden is no longer barred to us, and we can rediscover our vocation to live in it and work within it, and with it more responsibly. The sacramentality of where we are, and what we do, is again glimpsed and offered to us in the Liturgy of the World as a gift from God, as creator and redeemer. And this understanding of sacraments predates all that was to happen

---

[103] Mathew 27. 51

later, particularly in the Council of Trent in the great discussions about their number and way of working.

Of course, there have been many different kinds of theological and often tense debates about the classification and efficacy of sacraments, not least at that Council of Trent (1545-1563), convened by Paul 111 with about two hundred and fifty Catholic bishops and leaders present, producing no fewer than seventeen dogmatic decrees. Its concern was to stress the "objectivity" of the sacraments in response to the Reformation emphasis on dependency on faith alone. But right up until recent times, the debate has oscillated between two interrelated questions - the nature of the sacraments in terms, for example, of what really happens to the substance or "accidents" of the bread and wine in the process of what the Catholic Church calls "transubstantiation", and the authority/power of the priest to make this happen, to make them efficacious, or to use that legalistic term "valid".

So, it was often said by the formal decrees of the Catholic Church, and probably still is, that I, as an Anglican priest, cannot "validly" celebrate the objective presence of Christ in the Eucharist, whatever else I think I am doing, because I don't have the power/authority to do this. That validity hasn't been as it were "passed down" to me, because the line of apostolic succession has been broken by the Reformation and so the Bishop who ordained me wasn't in that line of succession-type linear authority. Therefore, ipso facto, my priesthood is invalid even if my "ministry" isn't! No, those words have been voiced aloud to me by a Catholic priest. Therefore, any Eucharistic sacramental service in the Anglican Church is invalid, although, they say, or at least sometimes they do, that of course all of this is up to God.

But this view of successive, linear, episcopal authority was broken a long time ago in the early church with disputes and divisions between different episcopal areas over doctrinal divisions and excommunications. In any case, it is surely far too transactional and literal an understanding of what happens in the Eucharist because of the "validity" passed down from bishop to priest; far too minimal to do justice to the way the Holy Spirit, acting in and through the whole service, and the whole congregation, (as well as the words and actions of the priest), is present in the "transformation" of the meaning of the bread and wine, not least through the "epiclesis" or invocation of the presence and work of that same Spirit over the elements of bread and wine. An Orthodox monk once told me that the epiclesis shouldn't just be seen as a moment in the Liturgy (at what we in the West strangely call the words of "Institution"[104]), but a dimension of everything in the Liturgy and of the meaning of Liturgy itself.

## LITURGY AS ECONOMIC AND SOCIAL CONTEXT

In my maximal understanding of liturgy, I'm stepping back from those transactional kinds of debates and their underlying assumptions and orientation. Suppose then, we shifted our emphasis away from the efficacy or categorization, or priestly authority behind sacraments, and turned instead to a bigger context within which we can view the meaning of a sacrament per se. Suppose we stepped back from the usual context of sacramental language and usage in the rituals and disputes of the church, and saw this through the lens of creation itself. The doctrinal definitions of sacraments have too often operated within a closed, looped circle of church context, and therefore it's perhaps not surprising to find that strange word "validity" popping up in the minds of some. But suppose the reference points to the presence of sacraments were seen as being part of the life of the world itself. Saint Augustine of Hippo applied the content of Eucharistic action to our human responsibilities and roles in the world in the following way,

*You are to incarnate the theme of your adoration. You are to be taken, blessed, broken, distributed that the work of the incarnation may go forward, that you may be the means of grace and the vehicles of eternal charity[105].*

And yes, our understanding of those reference points, and that presence, would come through the Liturgy of the Church. But this is notoriously divided and divisive territory. Yet, it is surely the focal

---

[104] A word many in the Orthodox world find strange given its other meanings.
[105] 4th Century. Easter sermon during the sack of Rome.

point of sacramental experience for faithful congregations; a focal point that, in many contemporary liturgies, directs our gaze to the wider context of creation in key words that begin the Eucharistic prayer in many Western Churches.

*Blessed are you, Lord God of all creation, through your goodness we have this bread to offer: fruit of the earth and work of human hands, it will become for us the bread of life. Blessed are you Lord God of all creation, Through your goodness we have this wine to offer, Fruit of the wine and work of human hands. It will become our spiritual drink.*

In those short phrases, our attention is focused on the whole complicated economic and social processes behind the production of bread and wine. This includes the sowing of seeds, research and development into different varieties and types, the agricultural tending of the land, the fertilisers used or not used in the growing of the wheat and the vines, their harvesting, production, transport and distribution, marketing and management, financing and consumption choices. All of these things are brought "objectively" into the inclusive sacramental presence of bread and wine on the altar. They are part of the human process of managing the things of creation which are now offered sacramentally in the Eucharist, because we are re-membering the words of Jesus as recorded in one of the earliest Christian letters.

*This is my body broken for you. Do this in remembrance of me. And in the same way also he took the cup, after supper, saying, "This cup is the new covenant in my blood. Do this, as often as you drink it, in remembrance of me." 1 Corinthians 11. 24-28*

The Orthodox, maximal understanding of liturgy gives us the opportunity for a similar orientation in all churches, which may, in turn, give us something more spiritually and theologically fertile, creative and inclusive, something that overflows its meaning and inspiration beyond the boundaries of our Church expectations and interpretations. It is so easy for us to view sacraments exclusively from within the traditions of service and devotion that happen "in church". Bethlehem and Calvary did not happen in a church service, but now what happens in church services point people back to experience their meaning in the world. Redemption didn't happen in the Temple or a synagogue service of worship, but the human life of Jesus situated in real history, and in real circumstances, and in a real human birth and life ending in a criminal, public execution. And if Christians shine or reflect the focus of the light of Christ on real human circumstances, in the real life and work of the world, they are but following the movement of God in that direction as revealed in Jesus. And that is the context of our worship and its purpose. And although we too often experience the reality of the world as a place of struggle and suffering, contradictions and confusions, that no longer precludes the way God has been en-fleshed within it, so that we may discern the things of God which are transcendent of it.

For, if the cross of Jesus's suffering takes place in the heart of creation, then so does its meaning as revealed in the One who appeared to Mary as the gardener she didn't at first recognize, the gardener who knew her and named her as she was, and would become. The world is not as it appears to be ,if we enter into the Liturgy of the World and know the place differently, shot through with the grace that can transform us with the light of new perception, recognition and understanding, the grace that illuminates our understanding of who we are, and where we are. This is the bounteous grace that names us and our potential as co-creating, co-labouring, co-shaping, co-stewarding and co-operating human beings in the transforming of the Garden of Eden that is our human home.

If the Liturgy of the Church celebrates and calls us to this vocation, this return, this transformation, then, because of that, it takes place in the ordinary life of the Liturgy of the World, where we have to help each other work this out, and work towards and with the Kingdom of God, invisibly present in that Liturgy of the World. And this is good news indeed for those who have never found the Liturgy of the Church accessible or meaningful, or who have dismissed it as irrelevant ritual because it doesn't connect with their everyday lives. But we know that an encounter with God can happen anywhere, and everywhere, and certainly it happens in the ordinary experiences of everyday life in the world - that which is sometimes called "secular" by religious people, so dismissing any possibility that it might in fact be holy. For example, Teilhard De Chardin, somewhere, once said, *Do not forget that the value and interest of life is not so much to do conspicuous things...as to do ordinary things with the perception of their enormous value.*

## ORDINARY THINGS OUTSIDE-IN OR INSIDE-OUT

From the very beginning of all things, God communicated his goodness through ordinary things. So why wouldn't we expect to find God's goodness in ordinary things, and even an encounter with the holiness of God through ordinary things, and ordinary experiences, though the epithet "ordinary" seems something now of a blasphemy. For nothing God has made should be called ordinary, even though those things are ubiquitous and often taken for granted, and certainly often misused and misunderstood. Many of the great poets and painters, as well as great scientists, have inspired us to look more carefully and to probe beneath the surface of "ordinary" things; to discover more about them by exploring their territory and significance. Some artists and scientists, like the mystics of the early church, have talked about unveiling the ordinary to uncover the unknown which is just there, hidden in plain sight, although veiled by the things we take for granted and with which we have become over "familiar", so that we no longer see what we are looking at.

The incarnation can inspire us to look again under the stone, under the surface of things, including our own nature, to see something rather wonderful and holy in the capacity of our humanity to encounter and uncover something of a reflection, at least, however distorted, of its created self. And that selfhood contains the latency to feel again the deepest origin, memory, identity of the divine, which is the creative presence of the image of God as revealed in Christ. And the scandal was not only in the crucifixion of this image, but in its birth within the human limits of that reflected image. And the scandal took flesh in the ordinary to show it could contain more than the ordinary, just as life itself could contain a reflection of the goodness of its creation, and be a sacrament of that goodness, waiting to be uncovered as only Jesus could, in the way he related to ordinary people.

And perhaps it is towards the sacramental significance of the ordinary that we must learn to look and return, in order to recognise and reaffirm its potential for created goodness, remembering that all of creation is, or would be, profoundly affected. So, we might look for, and expect, that what happens within the Liturgy of the Church makes re-orientates us towards what happens within the Liturgy of the World, everywhere in the world. And perhaps that orientation is its own form of evangelization, not to impose from without some kind of divine template, but to rediscover it from within. For that which is ordinary has been given as a sacrament of that which is implicitly if not explicitly sublime. For that which is kenosis, in its self-emptying, is kenotically ek-static in its emanating dimensions of self-revealing, outside of itself in order to express or be it-self. For that which is inside is implicitly Inside-Out in order to stand outside itself of itself in our perception from the outside in of its meaning and significance!

If God's grace only worked in the worship of the Liturgy of the Church, and in beautiful church buildings, then indeed ordinary things might be described as "ordinary", "mundane" or secular, by comparison. But, if the ordinary has been, and is, the place of an encounter, epiphany, liberation, transformation, revelation of new understanding and perception of the holiness of God, then we might equally call it extra-ordinary. And there is much to discover within the ordinary that is of the nature of the extra-ordinary, as poets and painters, architects, designers, engineers and makers of things have demonstrated in their search for ways to contemplate it, re-produce, re-present or understand and comment on their perception of it.

## ART; THE EPIPHANY OF SIGNIFICANCE

In the Liturgy of the World, art is only a partial expression of the way we shape and design our environment. But in its maximal sense, it not only includes architecture and engineering, but the way we order our production of any goods and services to the best of our ability, and as an expression of human work purposefully and carefully done. High art may be the expression of a civilising culture, but, in situations of hardship and crisis, it may be a luxury compared to the art of survival. Yet, art seems to have appeared in early human societies, and continued right through different eras of social and political change in all cultures. Cave art, with hand stencilling, goes back to at least 37,900 B.C. The Sulawesi cave paintings of that date follow the El Castillo cave paintings of around 39,000 B.C. When it comes to sculpture, the ivory carving of a female form known as the Venus of Hohle Fels, or the Venus of Schelklingen, discovered in 2008, goes back to between 38,000 and 33,000 B.C. The Lion Man of Hohlenstein Stadel is the oldest carving of a male animal figure, dating back to 38,000 B.C. It was only discovered as late as 1939. Even older, in a Neanderthal occupied cave in France, is the "cupule" (hemispherical petroglyph made by repeated knocking on a rock surface with an instrument) rock art that can be dated back to between 70,000 and 40,000 B.C. Abstract crosshatching and geometric shapes found on an eggshell in Diepklook, South Africa probably go back to 60,000 B.C. In this earliest form of art, it is thought that, whatever its purpose was, it had to be cultural as well as utilitarian. In some cases, there may have been some kind of association with certain religious beliefs, but this is hard to prove.

The language of death and life, birth and rebirth is very common in the arts, and takes on many forms. Different artists, using different media, including of course the novel, move in and out of the implicit and explicit descriptions of reality, often through the use of metaphors and symbols to express the inexpressible about situations of crisis, tragedy, degradation, despair, love, restoration, reconciliation and social transformation. For ten years or more, I was on the Board of Artes Mundi, based in Wales. Whereas the Turner prize was primarily for British artists, our short-listed artists came from all over the world, as did our judges. It was a rare privilege to meet and talk with the artists at the time of the dinner for the prize winner. Their art often straddled the representation of particular situations of the "human condition" in their own countries, mixed with an awareness of different international perspectives on the issues involved. While, sometimes, the language used to describe a work of art can be over-reaching, the experience of looking harder, or differently, at the world through the lens of art can be a revelatory experience.

Art represents a journey into the space of incompletion, in our yearning for completion, connectivity, communion, and fulfilment. The artist feels inspired or compelled not only to reflect and think intelligently about what she feels or experiences inside, but to pick up some tool, instrument or material to attempt to represent its spiritual, "sacramental", and ultimately its liturgical significance in the doing of public works through the expressing of personal work. None of this language may be used in the process, but may be inferred when we consider the nature of its significance from a liturgical point of view. The artistic calling is to a material, transformative expression or manifestation, of some thing, as a vehicle for something else, something inward and/or beyond, that makes an ek-static connection as a dimension of that expression, moving outwards in the direction of something else and something more. In the process of that expression, something invisible becomes visible, something intangible becomes tangible as a self-extension of the artist's vision or experience, an overflowing of the self into an external connection. In this sense, it contains a comparable yearning to the experience of eros, that sense of being connected outside of one's self, in order to be more of one's self, or to find one's self in a communing relationship with the physical and emotional other, so that the mutuality of the connection may come alive and lead to a sense of completion in the midst of incompletion.

## ART; RE-PRESENTING PERCEPTION-EXPERIENCE

Artists seek to re-present and reflect different experiences of different kinds of reality, knowing that perception is everything, but that perception takes place through the filter of our human nature, experience and knowledge. That process and experience of perception broadens the dogmas of knowledge which have been locked up in the post-Enlightenment world of rational evidence and "data" as the dominant cultural assumptions of our times. In the process of working on art, the artist has to reflect, reveal, and then struggle with their own idea of how their media can re-present what they see, in their imaginative mind's eye, or, physically, in visual reality. And what they see or how they see it, comes from assumptions and ideas picked up from the culture they've inherited or are in the process of changing.

One dimension of 18th century Enlightenment ideas in England and Scotland, was the need to challenge the pomposity of establishment values by the use of satirical humour. In its way, this was part of the new humanism of critical and sceptical rationality. In Scotland, Robert Burns used local language, common sense and honest, humorous, critical contempt to promote a disdainful and celebratory, Enlightenment egalitarianism. In England, Hogarth was doing something similar with his vivid, graphic cartoons. This was a century of rapid economic, scientific and artistic progress, all too often built on the wealth predicated on slavery and imports from the colonies. Fortunes were made out of sugar, tea and coffee production – luxuries used in the coffee houses to inspire Enlightenment discussion and ideas. Entrepreneurs like Josiah Wedgewood joined the early opposition to slavery and yet, at the same time, made crockery and ceramics for the monarchs of Russia and Europe[106]. The monarchy and the gentry were lampooned as having feet of clay in this world of more open discussion, pamphleteering and satire. Tensions increased because of soaring inequalities and the upwardly mobile and landed gentry used a culture of manners and fashion to highlight their distance from the lower classes and the poor on the streets. Some artists were fearless in representing the worst of their contemporary culture's bad ideas and habits. In so doing they not only struck a nerve but attracted popular support for the issues they represented.

"Re-presentation", in this sense, is an activity of Liturgy in the realities of the world. Artists work within particular traditions or genres of representation to some extent, and through creative innovation and new ideas to another extent, with the relationship between them not always feeling as if it is within obviously, conscious control. And what artist end up with at the end of the artistic process may be different from what they started out to

---

[106] And did a lot of entrepreneurial "levelling up" in is part of the Midlands without Government Assistance Grants or subsidies.

produce. The experience of the process of the production of a work of art is often a surprise to the artist, as things happen as if of their own accord, or when, in the doing of something, it is discovered that one thing leads naturally to something unexpected, but which feels right at the time, even though it wasn't in the plan or orbit of the original, design intention.

This experience can be more than just "use redesigning design assumptions and philosophy". That often happens and adjustments and readjustments are made which make things work out better in the long run. That is of the essence of different engineering and technological processes as well artistic ones. The process becomes its own teacher, and we learn, by doing, how to make things look, or work, better. We learn how to compensate for or correct mistakes made in the process. That learning can force us back to the original thought or design to either start again, or make certain alternations based on experience. But then, there may be something else at work in the process of doing and making.

## ART AS CREATIVE TRUST

I have often found that to be true, in my own pathetic attempts at painting, and certainly in writing novels. It's more about trust than design. One brush of paint leads to the next, which inspires something unplanned to happen. One sentence seems to lead to the next, unexpected sentence, if I can only get out of its way, and trust that what is happening has its own validity, whatever I may have originally set out to write. In fact, it often seems as if the novel writes itself, sentence by sentence, and chapter by chapter, if only I have the courage to allow a certain part of my brain to send its own messages directly to my fingers on the keyboard keys. So, what exactly is that about? What is it that gets in the way of true creativity, and exactly which part of the chemistry in our brains is doing the creatively new or unexpected thing, as if on its own accord? And is this kind of creativity part of the Liturgical work and processes involved in the way humans react to different ideas, stimuli and new perspectives, in the art of doing, making and living?

The very idea of creating something new, to re-present something that already exists as a thing or person (via both close observation and wide-ranging, freed up imagination), can itself be an experience of epiphany or revelation in the Liturgy of the World. It is a very direct way of handling, touching, managing, a representative form of life in another form or media, which then creates something new in the process which hasn't existed before.

The word "new" can not only have many meanings, based on different belief assumptions, but can of course be overdone. The Old Testament Hebrew word "bara" to create, is mostly used in the Genesis creation accounts, as if it is reserved for God's act of creation, not for human fashioning, production, copying, making, for which there are other words in those ancient texts. The other words all re-present, in a secondary way, the meaning of "bara". Making and creating, in that sense, is an essential part of being human which may reflect something deeper and spiritual, present in the way creation works in the processes of making itself. The designing, making, handling, and management of things is the basis of human work, and it is through work that humans fashion the content of not only the "things" they need and use, but the very form and functioning of society itself, and everything around them in their home and work environments. I believe this "work" is part of the meaning of Liturgy, and it links the individual with their networked relationships in communities of complex societies, as well as with nature itself. The making of "works" of art then, is part of this larger understanding of Liturgy and indeed the Greek word for "work" in contained within the Greek word for Liturgy. We might well say, as 20th century artists like DuChamp pointed out, that all productive "work", and all things produced by human hands, could, when placed in an art gallery, be seen as works of art. Museums like the Victoria and Albert in London demonstrate how we can look back on ordinary "things", made in different, historical periods, as being just that, ceramics, fashion, clocks, buildings, industrial and agricultural tools etc.

The creation of each art work is of course creating or introducing something new into the world, even when it is copying some object, view, or person, or combination of things that already exist in the world. And that is the case even when it is a copy-forgery of some painting that already exists. In each attempt to re-present something, we are fashioning something that didn't exist before, however miniscule the differences might be to what already has been done or has gone before, or whatever else might be involved in the object of our attention. But what is the relationship between a thing, and a re-presentation of the thing? Why the human compulsion to try and achieve that in so many different ways?

Again, two things seem to be true at the same time. A re-presentation of a thing communicates a thing, but is not the thing. In this sense, a re-presentation of something is like an image or icon of a thing. At the very least, in the work of re-presenting, it is bringing something forward for our attentiveness, or transforming its nature across from one state to another, fashioning something of the nature of a thing into a different version of itself, or what it represents, using a different material or medium. At the least, it is a reminder of a thing, by making something that symbolically stands for it, or rather some aspect of it, in the perception of the artist.

And an artist may also have the viewer's perception in mind and the assumptions they might bring to that viewing. Some artists might say they don't concern themselves with how others perceive what they produce, either in its own right, or what it is re-presenting to and for them. Others are very conscious of the possible future audience of their re-presentation, particularly if a commission, contract, or design request is involved. Liturgy works within the complexity of different perceptions of the nature of the world, and how other things, all things, fit within it, in relationship to those different perceptions and different uses of ordinary things, day by day. Ordinary things designed or made by human hands to become important, useful or beautiful in the perception of those who use them, as well as in the perception of the artist or manufacturer themselves.

## THE IMAGE OF APPEARANCE AND REALITY

The ambiguity of this question of perception - multiple layers of perception in fact - might be seen as an echo of the contradictory nature of different reports of the appearances of Jesus after his resurrection. He is the same but different. These two, contradictory things are both true at the same time. He is seen to be different than he was, but a certain similarity with what he was, remains as part of the "appearance". Appearances depend on the perception of appearances, and the look of what is re-presented, and also what is assumed by and about the appearance. In the Gospel accounts, the appearance isn't recognised at first. In John, for example, the "appearance" of Jesus is confused with the appearance or presence of what is assumed to be the gardener, by the Mary who knew Jesus at least as well, face to face, as anyone else. And then, suddenly, he is recognised, because he has done or said something that shifts her perception as it was influenced by her assumptions and beliefs.

Two disciples walk and talk with the risen Jesus on the road to Emmaus outside Jerusalem, as if he is a complete stranger to them, and then only recognise him when they offer hospitality and invite him to share their table. He breaks bread and somehow, in the act, he is recognised, just before he disappears from their view, their sight, their understanding. The writer might be working backwards from what he knew of the early church's perception of the presence of Jesus in the Eucharistic act of breaking bread, back to the physical appearance of a stranger who suddenly appears and then is known as the resurrected Jesus. The physical look of Jesus is that of a stranger, until that "appearance" moment is perceived and understood through that Eucharistic lens. A connection is then made between the Jesus of that act, and the risen Jesus who appears before them. But the story is told as if the other way around. The stranger appears first, but is not recognised, and then becomes the risen Christ re-presented as being with them through the act.

In the Liturgy of the World, the arts, over time, have explored so many different ways of re-presenting the image of something, in order to communicate the presence of something or someone, and how the significance of that meaning affects them. The image has to be fashioned in such a way as to communicate something about that "object" or "person" to those who take the trouble to really look at it. What it communicates, to its observer, may well vary from person to person, even though they are looking at something well known, like objects in a still life painting, or a person who was well known to them, as in a portrait painting. In more abstracted or impressionistic forms of art, it is surprising how the appearance of a thing, a view, or a person can still be communicated, even though it is fractured and distorted, or obscured by the style of re-presentation. In fact, this new view of a person or a thing may draw out something not seen before in certain on-lookers and so become its own form of epiphany.

And then we come across a painting, or piece of art in a gallery or public space, which holds our attention, not because it represents any thing, or any one, but because it has its own intrinsic, internal quality; one that is achieved either by a harmonious balance of shapes and colour, or because of the opposite - a certain dissonance which somehow reaches down into that part of our perception which appreciates those things. A Jackson Pollock, for example, or a Rothko, might do this as much as a less successful, abstract painting. The idea of abstraction implies that something has been radically changed, distorted, muddled up, or taken away from the natural appearance of things. But in fact, the shapes in nature include many different types of abstract "pattern" which form their own symmetrical or asymmetrical structure and appearance. If, for example, we take a close-up photo of the bark of a tree, it can have a significant appeal all of its own, but from another perspective or standpoint, looked at from outside the context of it being part of a tree. Now it reminds us of an abstract painting of nothing in particular. So, nature, in all its diversity of forms, includes its own abstract patterns, often unseen when we look with the assumption of finding what, in the art world, might be called realism or naturalism. The question then arises as to what extent we can ever paint something whose internal structure makes no kind of sense at all, and includes no obvious patterns, even of a disconnected ordering, and yet can work with something inside our brains which finds that particular combination of positive and negative shapes satisfying.

## LANGUAGE INSIDE-OUT

In the Liturgy of the World, things are invented to solve old or new problems; things are created to be useful or aesthetically pleasing in our relationship with our environment, and all this and more is happening through the way we produce and reproduce our re-presentations of reality or functions within reality. And all the time we are relating to things we have made, produced, used and consumed, we are using names about things and about people, naming type nouns, qualified by adjectives and verbs, to communicate our perception of them, and our understanding of how they work in their place and meaning. And these words are so endemic and embedded in our daily usage, that we don't always realise they are re-presenting the thing, or the person re-presented, to the extent that they become so associated, symbolically, with that thing or person, that it is hard to distinguish between them. A thing whose size, shape, colours and texture is well described by adjectives as well as a noun, and by their context in the sentence we are using, almost becomes equal to that thing in our minds. When we are talking about a small, black coffee table with four, red legs on a blue carpet in the centre of a room, we are communicating the appearance of that table as if indeed it were present in our mind's eye. The re-presentation has already "appeared" in our perception of something because of the language used about it. When we come to see the actual table, it might be larger or smaller than we'd thought, and its legs might be a brighter or darker red making the carpet seem more or less blue and vice versa, but we recognise that it is the thing previously described or talked about. And we seem, as humans, to be able to manoeuvre smoothly and quickly through both the physical reality and the language portraying, symbolising, describing, and communicating the reality, with perhaps only minor adjustments to our perception in relation to the appearance of the thing in reality.

A painting or a photo of reality, in their different ways, are things people enjoy or value looking at. When our daughter visits us after a holiday, she gets out her phone to show us photos of some of the places she's visited, and some of the things she and her family have been doing. And it's almost as if we are seeing those places, rather than just a photo re-presentation of them. And while she is there, she might well have sent us a WhatsApp video of them doing this or that. And then it really is, almost as if we are there, with her, in real time, across whatever distances are involved, looking at them walking through a forest, sitting down to eat with friends, or watching a new baby of one of their friends reach out her hands to one of them, or even to us. And if our daughter, or one of her friends, suddenly looks at us and says hi and waves to us on the video, it is almost the same as the appearance in the flesh of that person speaking and doing that same gesture, at least in the way we perceive it.

But it is, in fact, only a video representation of that appearance making it seem real to us. In the Liturgy of the World, in a digital age, appearances, representations of appearances, and the meaning of things are all part of our human experience, and a perception of our environment which we mostly take for granted, until perhaps we walk into an art gallery to look more intently at some photos or videos of reality, or paintings, and notice the difference and the similarity in our perception, or re-presentation of an appearance, as if both are possible at the same time.

In attempting to capture the representation, or resonance, or remembrance of something, the idea of an image is useful in describing the gap or space between reality and the representation of reality, but also their connection. In the Liturgy of the Church, this is the case in the Eucharistic anamnesis, its memorial or re-membering of what happened in the past, so that it can be experienced in the present. The gap remains, but a connection is made as we cross over that gap through the anamnesis. The combination of a connection and a gap both being true at the same time, expresses something about the inclusion of contradictions in some central, Christian themes. For example, Jesus is human and divine, both at the same time. There is a difference and a connection both at the same time. The radical experience of the suffering and death of Jesus is the radical source of the new life that appears as a resurrected Christ, who shows the holes of the nails of suffering at the same time as his resurrected appearance, an appearing that can suddenly come and then disappear again.

When we talk about creation as being the same as, but, in some way more than, the nature of nature, or when we try to map that which is sacramental or sacred onto that which is material and "ordinary", how shall we explain the gap and the connection between those things, or rather how the connection works across the gap? Again, we are asserting that both are true at the same time, if one accepts the veracity of the belief or perception that this is possible, and is, in fact, the case. In other words, we may choose to perceive something as ordinary, and, at the same time choose to perceive it as ordinary and more than ordinary. There are different kinds of language we can use to articulate the connection between the two. But what seems to be important is that, by using the language of sacramental or the sacred significance, we don't ignore or deny the ordinary nature of a thing. That ordinary nature, might be perceived, scientifically or artistically, as more than the word ordinary usually conveys or implies. We might invest into the language of the ordinary perceptions that make explicit the "something more" and challenge any reduction to something less.

Our language might easily break down at some point in this process, when we want to do justice to two things being true at the same time, without allowing either view to diminish the significance or status of the other. We may still hold on to the experience that we can relate to the "something more" even if the appearance remains ordinary, and even when, though our scientific understanding of its nature, we claim that truly extraordinary levels of complexity are revealed within it, or our artistic perception sees through the associations of the ordinary to something more than ordinary. And this same dilemma occurs when we search for ways of describing what difference it makes to talk about nature as creation, apart, that is, from our belief systems that hold fast to a faith in a Creator of nature or its processes even when we are convinced they work from within their own nature. And this same dilemma occurs when we search for ways of describing what difference it makes to talk about some thing in, or some aspect of, Jesus' humanity, as being also an expression of the divine or that which transcends that human nature. And this same dilemma occurs when we place the template of the

Liturgy of the Church over one of the Liturgy of the World, or when we attempt to represent how an Inside-Out understanding of Liturgy, in itself, can be possible in a world of thought and belief systems that make no formal allowance for a Liturgy of the Church as having anything relevant to do or say about the reality of the world

This dilemma will always sound impossible by its very nature, whatever philosophical systems we appeal to as part of possible explanations. But, although it remains highly appropriate to depend on words like faith and belief in our perception of the dilemma, and in the connections we choose to make or posit across the contradictory gap, this should not be taken to assume that no use at all of spiritual or other forms of intelligence about the nature of our perception of reality are possible. Belief is not, as such, anti-rational or anti-reasoning. It must include such things, but nor should it be confined by them, or reduced by them, in its insistence that there might be aspects of reality that transcend them. And if that is our experimental experience of reality, then it should not lightly be dismissed just because it uses a different kind of perceptual language.

It is not surprising that language has its limits here, as do ideas behind our use of language. From within those limits, it may well be possible to describe our perception, if not explain it. There are many paradoxes involved in attempting even to experience, describe or represent the presence of something spiritually significant, let alone sacred. The Russian Orthodox Church has a literary and theological tradition of the Holy Fool. On the one hand, acting the Holy Fool, with all the unexpected and inexplicable behaviours involved, was seen as its own form of ascesis, indicating some kind of special relationship with the unpredictable nature of holiness. But in the very act of being a Holy Fool, in order to prevent the risk of revealing anything as serious as saintliness, the danger was that the act itself expressed a certain egotistical, attention drawing, which undermined the very holiness involved. Sometimes, the foolishness of the Holy Fool hid this holiness through a veil of genuine humility as an expression of the limits of human capability. Too extreme a form of humility however, so hid any signs of saintly calling or aspiration, that it came across as just a simple foolishness.

During my year in Romania, a woman at the Cathedral regularly moved right to the front and would stand in front of an icon on the iconostasis for a long time, stand and bow with tears and sometimes making a wailing sound. She kept apart from everyone else and to be honest it seems they kept apart from her. Occasionally she would go and sit on the Patriarch's throne. Her movements were clearly unpredictable and my first thought was she was suffering from some kind of mental health problem and needed help. My second thought was that if this unpredictable and sometimes disturbing behaviour happened in Westminster Abbey in front of the Archbishop at a large formal occasion, officials would courteously escort go up to her and move her away from the altar area and even take her into another part of the Abbey complex, or even encourage her to leave. Granted that services in the Abbey had a more ordered and static atmosphere that the general movement and sheer numbers in the Patriarchal Cathedral in Bucharest. But even there, in the crush of bodies she stood out with her erratic and definitely unpredictable behaviour. And nobody went up to her to warn her or escort her out. They simply left her alone. I discovered later that at a meeting of the Holy Synod no less they had discussed her case. The majority view was that they dare not interfere to prevent her doing what she did. Apparently, some of the Bishops said we dare not touch her because she may be a charismatic gift from the Holy Spirit to teach us something. This caution or humility in the face of erratic behaviour draws I think, upon the Holy Fool tradition. The woman was not acting a part, this was who she was. She may not have been aware that her behaviour was unusual. She may indeed have had some kind of mental health problem resulting in a behavioural separation or isolation from the "norm".

By contrast, for a year or two, I used to take on the role of the Pierrot, white faced, silent clown, and be invited to take services in churches, at conferences, and yes in one or two cathedrals. My daughter would play the flute to accompany me, and we would involve as many local people as possible in the Liturgy which meant considerable planning and organisation beforehand. I'd be impressed by the clown priests in England who had taken up the Holy Fool tradition. Pierrot was silent, and in the Commedia tradition, suffered as a victim of other people's power and pomposity. His task was to register, point to, others rather than himself. In putting others centre stage, he was the humble one in the liturgical drama. He was, as it were, mimicking the silence of the suffering Christ before Pilate. In this role, it was possible to celebrate a Eucharist using mime actions alone, inviting others and the congregation to say many of the formal prayers. The silence accompanying the actions, meant, I think, that people could experience something different, something perhaps quite powerful in the simplicity and "poverty" of the miming at certain key points in the service, and with the bread and wine. It was possible, for example, to mime certain actions with a baguet style loaf of bread that represented crucifixion suffering through a certain amount of pathos in the actions, emphasised by the silence, and the space and ambiguity it left for people to perceive it in their own way. I feel some allowance for this space for ambiguity is needed in understanding the gap and the connection between our ordinary human nature, and the presence of holiness, either in our reaction to others, or to the presence of God within us, if we dare put it like that. It is hard indeed to talk about this presence in relation to the spiritual perception of our own and others' humanity. Much caution is needed. We dare not simplistically dismiss its possibility in the most unlikely and unexpected of situations and people. It is part of that larger agenda of how we understand the world and things within the world, being careful not to dismiss them by the language of secularity if they bear the imprint of God's creating and creative presence. But there is no denying that the gap as well as the connection exists. In trying to make sense of that gap in relationship to a connection, when both might be true at the same time, some admission of the ambiguity is appropriate. And when words fail us in our apprehension of what might be involved some space for a Pierrot kind of silence is also helpful.

Pierrot moved the location of meaning from himself to others through his mime and the silence. I hope what I did in those

Liturgies may have been true to a dimension of the Holy Fool ethos, but clearly only through a representation of a tradition of performance "clowning" through which travelling players enacted some universal themes in local villages and towns. The tradition goes back a long way, and took many forms, but always with some stereotyped characterisation. That was very different from the Russian tradition of the saintly Holy Fool, whose unpredictable actions and words were seen to be a possible vehicle of the presence of the Holy Spirit bringing connection across the gap in their own way.

In discussing this Russian tradition, Rowan Williams points out the contradiction *between the deliberate concealment of holiness and the conspicuous display of it.*[107] Again it appears as a gap across a connection that is itself always some kind of paradox. We dare not pretend otherwise or attempt to falsely reduce the paradox of holiness. The challenge rather seems to be the way different individuals, in different kinds of Liturgical community, are called to live it in different ways. It goes to the heart of the nature of spirituality in both the Liturgy of the Church, and of the World. This is more than the health-based kind of spiritual exercise designed to improve or balance our internal wellbeing. It is not a spirituality that isolates us more in our narcissistic concerns but enlarges our horizons and community concerns to the presence of that which is of God in other others and in creation all around us. Rowan Williams comments,

*....this again shows how the convention of holy folly brings to light, deliberately or not, some basic paradoxes about holiness. The conscious refusal of conventional marks of holiness itself becomes a convention; transgressive inversions of piety acquire the same level of self-conscious or even self-serving ambiguity that attends the ordinary norms. Yet the phenomenon - even as a literary affair – of holy folly acts as a prompt to look for insight, spiritual discernment, in unlikely places, and to suspend judgement on apparently eccentric behaviour*[108].

---

[107] *Looking East in Winter* p 198
[108] Ibid p 201

He also points out the widespread appearance of a folklore dimension of this contradiction about the *mysterious and often counter-intuitive character of holiness* **found** in *Talmudic literature, in the Qur'an, in medieval Western romance and Russian secular narratives of the same period and survives in fairy tales from the Caucasus to the Celtic world. In essence, it is about the capacity of a supernatural being to perceive what others fail to see, a capacity that is shown in incomprehensible and initially offensive behaviour, inappropriate tears or (more often) laughter*[109].

## LOOKING THROUGH BOTH LENSES AT THE SAME TIME

Artists paint self-portraits, or portraits of other sitters. They talk about capturing the "essence" of the person as being something different from "just" a likeness. And in every attempt at a likeness, there is huge variety in the physical looks achieved by the same painter about the same sitter, or in different portraits of themselves. And when we watch several artists painting the same sitter we see a different truth captured about that sitter in each painting. In some cases, the likeness may be less good but something of the character is still captured and obviously present. In others the likeness might be superb but there is little of the character let alone the essence. Art navigates between different perceptions of the same thing or different things, showing us something we've never seen before in quite that way, or, as we sometimes say, quite that same light, as it were. In the challenge of painting, many artists have experienced a sense of failure when it comes to capturing, or representing, something that is more than just a superficial, physical likeness. They have carefully observed the appearance of a person in order to go deeper and in the process somehow "catch" something of the character or even the essence. That word is beautiful and evocative, as well as being beyond easy definitions. Yes, it comes from the Latin verb *esse* to be (and forms the heart of the word "essential"), which in turn came from the Greek *ousia* or being. But it suggests a state of being that cannot be simplistically related to different ways or expressions of being, without a reduction taking place. In the idea of

---

[109] Ibid p 199

essence, we already have the hint that, compared with its nature, everything else is some kind of expression of part of its nature. If we are to believe Pseudo Dionysius, and many of the early Christian writers and mystics, the essence is unknowable and that may be true in humans, as well as in God. Friends and family may think they know the character of a person and artists can put down paint or drawing marks which represent that character through a physical likeness and even beyond it. But even the person concerned might admit they do not fully know the essence of who they are, except to sense this is something more than their appearance can ever portray![110]

We might want to see this "something more" as something spiritual. This word may not always convey the truth or essence of the essence we are seeking, which is present in the uniqueness of every human, because that uniqueness comes, theologically, from its source as being the humanness which is not only the created gift of God, but a reflection of the uniqueness of God. And if we take the Liturgy of the World seriously, then we have to say that God in Christ has identified with this quality of humanness that is already there in everyone. The incarnation implies that Christ identifies his own humanness with our humanness in this respect. Ontologically speaking, it carries the reflection or representation of unique essence that is present in all humans even when not always expressed or sensed in any obvious way. Our likeness links us with the image of Christ as in the perfect image and likeness of the essence of God. Because that image of Christ enlightens everyone who comes into the world, his humanness, although unique in a unique way, inhabits the humanness of everyone and affirms that whatever character their unique essence takes, it is always something more than its

---

[110] And we note the (narcistic) obsession with "appearance" or likeness in contemporary culture, aided and encouraged by the technology of Tick Tock, Instagram, etc. Many young people spend disproportionate amounts of time sending each other photos of their appearance or activities from daily life. In Oscar Wilde's novel Dorian Grey, the hero wants to preserve his appearance from the effect of his debauchery which only appear in the physical likeness of his secret portrait.

appearance, however closely observed by the artist or come to that the scientist it might be.

Observers of a painter at work can pick up on this problem and affirm the likeness and yet want to see the "something more". There appears then to be a gap in the way a portrait represents a sitter and the sitter themselves. This gap is only sometimes crossed when the something more is perceived and represented effectively in the process of connecting it with a good likeness of the physical appearance of a sitter. The something more is of course always both ambiguous and illusive. This is the case not just in the perception of the painter but within the experience of the person themselves. There are cases where they would be the last person to ever admit to understanding or knowing something about their essence, certainly the essence that others might perceive or recognise as being at the heart of their being or even their character. And when attempting to understand, let alone paint this "something more", the artist or the observer might also admit that the failure might spring from their own lack of self-awareness or from the ambiguity they experience in their own perception of others, or from something far more basic which so many of the early theologians of the church insisted on. That the essence is unknowable in and of itself however much we sense that the appearance or likeness captures something of the character

This takes us back to the early accounts of resurrection appearances and what they try to say about the visions of the "appearance" of Jesus and the physicality of the resurrected form of the appearance. Technically, because the descriptions by Paul of his vision of the resurrected Jesus come first chronologically, it is tempting to say that the later, and contradictory, as well as complementary, Gospel written accounts are created in the spirit of that later experience, which has none of the physical detail - the empty tomb, the stone rolled away, the different kinds of young men or angels or figures in white giving different descriptions or instructions, the gardener, the stranger on the walk to the village of Emmaus, Thomas's need to see evidence of the humanity in the human suffering and so on. But the written Gospel accounts are based on oral tradition passed on from a much earlier stage, before Paul's visionary experience of Jesus. And if so, perhaps Paul knew them well enough, but then needed to stay true to his own, very different experience of Jesus which brought him into the orbit of the apostle's experience as a claimed witness of the resurrection.

It is extraordinary enough that we still have these different accounts which so obviously reflect the different perceptions of appearance reality, emanating from the experience of different individuals observing that reality, wondering about the issue of a representative likeness. If they were all the same, then we would know the texts had been edited more than they have been, and that might make us treat them differently from within our own attitudes to such things. It is salutary then to note how hard it was for those closest to him, in his life and ministry, to recognise "him" in those appearances. This may well have been an understandable result of their grief and confusion and the cognitive dissonance it created. It may also have been that what they expected as the "something more" to be, or look like, wasn't, in fact, what they saw. But nor was what they saw, recognisably like their memory of his physical likeness. His essence might have still been the source of his "appearance" but clearly the latter had changed sufficiently for it to no longer be an obvious likeness, even though it could still be observed as a human experience of his presence.

There truly are many graced moments in our lives when the ordinary encounters and experiences of life become extra-special, or take us well beyond what we think of as ordinary. Our vocabulary about them has changed over time. What we used to think of as a beautiful thing or moment is now known as "cool", "wicked" or even "insane". It is always awesome and wondrous. We photograph them, tell our friends about them, write something down in our diaries about them, and above all re-member them, and we re-present them and re-live them. And that happens in both the Liturgy of the Church and in the Liturgy of the World. And both overlap in the birth and paschal mysteries, where God is encountered in the life and death patterns of our experience. For the liturgy of both is the same liturgy, experienced through different lenses, like both sides of a pair of binoculars can be adjusted to focus together at the same time into one clear, circular whole, through which we view the world and bring that, which is far away, closer to us. And either of those two lenses can become misted over and both may need refocusing from time to time. So, it's not easy. Sometimes, it will be the Liturgy of the Church that most illuminates the Liturgy of the World, and sometimes it will be the other way around. Then, one day, we will realise that both can be focused together like a pair of high-quality binoculars. And, in all of this, we need to remember that the light entering our eyes comes from outside of our eyes to illuminate our vision. We might say it comes from the Outside-In (Liturgy of the World) to illuminate what we have seen and known from the Inside-Out (Liturgy of the Church). We may be able to adjust our focus, and develop our inner vision, but what we are seeing is really there, however much it overlaps with all that is ambiguous and uncertain in our perception of its nature.

It is pretty clear that those ancient, mystical writers of the early centuries saw this ambiguous uncertainty as part of our apophatic knowledge of God within which, that which is the outward expression of God's Love, takes very seriously the otherness of the cosmos and its propensity to exist and evolve. It also took that universe, that world, so seriously, that the same Love becomes emanated kenotically and ek-statically in the incarnation within that world. But all of that is part of the great mystery of God and God's nature as love moving away from itself, to be itself, in the Liturgy of the World.

## THE MYSTERION OF TRANSCENDENT IMMANENCE

*If transcendence is not something which we practice on the side as a metaphysical luxury of our intellectual existence, but if this transcendence is rather the plainest most obvious and most necessary condition of possibility for all spiritual understanding and comprehension, then the holy mystery really is the one thing that is self-evident, the one thing which is ground in itself even from our point of view. For all other understanding however clear it might appear is grounded in this transcendence. All clear understanding is grounded in the darkness of God.* **Karl Rahner**[111].

Even their use of that word "mystery" is a clue to the way those early mystics understood the incarnation. For this was no detective type mystery story, where the answer would finally be revealed only at the end of the book. And there were, around the Mediterranean several mystery religious and cults to tempt them with their thinking. The "mysterion" was the incarnation, understood within the context of a God who creates as the source of all creation. The mysterion was that movement of God emanating out of the "Otherness" or the Holiness of the unknowable nature of God's Otherness in the direction of our otherness, as cosmos, within which human life became possible. And the Otherness of God's mysterion, and its self-giving, can be seen in the same direction of travel, away from its self to benefit the otherness of human life in and through the self-giving Love seen in the Son. For this is the revelation of the movement of Love within the holy Otherness of the society of God (perichoresis in the Trinity) in our direction, making possible the possibility and propensity of our otherness to come into being, and making possible our accessibility to a relationship with this emanating God in Jesus. The early church's mystical writers expanded on this crude and basic statement in so many rich and creative ways, attempting to understand and receive the mysterion at the heart of it, as revealed by the incarnation of God.

The mystery then is not about our religious movement away from being human in the religious direction of seeking God, but the reverse of that, in the self-giving, kenotic movement of God away from the nature of God in the direction of the other which is the cosmos, and in the other, who is the Second Person of the Holy Trinity, and an expression of the ek-static nature of God in human terms. The Mysterion is that ek-stasis, that standing outside of its own nature or existence[112], to express that nature even though that

---

[111] *Foundations of Christian Faith.* p 21-22.

[112] A word with an interesting etymology - present participle of Latin existere/exsistere "stand forth, come out, emerge; appear, be visible, come to light; arise, be produced; turn into," and, as a secondary meaning, "exist, be;"

nature, in its own being, is unknowable. And we might even want to say, once we have reflected on the original meaning of "liturgy" in the next chapter, that it has a meaning applicable to the very nature of this mysterion. And when, or if, any use of "liturgy" slips anchor from this mystery, and sets us off in a different direction, it stops being liturgy, and no longer communicates or attempts to communicate the mystery of the incarnation on which it totally depends for its veracity and capacity.

So we pause on these words about liturgy, as the vehicle of the mystery of the incarnation, to take in something of their significance. And it can, by definition, only ever be an attempt at something, and not everything, and the risk is that, in attempting even that, we can so easily mar the beauty, or significance, or truth, behind its meaning by the clumsiness of our attempt at finding the right words. And there are many different kinds of beauty, significance and truth. "Truth" can have statistical and factual, moral and personal, historical, legal and political dimensions and aspects to ways of being what it is claimed to be. And these are just words about assumptions and systems of truth, and people use words in many different encultured ways. Words can only approximate themselves to the meaning of something that is beyond words. The Word of Life may have become flesh and dwelt among us. But that was in more than words, even though the Word can also inhabit our words, that is our cultures, our different ways of relating through language, understanding more about creation and humanity through language's utility in examining and expressing our beliefs and ideas. The Word is also encultured, because that too is part of the way the incarnation surely works, available and accessible in all cultures, and, come to that, all times, during which the meaning of words changes so much as well as all our stumbling attempts at expressing meaning within different languages and even the idea of language as such. So words themselves, in whatever culture, are, or function as, changing metaphors of experience, and this is especially so of spiritual experience. And by spiritual, I don't mean religious, or religious in an

from ex "forth" (see ex-) + sistere "cause to stand…"

alien or exclusive and separate sense. I mean something essentially human, however locked up in the warps and distortions of our human condition, our different ways of being human in all their fallibility and finitude.

And yet it is through that very finitude, which is implicit in the diversity of our human experience and human nature, that we experience and share that which is transcendent of the way normal language articulates meaning about experience. And when that happens to us, we experience a sense of spiritual connection that is often a plenitude of new experience in itself. And so, occasionally, we meet concoctions of words shaped in ways that produce a sculptural representation of meaning, that strikes us as imaginative, or beautiful, or meaningful, or having its own wisdom and truth to tell. And that can lift us up and beyond the framework of those same words into a new insight, inspiration, and intuition.

## IDENTITY NARRATIVE INSIDE-OUT

And then we realise that we are in the presence of something truly significant, significant enough to be transcendent of the passing, temporal and metaphorical meaning of the words we use in our prose, and even in our poetry, novels, plays, scripts that contribute to the narrative we think we are using to understand what we perceive of as meaning in the experience of living and our existent part in it. And that narrative shapes our experience and use of words, which then, in turn, slightly, or more significantly, shape that narrative itself. And the post-modernists have taught us much about the existence of the "narrative" in a world they claim can only exist as being made up of different, individual narratives, rather than one overarching meta-narrative. For the latter, they point out, so easily became oppressive of individual experience and its articulation and legitimacy. And some have gone so far as to suggest that an individual's narrative of the world creates and shapes the nature of that world in itself, for the narrative is everything and everything is a narrative. And these insights should not lightly be dismissed, for they may well contain important and significant parts of a changing cultural experience of the meaning of experience.

But, of course, that leaves us with a quandary. It begins to look as if individuals live in isolated, separate and separating bubbles of their own identity narratives, which divide into separate rights, categories and labels (not least about race, sexuality and gender). It is as if they are all, subliminally, following Margaret Thatcher's claim that there really is no such thing as society only individuals and individual groupings around particular identities. If there isn't anything significant about the commonality of society, then we owe primary allegiance only to our own integrity and choices, based on a rather excluding claim about our own human rights, as if there were no human responsibilities, and no possibility of human communion across the diverse categories of our human condition. It's as if the idea of a human race is itself exploded into atomized conditions and compartments, each with its own separating label and claims. It's as if this atomisation means I am suddenly just black, or trans, or gay, or old, or disabled, and because that is the nature of my being, I present myself to society in that way, asking society to recognise those labels as expressive of my full identity. And this, one might argue, is a logical extension of all that was good about the Enlightenment revolution which established the priority of the individual and who would want to oppose the rights of the individual.

There is of course a great virtue emerging from this "narrative" in affirming the value of each personality and the precious individuality and therefore diversity of each personality. But, paradoxically, it has largely overturned what we thought we had in common, alongside and within our connected diversity, and replaced it with separating divisions and categories of human being, which risk doing the very thing its supporters had fought against. They had fought against the belief, implicit or explicit, in the beliefs of those times, that the other is something alien, that the differences between us divides us into separate levels of status and value significance in society. Then, somehow in challenging all of that and replacing it with the value of each separate individual whatever the nature of their otherness, and in the very act of affirming those differences, down to their smallest constituent parts and sub-categories (particularly with gender identities), we are honouring the rights of others. And, perhaps inevitably, certain minority rights supporters having, fought painful and costly battles for their rightful recognition and resources then group together and accrue to themselves a separate value system in order to protect and assert their identity, in this or that particular minority identity. *I am what I am* of Exodus 3 has become *I am my particular minority or majority identity* and that is what I am because it defines me over and against other group or individual identities. And, not surprisingly, people adopting this creed are proud of that defining identity. And if they don't recognise any "something more" about human identity per se, or an overarching human meta-narrative above the separate identity narrative, we do end up with an atomising kind of society with all the obvious risks of fracturing, competition for resources or attention, and divisions.

But I would argue against this narrative about the separate excluding narrative of each, because it so evidently seems to reduce or deny what we have in common as human beings and the "something more" that constitutes the nature of each of us even though it may be ambiguous and confused if not confusing. The individualised identity narrative sets one against the other. It turns the rights discourse into a hyperbole of itself, where, perhaps inevitably, individuals affirm their rights by opposing the rights of their divided others, at least by implication, as one group tries to shout louder to claim the attention of all. I remember attending various community meetings where one powerful sub-category group, say of disabled people, or of black people, of young or of elderly would shout down the claims of another less vocal, and sometimes more vulnerable group of people, at least when it came to accessing limited grants and resources.

And so, the "narrative" narrative became an ideology that, in post-modernist hands, broke apart the value we believe we have in common, to allocate separate value, affirmed in separate categories of identity, which themselves reduced the nature of human beings once they were adopted as "identities". The idea of human value allows for individual differences, but identity value can so easily define itself, in my case and for me, in ways that exclude the value claims of others. Human value implies the inclusion of others, as well as me, in some kind of relational experience of a commonly held and connected significance. It emphasises the connection, rather than the gap. It creates a humane framework for communication and understanding, not to say empathy, compassion, and sympathy. And where the gaps exist, they are experienced and celebrated as part of the rich variety of human value. Yes, this, it can be argued, is only true in an ideal sense of (a truly multicultural) human value, whereas, in practise, this is denied or undermined by contradictions, by a certain use of oppressive power, by prejudice, and by, most tellingly, the evidence of history. It is also undermined, paradoxically, by those most concerned to affirm the differences but in an ideological way which accrues to itself unintended negative consequences for others. Then, what could have been seen as a connecting human value becomes a divisive one. Where that happens, lo and behold, the sense of a gap increases rather than reduces. And perception is of course everything, such that it too can become exaggerated and in that sense damaging.

There may be such things, legally speaking, as different forms of identity status, such as for example married or divorced. And we are asked to own and sometimes carry with us certain kinds of identity papers which lock the meaning and legitimacy of our identity into a photograph, date of birth and address. Apart from our date of birth, these kinds of identifying details may be problematic, because of their temporary nature. Some go further and include blood group or might in the future include other medical descriptions of our identity. The police use identity parades to identify our identity by how we look in the perception of others. And indeed, we can be recognised and identified by how we look, because every individual looks slightly different, in some respect, apart from identical twins. But, in common usage, we tend to identify our identity with more than any of this. We think of ourselves as more than our work identity, or job title, and even our married status and sex. We identify something about our inner identity with our name, the name and understanding of our-selves that comes from within ourselves, as a collection of accumulated experiences of ourselves and what we think and how we feel and how we react in different situations about that or because of that.

We need to rediscover a narrative about the nature of human beings that is greater than their individual identity narratives, at least those which then separate one from another and, in the process, redefine and reduce human uniqueness into exclusive identity identities, based on colour, language, sexuality, class, religious belief, disability etc.

The mystery of the human person, every individual person, is surely more than any of this. So perhaps we need a new narrative that corrects this reduction by clearly asserting that I am more than my LGBTQ plus plus, or other labelled identities. I am more than my disability, however much it affects my life and therefore my understanding of who I am. I am more than my skin colour, and the nature of this "more" enables me to rediscover my unlabelled and uncategorized value part in the human race, and therefore what I have in common with other people, rather than what separates me from them across the different kinds of ideological identity gaps.

And I think this can be done without forgetting the value of difference, but avoiding the ideologies which turn difference into division, sometimes in such a radical way that division produces opposition and tensions, competition and exclusions, and even, sometimes, certain sociological ideologies built on those things which turn differences into illusions and theories of superiority. And this was a driving force behind the horrors of National Socialism and the racial theory it used to support those horrors.

Surely, wherever and whenever this happens in the equal opportunities type definitions of separate labelling, it is something of a paradox, because in asserting the rights of everyone to be affirmed and valued, the last thing anyone wanted to do was to ideologically define the values of others as not only separate and different, but divided from me, and, in the worst cases, inferior or superior to me. If this is what the values of diversity culture end up evoking, then we should note how destructive that can be, and show caution in colluding with the causes or symptoms of its excesses.

There are many ways of approaching how we might talk about

the "more" factor when it comes to understanding the human person within the narrative of the Liturgy of the Church or of the World. There is so much that can be said about the human person in terms of capacities - and not least spiritual ones – as well as needs. Tragically, too many people feel all sense of worth and value has been knocked out of them by poor parenting and educational experiences. So, we need to help each other discover more about ourselves than the narrative we ourselves have chosen to nourish over time, or worse, have been given and made to identify with, because of images imposed on us from others, for example the teachers or parents who have said to us that we will never be capable of ..., or that we are hopeless at being or doing... And when that has happened - and one hears stories of it happening quite frequently (yes it happened to me too) - it is perhaps not surprising that individuals spend much of the rest of their lives living up to, or down to, that imposed judgement.

# CHAPTER TWELVE

## 12    THE LITURGY OF PUBLIC WORKS

*Liturgical action is, we might say, "saturated" with the meaning God gives to the material process of the world. Thus we must say that, instead of providing a route out of the actual world into a sort of religious virtual reality, these actions uncover meanings that are always latent in the world we know.... The point of liturgy is that we should "know the place for the first time" as T. S. Eliot says of spiritual activity in the "Four Quartets". We are returned to where we actually are in God's eyes; in relation, in communion with God, with one another, with the creation.* Rowan Williams.[113]

## THE "APPEARANCE" OF THE IDEA OF LITURGY

Now we come close to the heart of the matter, as found in the meaning of that word "Liturgy", which has been passed down through the centuries and which is addressed in such a profound way in Rowan Williams' *Looking East in Winter*. The discussion in my previous chapter isn't a digression from our subject of liturgy, but an introduction into its significance in public and civic society, in culture, and civilization, or the things that make for civilization. But for those who haven't thought about it that much, there may be a surprise coming, once we unpack that context, and once we stare, in the face, the significance of the basic and material associations and orientation of Liturgy, as Rowan Williams has pointed out. And to see the point of that significance, we might well start as far back as we can go, with the appearance of the meaning of the word Liturgy, or, in the Greek, *leitourgia*.

This is where we start from in order to understand how this word later came to be associated with worship, or worship with it! It was probably something that happened in both directions and that is typical of this word and its reference points of meaning which have a tendency to manifest themselves from the inside-out and then from the outside-in. And, without being too pedantic, but to unveil a meaning, we can break that word down into its two constituent parts, ~~laos and ergos. And there~~ we have it! There it is, staring us in the face,

[113] *Looking East in Winter.* Bloomsbury Continuum. 2021 p. 151

asking us to appreciate the implications of its meaning, and to realise that this wasn't lost on the early Christians, and those involved in its adoption for Christian worship and theology over time.

And what did it once mean? It meant literally the work of the people. "People's work"! Public works in fact, for that was the original context of the meaning Looking East in Winter of liturgy, and, yes, there were people called *liturgists* responsible for public works, for paying for public works, for creating and maintaining and encouraging public works of civil engineering like drains and bridges. And there were other kinds of liturgist who were responsible for ensuring that others helped to contribute to these things in their different ways, to make Liturgy work well. And they set all of this in the context of an offering to the Gods, knowing that making and maintaining public works was a civic, but also a religious duty. I like to imagine hearing a group of people standing around in one of those early cities discussing "Liturgy" but thinking of the drains or bridges or the material infrastructure needed to keep things going and to make things work. As I once walked down a street in Pompey, I thought I saw, scratched into the wall of a house, the word Liturgy meaning that this was a place where you could call for help in the making or maintenance of public works of this kind.

Liturgy, then, as Public Works. This is how city states of the 5th century B.C. onwards, worked in Greece and in Greek speaking areas. There was no welfare state as we know it now, but there was the expectation that certain citizens - as far as we can tell, at least twenty per cent of the population - took responsibility for ensuring the working of the physical infrastructure of the state, the society, which, in turn, contributed to the wellbeing (as we might now say) of the citizens' experience of living in that state. And we remember they were, at the same time, developing ideas about the nature of the people living in a city state as the *polis* within which individuals became more than individuals, responsible citizens with a shared sense of public responsibility for the decisions made in the *demos* that benefitted or harmed other citizens. Public works then, *Leitourgeia*, for the *polis* to work well for the sake of the *demos*.

And we still have the echo of that in our modern societies. And one of the big divides in our world is between those societies run with some kind of democratic system (for all its limitations) and other societies run by centrally controlled systems (and dictators). And any democratic system will feel a responsibility for facilitating, if not directly providing, the kind of human and physical infrastructure which makes society work well. And, within that broad brief, we have been struggling over time to bring the best values and potential to the surface, and to restrict the worst. We have been struggling, through democratic processes of debate and policy making, to improve the opportunities of individuals through better education, good parenting, social mobility and skill development. We have been attempting to balance individual and economic freedoms with a well-organized and well managed society. And there is always the potential for failure all around in the delivery of such policy goals and in the poor functioning of our social and physical infrastructure. None of this "liturgical" effort and activity is easy.

And from the inscriptions and other evidence we have, although I am far from being an expert on this, liturgists in those ancient Greek societies were well respected, although when they came calling to encourage other well-off citizens to become more publically minded, I suspect they were hardly welcomed with great joy. For to become a liturgist, responsible for the liturgy of public works was a costly business, and we have all sorts of other descriptive words and titles for the different roles involved now. But the basics of Liturgy are important for our purposes, not so much the details. Without a contribution to public works, you could hardly be expected to be a highly valued citizen of the *civis* of the *polis* that we, or rather they, knew as the *demos* in the state, the city state. And it was from within that maelstrom of creative ideas that the idea of democracy was born, although by our standards a very limited form of democracy, because not everyone could be a citizen participating in the agora-market place discussion of decisions that had to be made. And not every citizen could contribute equally to the funding of liturgy or public works that was the responsibility of every liturgist, committed, or press ganged, into creating the liturgy of the state which enabled ordinary citizens to feel they belonged to something bigger than themselves, but in which they were valued, individual members, all with their own civic responsibilities.

We know that the holder of a liturgical responsibility was not taxed a specific sum. It has not yet become the basis of a formal taxation system but it was intrinsic within the functioning of their economic systems. It became associated with civic religion as embodied in the formal festivals of the State. We are told that in the time of Demosthenes, there were at least 97 liturgical appointments in Athens alone, responsible for managing the public affairs of the festivals. The rich clearly took the burden of the cost of civic amenities and public works. In the Roman empire such obligations were known as munera, which sometimes became an expensive burden whatever social kudos it gave to the donors. The munera covered a wide range of civic amenities apart from roads, bridges and aqueduct building and repairs. It included some of the cost of raw materials provided in what we would now call supply chains, and surprising things like providing the bread and basic food for troops. It also had to cover the cost of public drama, music, poetry contests and religious festivals, so it entailed high culture as part of public works as well. Liturgy - as the delivery of quality public works and public culture.

Suddenly then, the designers, architects, builders and artists of these things are Liturgically important. One thinks of the medieval and contemporary guilds of the makers of ordinary things, of the art and craft of making, of the technical training and qualifications, of the hard, cultural work of envisioning, and the hard physical and manual work of making and building anything from great cathedrals and public buildings to the humblest home. As we look out of our windows at the cranes erecting tall buildings in our cities, or a brick layer building a wall in our back garden, or a new public statue being erected, a bridge or road being built, or a drain cleared, then perhaps we could look again and see something of the nature of Liturgy in action through "ordinary" work, as understood in those early times.

And all of this was, after all, a significant moment in the development of an idea. And this was not only the development of the polis, the democratic polis, or political unit and system (as opposed to the *oikos* or the family unit) which ensured as smooth a running of affairs as possible, which was in turn part of the *oikumene*, the gathered economic and social community, which was in turn part of the *cosmos*, the divinely created and loosely governed creation of everything. But this kind of citizenship was a form of new civilization, and, at the time, I have no doubt there were many who saw it as a civilizing form of civilization, despite all the pressures, challenges, and threats that realistically and practically existed, from within, as well as from without. So the value and practical experience of citizenship depended on quality public works and public culture and effective, not corrupt, public demos to to promote the wellbeing of the oikumene within the nature of the cosmos so that every oikos or household could get on with managing its affairs in as much stability and peace as possible.

And holding it all together, its framework and its details, was a word for an idea that somehow extended itself into early, or not so early, Christian usage. And the link was probably a religious one. The liturgist and the liturgy of those early Greek states dedicated their public works and public culture as an offering to the Gods. Perhaps such an offering was prompted by the hope of divine help with the success and maintenance of those roads and bridges, buildings and drains, and civil engineering works, those public ceremonies and festivals and art. Perhaps this was all an understandable thing to offer to the Gods as the work of their hands and their wealth, in order to do some kind of deal that all would be well for the citizens of the state, and their lasting reputation within it. For the financial and other costs involved were indeed high. And when the liturgist and his cohorts had "persuaded" you to contribute to the liturgy of the state or the civis in this way, then you probably had little choice, at least in some cases. In others, perhaps it was an aspiration one rose to, the privilege and responsibility of contributing to the common good of all. Or it was just a further opportunity for self-aggrandisement. And that is still a tension present today in public service and political life.

Now that phrase "common good" is often used today. It is presented as a symbol to bring together all that is disparate and divisive in human and political experience, especially in a post-modernist context where the metanarrative seems to have been broken down into separate and individualist or group stories about categories of human value and worth, if not human experience. And church leaders have often drawn on it when searching to use a middle axiom, half-way, pivotal point between Christian language and so-called "secular" language about what might, after all, unite us beyond that which divides us. But I confess I have never heard a church leader call society back to what really matters and connects through an appeal to "liturgy". Yet, back then, from whatever time, and however it was done, the idea of liturgy, in this sense, was accommodated for Christian worship and for the very essence and expression of the common good, in material and political and artistic and spiritual terms. And not only that, but a public good that could be offered to the Gods and made sense of because of the Gods.

It's difficult to know when this first happened or how. It might not have fully entrenched itself and its use until centuries after the life of Jesus. And it was lost and rediscovered over longer periods of time, and that is still the case, certainly in the major differences between Western and Eastern Christianity. But there is something truly significant in the way this maximal understanding developed, which may well have benefits for our times and the way Christians think about their worship and its orientation, reference points and meaning. There has to be something maximal in our understanding of the Christian message if it is to mean something more than just another religious group or cult. If it is to be earthed in the needs and opportunities and reach of human society, then it has to have the natural capacity to reach out to its very edges and depths, its questions and quandaries about its nature and meaning within creation. It has to touch the common good of all, even in the most heterogenous complexity of multicultural societies. It has to put its roots down in the very depths of our shared concerns and divided attitudes to our total environment, including our relationships with each other across the reality of tensions and disagreements. It has to touch or emerge from the realities of the workplace as well as the home. It has to speak a language that inspires new attitudes to major crises and normal every day realities. Christian belief and hope are centred on the reality of the Incarnation in the reality of creation and the human societies that have evolved over time within it, with all their positive learning and negative behaviours. It has to be part of a cosmic covenant and context within which Christians make extraordinary claims about a creator and the nature of the being of God as revealed in the Word made flesh which and who dwelt among us. The mystery of the incarnation is the focus of this understanding of the liturgy and, because of that, its reference points are maximal and inclusive. They are part of the ontology, the very nature of the being of things, rather than just our existential self-awareness of the human condition within it.

## LITURGY AS VISION AND PRAXIS

But presumably so far have we travelled, over time, in the divisions and schisms of the Christian church, and in our Christian discourse about worship, that we have forgotten that worship for those early, Greek encultured Christians was, in fact, a theological outworking of the meaning of "leitourgia" as public culture and public works, as "work" that benefits the public and common good of all in communities and society as a whole. And more, that in historical terms, though much has changed in the meaning of all words, liturgy would be a natural word to use when wanting to talk about any offering to God for, and of, all that we do, and hope to contribute, towards the common and public good of all. And, theologically, those early Greek, mystical writers would have added that the meaning of liturgy includes the idea of an offering to God of our participation in the work of God, through human hands, as if we are nothing less than co-creators in the work or ergos of creation itself, in which, and through which, the laos or people of God experience their relationship with everything in creation, and everyone else in creation, and their work, their ergos, their energy, as an offering of their responsibility within it, and for its responsible "management" in the oikos, the polis and the whole oikumene.

In that sense, any exploration of the meaning of liturgy takes us straight into the world of work and our workplaces, including domestic ones, and certainly unpaid voluntary and caring work as well as the public and private sectors. For through that "liturgical" engagement, we are continuing the work of creation by helping to use ordinary things in ways that bring order out of disorder, that fill the void of formlessness with new or changing forms, fashioned by the skill of human hands and ingenuity. Liturgy takes of natural raw materials and brings them into the shaping of human production for human utility, aesthetics, and the common good, with all the ethical questions involved in the shaping of public culture and values.

And there have been many misuses and harms to the Liturgy of creation and production, and in public affairs over the centuries, as each age discovers new technology and new ways of using it, too often in ways that damage and harm God's good creation and other species and other humans within it. For, some things that are produced, shouldn't be produced at all. They are a risk to the common good of creation. They are a danger to the public works people need, to public values, and to the people involved in the production and consumption processes. Many things that are produced, should be produced and consumed in different, better ways to ennoble and enable those involved, rather than the opposite. And in the polis, those responsible for shaping the polity of society are called to be good liturgists themselves and to help others to do the same. That is the calling to which they should constantly feel a huge sense of responsibility, so that the offering of a good society can be the "work" of their hands, their minds, and their value system.

But, as artists and architects know, there can be a wondrous relationship between beauty and utility, not only in the design and manufacture of ordinary things, but in the way we perceive and handle them. And great art has often demonstrated this in different ways, teaching us to value things in new ways, as part of our role as liturgists in the liturgy of creation, where we are called to be priests in the way we take, and offer, and then use ordinary things as a blessing or a curse to ourselves and to others.

For when the early Christians meditated about the ever-present meaning of liturgy in its formative and normative use in cities and places influenced by Greek culture and thinking, (as most were around the Mediterranean area, including in the Roman and Jewish worlds of the time) it was probably quite natural to think of "leitourgia" as that act of cooperation with God in God's divine "ergon" of creation and creativity and as revealed in Jesus the Christ, so that united with Him, in the mystery of the incarnation, and its redemptive, putting right, suffering presence of words and deeds, all citizens of the Kingdom of God could relate to each other as servants of others in the public acts of their witness, and their public works of self-giving love...for the good of the whole of creation and the common good of all humanity. What a vision that was! How wide were its horizons, and how profound its implications! However much it slipped in practise, what a responsibility the church community must have felt in calling themselves and others back to the authentic performance and fulfilment of that vision.

We know that the early Councils of the Church channelled their thinking about this broad vision of the nature of the divine, and our response to the divine in relationship to all creation, into the difficult questions about how the incarnation of Jesus could be both human and divine. And that channelling took many forms over the first six or so centuries, as Councils and bishops and theologians, and different divided and divisive movements of thinking came and went. And some of those individuals and movements were derided as heretics and heretical by the Emperors and their Patriarchs and leading Bishops, and so there was violence done in the human relationships involved. Right up to the eighth century when the fault lines of the Great Schism between the Eastern and Western Empire began to appear and then were crystalised in 1054 by the Bull from the Vatican excommunicating the Patriarch of Constantinople. And then, of course, the Reformation was to follow where both the Catholic and Protestant divisions excommunicated each other and then turned to the violence of Inquisition and war against each other all across the continent of Europe, tearing nations and communities apart.

And although worship continued to develop in the West, through times of dispute and division, the focus of attention moved away from the public works and significance of Liturgy in its maximal sense. It settled down into the praxis of worship as a denominational, confessional, sectarian expression of congregational and community identity around the worship of God, or, in the case of many, modern Church movements, the praise and worship of Jesus as if in a personal relationship individual to individual.

And in the process, the maximal meaning of Word and Sacrament as living symbols of the presence of God everywhere, in and through Liturgy, was slowly reduced, changed or lost. Both Word and Sacrament lost their Inside-Out, broader reference points and contexts in a slow process of increasing reductions moving Outside-In. On the one hand, the Word of God was reduced to a literal interpretation of the Bible under the authority of fundamentalist interpreters, using their power as ministers of the Word to sometimes dominate people and control their thinking. And on the other hand sacraments were reduced to a literal interpretation of certain, church rites and rituals under the authority of the hierarchy of the Church. Of course, reductions can lead to their own compelling and interesting, new forms of development and expansion, which may creatively enhance the nature of the reduction, or of something new with its own creativity and value. But, on the other hand, something that might have been, and become, even more precious can be lost over time, through knowing or unknowing, small, or larger changes.

And in asserting this, it is important to note the danger of one group or individual (like this book) pointing out the reduction taking place, as if it were only taking place in the "other" group, when the truth is that, within certain relative parabolas, all have developed and changed their understanding over time of the tradition handed down to them, even those most committed to defending that tradition against development. And tragically, a one-sided aspect of tradition or just its externals is sometimes defended against all else, and all comers, or it is defended for the sake of defending or conserving, with little awareness of the wider meaning and implications of the content of that tradition. For that too may be a sin against the Holy Spirit's mission to lead us into all truth. And that extraordinary and challenging belief implies a future, as well as a past tense, as a source of the ongoing present task.

The risk was always going to be, in the orientation of both main branches of Western Church theology, that the more extreme forms of each became ghettoised within their own narrow interpretations of each other. In reacting and counter-reacting, rejecting the value of the other by default or intent, they may not always have noticed what this was doing to reduce the scope and horizons of both Word and Sacrament considered separately or together within a Church context. And so, the Word of Life was somehow forced into the limited framework of a textually literal focus, and the Sacrament of life was somehow forced into the limited and literal framework of a dogmatically and doctrinally defined series of church-based statements, authorized and controlled by episcopal power. And, in the process, both forgot or slowly overwrote the more maximal significance, horizons and reference points of *Leitourgia* and its earthing in the public works of the Kingdom of God in the world. Slowly, a wider awareness of the sacramental presence and significance of Liturgy in the whole world of divine creation, was turned into a focus on internal, sacramental and priestly activity which accrued around itself a new set of churchy and clerical pathologies.

Meanwhile, of course, many traces and echoes of the maximal meaning of Liturgy remained and were, from time to time, called forth by individual theologians, church leaders, monastic communities, or groups of very spiritual and active lay people. Despite this, general trend, of an inward facing church, was to defend their boundaries against a world they increasingly labelled as secular, political, corrupt, evil and so on, partly to booster a sense of their own significance and from there to view those things as the mission field of their own interventions. Of course, the story is more complicated than these simplistic sentences imply. At any stage in this story, Christians acted or thought they were acting out of the faithful vision they had received or passed on. There were also good reasons for them to believe the church had something of eternal and immediate value to share with others, something to work for in different ways, out of their calling to express Christian charity for the real and urgent needs of others. And there were always such needs all around the gathering of local church communities. Churches and individual Christians found new purpose and renewal in responding to those needs, in the work of providing education, health services, social care, social justice and what they saw as civilised values to other parts of the world. And few would doubt their sincerity and certainly, nor the widespread need, whatever the concomitant and conflictual results which in some cases ensued from the Churches' engagements. And the need will always be there and so remains a major part of many churches' local and national activity across the world. And such work forms its own crucial role and just cause in the wider Liturgy of the Church, for, without it, our Christian calling would have little practical or even spiritual meaning. No one should doubt the calling to do good works in response to a neighbour's need for it comes from Jesus himself in many of his parables and the way he lived his life. But, increasingly, few saw it as part of the mainstream "Liturgy" of the Church, and few would want to stretch the meaning of the word "Liturgy" to include all the good, miraculous work that is being done in the Liturgy of the World by so many agencies and individuals. And so, it is perhaps predictable and even understandable that the church may have lost its vision of all life being the focus and context of the sacramental significance of the incarnation of God in the humanity of Jesus, who was and is the Word of Life, so that we may glimpse that abundant life he talked about.

And it may well be that adding a labelling word like "Liturgy" to the good work being done adds nothing, by and of itself, to its intrinsic value. Where there is loving self-giving for the sake of others, no more needs to be said, certainly not more strange, churchy sounding words that few really understand. On the other hand, to unpack the meaning of those words and show how they can help a dynamic connection to be made across the gap, obvious now in all political cultures between the Liturgy of the Church and the Liturgy of the World, just might refresh our vision and affirm what needs to be affirmed on both sides of that gap. For to affirm the spiritual significance of either, to the exclusion of the other, is to denigrate the truth contained in, and claimed for, both in central Christian beliefs about the world and in the very core of the meaning of Liturgy.

And so we can see how, within this maximal understanding of the meaning of Liturgy, there is an orientation which draws into itself other key words with their own particular meanings. And these are meanings that have changed over time, through use in different contexts. So, the way we understand them now may bear little relationship with their early usage, which, in turn, depended on their positioning within an even earlier, pre-Christian usage, drawing on not only the cultural assumptions of mainstream Judaism, but the dominant values and viewpoints of the Roman and Greek and even Persian and Middle Eastern worlds. For it was within the cauldron of religions and cultures, in that part of the world, that the incarnation encultured itself within the meaning and perceptions of those times, where, for example, expressions like Son of God, Son of Man, Word of God were current within their own particular histories. We have already noted the difference between an early Christian understanding of mysterion, and our contemporary interest in mysteries. We might pause now to consider another significant idea within the wider reference points of liturgy and liturgical time.

But before that, I pause just "to be clear", as the politicians like to say, when they aren't always being clear. And it may be that I am being far from clear, as there is an inbuilt tautology of related meanings in the big words we are considering. So just in case I really am being obtusely unclear, let me say that I am using the phrase "Liturgy of the World" in a particular way to symbolically represent the application of *Leitourgeia* as public works, culture and value, offered to God through the contribution of human beings to the greater common good of others or of all. So, I come to the phrase via a prior belief that the early Christians appropriated and adopted this idea of liturgy and no doubt adjusted its meaning for their own theological and mystical purposes.

In this adoption inwards within the Liturgy of the Church, they provided an opportunity, paradoxically, for the meaning to move outwards again. This Inside-Out movement was understood to be within the wider canvas of God's action in the world, as Creator to creation, and, at its heart, the coming of God's action and presence in Jesus with the implication that what had been understood as religious hope and purpose was connected in meaning with the Liturgy of the World. And they sensed that the Spirit moving over the void and the waters of creation at the beginning, was the life–giver in creation, bringing what the Hebrews called breath, life and spirit to *all* of its processes, all contained in the one word, *ruach*, the equivalent perhaps of the breadth of meaning contained in the Greek word *pneuma*. And the pneumatological event at Pentecost seemed to bring fresh *breath* and *life* into the idea of creation itself, along with the creativity of human communication, through languages and mutual understanding and relationships within it. And that quality of communication in turn promised much for how human structures and organisations could be in-spired, (or spirit filled) across a huge diversity of human cultures.

## PUBLIC WORKS OR SOCIETAL FRACTURE

The vision appeared to be that the Spirit who moved Outside-In as gift, could also work Inside-Out in the gifted realities of communicating hope, purpose and wellbeing in people's daily lives, work and responsibilities. And, indeed, there are people in organisations today specifically charged with ensuring that that which is *Inside* serves that which is *Outside*; that internal customer and external customer values match; that the strategic and HR wellbeing inside, serves the needs of those outside. And strangely, when we unpack what any of that means in practise, it refers to pretty much everything that organisations do in society through their inside activities stretching out through services, supply chains, political and social environments to contribute to the Liturgical wellbeing of public works, culture and value. And none of this happens by chance and, no, sometimes none of it works very well at all. Companies fail. Internal management betrays the trust of employees, groups of employees can frustrate strategic goals, undermining leadership and company reputation. Customers can be, and feel, let down and treated inhumanely by systems designed to meet internal, organisational needs, more than theirs[114]. Frustrations increase and no matter how

---

[114] As everyone now seems to know when making a telephone call to a utility

many reviews, commissions and enquiries take place (eventually) one can't help but wonder why success, wellbeing, safety and satisfaction are so often blocked by bureaucratic stupidity and poor management. Governments can inappropriately interfere, or helpfully contribute better policy frameworks in the public square and for the public good. And, in any complex system, it is easy to hide the small acts of irresponsibility or poor-quality management performance that add up to break downs in the whole.

It turns out that the small things matter and therefore in addition to good strategic vision and leadership, organisations need to enhance not undermine the qualities of care, concern, helpfulness, kindness, support, positivity, creativity, loyalty, reliability that are the very life blood of any organisation, at any level. In other words, as I so often found as an Industrial Chaplain, if the gap between macro level, Board quality decisions and micro level management grows too big, people in organisation can very quickly lose their sense of confidence, motivation and respect[115]. Divisions between different levels and groups in organisations can be as negative a force as tribal divisions in a county. Perhaps that is why many Ukrainians who fled the country are now returning to fight in response to the call for solidarity in and for that nation. This didn't happen in the

---

company or a large public sector organisation. The language used about "you call being important to us" appears in inverse proportion to the design of the behaviour.

[115] The examples of this are endless, and found in the private as well as the public sector. I remember a conversation with a Chief Executive one day who was proud of how well things were going until I pointed out how unhappy the receptionist was because her manager undermined her abilities and restricted her initiatives. She knew better than he did when more ordinary things like paperclips were needed, but he never made allowed her to order more. Her frustration was inevitably communicated to senior visitors and customers passing her at reception. A few weeks later I was on a panel discussion on strategic leadership hosted by a global chemical company. Ohers spoke, as I would have done, about top level and top-down cultural change but instead I found myself talking about bottom up "paper clip" type issues that caused so much unnecessary frustration in different sectors. In all sectors the Liturgy of public good and public culture can so easily and far too often be undermined or blocked.

tribalism of the Yemen, the fractured groupings in Lebanon, Syria or Afghanistan. In those and other places, times of crisis seem to send people scurrying back into their narrow tribal boundaries, where inevitably, perhaps, divisions of tribal loyalty undermine the meaning of the nation.

In Britain we know how long it took for Romans, Normans, Saxons, Celts, Anglo Saxons, Brigantes, and many others sub-groups to sense they were part of something bigger with the potential to be better because of that. There were still the tribal divisions of the English civil war tearing our nation apart and many of these are still represented by place names and emotional attachments. A Christian ban on cousin or relative marriage, plus the later development of common tax and legal systems may have helped reduce the power of that tribalism, where it hasn't in other places. In Syria, the Arab Spring (and Basshar Al Assad's reaction to it), led to increased not less sectarian tribalism – different kinds of Sunni and Shia, Kurds, Arabs, Druze, too many Muslim and Christian sub-groups into which of course fundamentalist and extremist Islam could get an even firmer foothold. And because of this tendency to sectarian fracture, we clearly need immigration policies that are just and humane, but careful not to import more groups of people who make loyalty to their tribal boundaries the priority and therefore potentially disruptive of the common good of public works and public culture. Some forms of multicultural ideology have indeed only increased ghettoed, tribal loyalties and sectarian behaviours, which far from enriching society, have only further endangered it as we still see in Northern Island. And of course, nationalism can become its own form of tribalism and the cause of inter-national divisions.

So, if public works, public culture and public value are important for our understanding of Liturgy, then it really matters how those "works" work in practice. And that depends on how well they are designed, led or choreographed, to increase effectiveness and belonging across divisions, to reduce fracture and friction rather than increase it, so undermining the nature, meaning and value of public works and culture. And this is as true in some organisations as it is in countries. It appears that in public culture, we are currently seeing far too much fracturing in recent times. There seem to be cultural warriors everywhere, wanting and willing to dismantle what they disagree with, even if it means breaking those invisible bonds which hold society together. And that may be the unintended result of their virtuous concern to rid society of its historical faults, and in particular the symbols of those faults in anything from statues to place names, books, Foundations, stately homes, university buildings and educational curricula. So, depending on the leadership assumptions and skills in all sectors, politics, the media, civil society, religion, we have to say that the way public works and public culture are organised really does matter, not just to the quality of specific "works", but as to whether and how society itself can work across the potential divisions and disagreements that are always present, and either suppressed in dictatorships, or managed well or badly in democracies.

And it is to that subject of making "work" work well, that I now turn to extend our understanding of Public Works in the Liturgy of the World to include an understanding of choreography and design that seem to be ubiquitous in all human endeavours.

## LITURGY AS CHOREOGRAPHY

All liturgy has shape and form. Like a group dance, its choreography is worked out over time through trial and error, and learnt movements are shaped and practised to create and experience the intended meaning, the content and symbols of that meaning, in ways that communicate it with those involved and those who watch and witness it. And the shape and the content of every movement, within the choreography, has to contribute to the theme or themes of that meaning. And it is through physical acts and relationships that meaning is discovered and conveyed within the symbolic landscape of a particular culture.

The meaning is designed to be explored, carried and expressed through the design and delivery of the choreography. And over time, traditions developed in the great ballet and dance centres of the world, which were then passed on to the next generation to learn and to use, and sometimes to shape in new ways, as a famous conductor will be known for something distinctive she did in the performance of a certain symphony, with a particular Orchestra; or a famous theatre director will be associated with her or his production of a particular play. A Kenneth McMillan performance of *Manon* for example, Mathew Bourne's *Swan Lake*, a Solti performance of *Mahler's Second*, Peter Brooke's *Midsummer Night's Dream*. The list goes on and on as new choreographers, conductors and directors of the arts are constantly appearing.

Liturgy is its own form of all these things, where choreography, conducting, directing and participation happen to communicate "something more". And they happen in all parts of life, not just in the arts. They happen in the running of schools, hospitals, businesses, and societies, as organisations, small and large, are shaped to meet the needs of those who benefit from them, and serve them, in all the different roles involved, inside or outside the organisation. For, in Liturgy, that primal relationship between inside and outside is always present. In the best organisations, there is a coherence of quality and values for both inside and outside "customers" of what takes place, and what is made, and how it is delivered[116]. Organisations that are organised in ways that treat the relationships between individual staff well, are more likely to treat outside users or customers of their goods and services well. The processes used, to ensure this happens, are part of the systemic, social organisation designed and choreographed to facilitate this. And that's first about the quality of the leadership and its capacity to involve the motivation, skills and contribution of everyone involved and then to pay attention to the details. There is choreographic design at all levels of decision making and human relationships from the top to the bottom of human societies. And. without that, the Liturgy of the World would not be possible, and even with it, sometimes terrible

---

[116] In saying this I was very influenced by Peter Drucker when I met him at a conference in Washington. At the time I was chairman of a Housing and Homeless Centre in Derby (as part of my work as Principal Social Responsibility Officer for that Diocese). He changed my thinking about how we thought about customer choice in the Third Sector.

mistakes are made in the attitudes developed and the decisions taken which drastically affect the culture of organisations and their public value.

And this began a long time ago in the history of our species. It began in the discovery and ordering of the social movement of human sapiens, but also in their response to the management and design of their external environment in its great bounty and in its great threats. Look at any great piece of architecture and imagine, through the ages, how we have shaped our shelters and public buildings according to changing social and cultural need. Design is everywhere. There is no single manufactured, human shaped object where design is not present. Design is about ordering, shaping, constructing, changing and maintaining the way humans use raw materials and organise their environment. Every single thing that is not exclusively natural, untouched by human hand, has been designed by human brains and human hands.

Design includes many subsets of its own production aesthetic and utility. Questions stimulate new thinking. Questions like, how does this work? How could we make it work better? What is this thing being used for, and in what contexts, and in whose interests, and for what purpose? These are strategic, teleological questions that have to answered as clearly as possible. How does it look to us? Could we make it more pleasing and beautiful, more compelling and attractive? Could we rethink, re-design, reshape and re-engineer this thing, so that it works better? How could we invent a different way of doing things, according to changing need and knowledge? Would this medicine work better if we re-engineered its internal, biochemical structure? Would this aeroplane fly faster and more efficiently if we smoothed its design? Would this colour scheme work better alongside that one? How can we build this washing machine to use less electricity and last longer? If the shape and colour of this tool, this phone, this cup, this sofa, this suit, this house, this pen, this computer, this chair, this factory, this hospital, this nursery, this estate, this city were designed differently, would it work better. Would people enjoy using it more, or being there much more?

And design doesn't just apply to the shaping of things. It works for the organisations of events and meetings. Does this way of organising this project, this meeting, this decision, this group, this society, work better than before? How could we do this differently with better results for everyone involved? How should we organise the way we organise things? Everything we do is affected by the attitudes and beliefs we bring to the processes involved, effected by how we think, and what we think about, what our personal experience and skills and training tell us about it. And it is true that careful, comprehensive planning and preparation is not enough. There is nothing wrong with good planning so long as we are open to the "something more" unexpectedly happening. For it often does. We say that a good play takes off in ways we never expected or experienced at any of its rehearsals. And that happens in the choreography of Liturgy in the Church as well as the World. It happens because we are more than flip chart processes and pathways. We are handling living, dynamic reality that contains its own potency to reveal "something more".

## LITURGY AS SCIENCE.

If Liturgy is a dimension of the Liturgy of the World, then it includes questions raised under the attentiveness of different scientific disciplines dedicated to understanding how the world "works". If Liturgy is involved in public works, then it is involved in every level and way of understanding the nature of what makes for public works. The way we produce Public Works depends not just on art, design, financing, and building issues, but the nature of the materials and elements used in themselves. For without that nature, there would be no materials. And materials are part of the very nature of nature, and of our understanding of creation. These "natural" things are studied in material science and chemistry, which in turn depends on the forces and laws of physics, as we understand them empirically and through mathematical calculations.

We live in an extraordinary universe which invites us to study its processes and how it works. For its workings, or processes, are what constitutes or flows from its very nature, of which we are but a small part. We humans, who ask questions about the way things work and do such studies, live on and within a particular part of that larger universe which affects our lives. So, the science we are studying comes from the nature of our perception of ourselves, from within ourselves, within that object of study, inside-out as it were, because of the way things on the outside, have influenced us on the inside. This used to be called natural theology, and those who studied it in that way were known as natural philosophers, in other words, people who loved (philo) to understand the wisdom (sophia) of natural things, and how they "worked", and how they came to be like that.

The size and scale of the universe is both smaller and larger than we can see in our normal ways of looking without a microscope or telescope. So, what we see, is only a fraction of what we could perceive or know about the universe. The very small, in the world "down there", is too "far" away from us for us to see it, as it really is. It is like another universe. The very large is too "far" away to see it as it really is. We certainly can't see it as it is "now", because we are only seeing it as it was hundreds, thousands and millions of light years ago; we are only seeing the light waves from the objects that have taken that long to reach us.

Then, both the smaller and the larger become more strange when we see them on their own terms, and from within their own scale of being. Both are relative to each other and relative to their own scales of being. Both exist at the same relative "time", and within their own space-time, and both include the other. The larger includes all the smaller parts which make up the nature of the universe, with all its structures, forces and elements; the smaller includes the larger as the context for the part it plays as it has evolved within it. And compared with something really large, for example a sun hundreds of times bigger than our sun, our large sun may seem very small, even though it is hundreds of thousands of times bigger than something we can see under a microscope - something like an atom for example, or the beating cell of a beating heart muscle.

To say that things exist at the same "time" is an understandable assumption from our point of view. But time is one of those fundamental questions we need to revisit from time to time. The assumptions we make about the nature of things has to be occasionally revised, and new questions asked in the light of those revisions. Such assumptions can appear both familiar and strange at the same time. And revisiting them can involve theological, as well as scientific questions, both at the same time. And the questions we often ask are naturally based on our common-sense perception of things, but they may, at the same time, be more strangely complicated than we realise.

So, from that perception experience of time, we commonly ask "what is the time", not always realising we are on a planet spinning at about 650 miles per hour, or that travelling in an aircraft capable of going faster than that, we would see the normal passage of the passing of a day be reversed. As we travelled faster than the spinning earth, we would see the setting sun rise again. For it is the movement of the earth around the sun which constructs our experience of time, our way of measuring time. But our sun is but one star in a galaxy of billions of stars, in a universe with billions of galaxies, and it is all (a very big "all" indeed) moving away from itself. So, what does that do to "time"? And if Einstein is right about the fabric of the universe being made up of space-time, then we cannot talk about time without talking about distance, and, cosmologically speaking, distance affects time, because of the speed that light travels, which is measured in time in order to convey the distances involved.

Much of what we feel in our experience of the present time, is drawn from the past. When we think of the present, we believe we experience everything around us as being part of the same "now" that we perceive to be the now in which we exist and perceive things. But we perceive things within the light of our capacity to see them, within what we call the "now" of our experience of seeing them. But because the sun is 93 million miles away, it has taken the light from the sun which makes it possible for us to see things (as well as benefit from its heat) about eight minutes to reach us. During those eight minutes anything could have happened to the sun which we experience as shining on us now. It could have exploded, and we wouldn't know it for another eight minutes.

We can look back in time by photographing deep space in the night sky. The Hubble space telescope has taken photographs of ultra-deep space at distances which take us back millions of light years. Astronomy helps us look at the past as if it were the present. We cannot see beyond a certain point, because light from that moment in time hasn't reached us yet. So even Hubble can't see further back than about 500 million years. The universe is expanding and the further back we go, the more light is stretched or red shifted. In the future, we will be able to watch the formation of the first galaxies and structures in the early universe. But we can't see into the future, because time only flows in one direction, as explained by the law of entropy. Something that hasn't happened yet, cannot be perceived by waves of light coming from it.

Our brains can imagine the future in all sorts of creative ways, but that is not the same as our brains remembering memories from the past, even though creativity can be much involved in that process as well. Entropy is a measure of the way material things rearrange themselves. The more ways things can be rearranged without destroying themselves, the higher entropy a thing has. Objects in a more ordered state, with fewer ways of disordering their structure have lower entropy. Entropy always increases. According to the second law of thermodynamic, every thing tends to move from order to disorder. The paradox is that, in the past, the universe was more ordered, and, in the future, it will be less ordered. Increased complexity seems to introduce less order. This introduces a direction to time. But is this movement fully understood? Why were things in the past more ordered? In the state of transition from more to less order, how can more complicated, even beautiful, cosmological structures appear? And didn't Einstein make all of this apparently simple, linear perception of the movement of entropy from the past into the future more complicated? And doesn't our perception of the movement of time depend upon where we are standing? If we move very fast, then, apparently, we could theoretically see time ticking more slowly for someone we pass by. An experiment was done showing that people on planes travelling around the world in different directions will age differently, albeit only by an infinitesimal amount. And does that small amount prove very much if it doesn't make that much difference to the way people experience time? And, if our lives are a series of time moments like places on a map of time, why does our memory of those times, or those places, so affect our understanding of time? As time passes, and we inevitably get older with it, don't we reconsider the past and see what we thought we saw then differently? We can't return to those moments physically, and time travel of that kind looks very unlikely, but we can move through our memories of the past to the past, from within our present remembering of them, and all that has changed in the mean-time because of our different experiences of ourselves and others as time has passed. For liturgy is also, and always, about those relational experiences, and the way they affect our perceptions of the world.

## LITURGY AS SOCIAL EXPERIENCE

And we are essentially social animals. Homo Sapiens outlived Homo Erectus mostly because the latter species wasn't as good at working out supportive, cooperative, relationships. And our brains consume vast proportions of energy input to do that. And because of the pelvic paradox in humans, where large brains mean we are born at a less developed stage, necessitating a longer-term dependency need on the mother and the father, this, in turn, means that closer bonding is established over a longer time frame than with many animals. And homo sapiens has developed a greater capacity for empathy and altruism partly because of this, and more so than other social animals or primates. We are not unique in this respect, but other social animals are not so self-consciously articulate and self-aware about it. And while many social animals[117] (like ants and termites) live in extended groups, humans have evolved the ability to relate across kinship, tribal groupings and language barriers as well as within them. Humans have evolved and then developed and shaped the way we understand those relationship, and the way we

[117] I found Edward Wilson's book *The Social Conquest of the Earth*, Harvard, 2012 very helpful on this.

organise them to best effect for the sake of individual and public good, even when those things are in conflict with each other. And out of that conflict, and even its worst results, we have often been forced to learn our lessons and imagine, or hope, and work for a better future. Such are the ways and the processes of Liturgy in action in the World and those processes have significant and sacramental value to unravel and explore.

Where those "ways" of understanding human relationships communicate meaning and purpose, in individual and group human life, there is evidence of the choreographic effects of Liturgy bringing purpose and meaning into human experience through "public works". Liturgy isn't just involved in the provision of material, public works, but public communications and relationships[118] as part of public value. It is not just about the engineering and construction dimensions of public life. It includes the "work" involved in the development of human culture, as well as the work created and organised in human productivity. And in both we find the "work" involved in human relationships, which adds another dimension to the creativity and inspiration to make things well and to make things better. The culture of any society depends upon the work done to achieve good parenting, education, and the good ordering of society as a whole by those elected or trained for those purposes. So, yes, it does involve politics in the way we design and construct the constitutions and policies which then frame the way we choreograph our human relationships in economic, legal, moral and social life within any State. For ultimately, the State is made up of personal

---

[118] Just last night, in a car coming back from a concert in the Guildhall School of Music and Drama, where our grandchildren were playing, I had a lovely conversation with a person recently promoted to a senior role in a London University. She is now responsible for heading up external communication of the reputation of that institution, based on its internal wellbeing. We talked at some length about the link between good internal and external relationships. The former being the reality being communicated, in a world where the "reality was the comms" in the challenge to bring strategic, meaningful cohesion across any large, complex and sometimes fractured organisation, as so many seem to be for understandable reasons.

attitudes and behaviours in the way the culture of society is helped or hindered to express, encourage and support the best of those attitudes in individuals, organisations and informal groups, alongside the way it uses the law to fairly or unfairly, justly or unjustly, censor and punish those who exhibit the worst. And you can insist that all of this is political and secular, and hence not the place into which the Liturgy of the Church should trespass. Or you can choose to believe that all of this is part of the Liturgy of public works and public value in God's world, in which the Liturgy is already and always involved. And if you choose the latter perception, then the way public works function symbolically through public performance and ritualised ceremony will also matter as its own representation of its Liturgical values. For the Liturgy of the Church is not the only location for ceremony and symbolism.

## LITURGY AS PUBLIC CEREMONY

In the public mind, a popular understanding of what "secular" Liturgy might mean, as public organisation requiring careful choreography in the Liturgy of the World, can be seen in the kind of ceremonial which happens on, what we call in Britain, State Occasions. Dressing up and different kinds of processions and music are involved. This might remind some of the kind of thing they expect to happen in the Liturgy of special services in churches or a Cathedral. On a State occasion, we expect to see various State coaches, dating back to previous centuries and past traditions, processing down the Mall, to or from Buckingham Palace, accompanied by the Household Calvary in their polished and glittering uniforms, sitting on impeccably behaved horses. The sights and sounds of such a procession can be impressive indeed, lifting peoples' spirits during hard times or a major crisis. The Royal Family in Britain have a reputation for "being there" and "being seen" in ways that inspire hope, confidence, and nostalgic feelings which are hard to define. They represent the nation's traditions and remind us that the whole is greater than the parts, which, in some deep emotional way, holds it all together. In a constitutional monarchy, the Royal Family, however flawed, represent something more and hard to define in our national identity, certainly more than the Government or political parties. Despite the advantages of television and the internet, many still travel to see and be part of such occasions for themselves, to be there physically, lining the streets to see the appearance of those and whoever is riding in those coaches, waving back to them. Those who go to witness them not only soak up the atmosphere of the occasion they help to create it.

Yes, "processions" are often seen in the Liturgy of the Church as well, where the clergy might process into a service, fully vested in colourful robes of different liturgical colours, accompanied by their own household calvary in the form of a crucifer, acolytes, members of the choir, church wardens carrying their staffs, and junior clergy if there are any, plus visiting dignitaries like a Mayor, High Sheriff, Lord Lieutenant, and sometimes representatives of civil society and other faith communities. Usually, such processions are accompanied by rousing or moving music. In the Church of England, we are used to seeing well-rehearsed and well-performed processions in churches on State Occasions, involving not just royalty, but politicians as well. It is part of the nature of a State Church to know how to conduct the ceremony of such public occasions to the highest possible standard, putting the Liturgy of the Church at the "service" of the Liturgy of the World.

Processions, ceremony and ritual can communicate something more that goes deeper, something illusive that catches the spiritual significance of the occasion and makes the physical and visual action of the ritual come alive as meaningfully re-presentative. These ceremonies are carefully planned and prepared, but the quality of their liturgy in both Church and the World depends upon a certain inner attitude to inform and inspire its external appearance.

At the State Opening of Parliament, politicians from opposing parties can be seen walking in procession and standing close together, as a symbolic reminder of their place in wider society, governed by a Head of State and joined by leaders from other countries and civil society. There is a well-rehearsed ritual about where people should sit and in what order, as well as how they should process. Invitees in congregations usually dress up to look their best and where there is commentary on the broadcast service, we are used to a note of dignity and respect whether the occasion is celebratory or sad. Care is taken for parts of processions which move outside the building to appear genuinely part of the ritual performed. It's as if the procession enlarges the territory and reach of its own content or carries the meaning expressed in the splendour of the occasion outside its main focus of ceremonial activity. Ceremony, procession, colour, dignity, carries the meaning of a special event through the public appearance of political and other leaders of a country, and provides opportunities for public participation in the event. Ceremonial rituals nourish and enlarge the sense and scope of public support for a national event. The sustenance of national identity needs such occasions, if it is not to wither away and be replaced by something else, something less accountable to public opinion. The enthusiastic waving of national flags and banners can be an enforced activity in dictatorships, or an expression of public delight and appreciation at a sports event or a national occasion. A constitutional monarchy that manages to steer a neutral path through political oscillations, and yet stand as a figurehead to represent the values and concerns of a nation, may inspire public support across political divisions. Its special occasions become surrogate and representative events for the whole nation, or at least a majority of it, to share in the celebration of something good, or public mourning as at Princess Diana's funeral. And such occasions can express the values of that nation, those that are obvious as, for example, intercontinental ballistic missiles being paraded through the Red Square in Moscow, or children dancing, or floats carrying examples of voluntary work. And sometimes such ceremony reaches down to something deeper that cannot be so obviously or easily expressed in the public Liturgy of public value. And sometimes such ceremony becomes empty or counter productive public theatre in places where public value is suppressed or fractured. Liturgy isn't only about good choreography but the content it stands for and represents.

A democratic leader has not only to win the largest number of votes, but to demonstrate they can re-present those who didn't vote for them, in order to minimise divisions and enmities and further societal progress. It is a fragile exercise. In difficult times, it is tempting even for the democratically elected leader, faced with growing opposition, to turn in the direction of more tightly imposed regulations and media messages to protect his/her own position and power, as well as to defend those who elected him/her against those who didn't. Flag waving rituals of pomp and ceremony can either reflect the continuity of national values and traditions re-presenting the greater public good, or be reduced to a forced or false adulation of the power of the individual leader. The right ceremonial ritual can help to nourish, sustain and propagate either the power of the political leader, or the value based tradition of the country, in ways that transcend the views of a particular leader in power, and pass on an inherited and widely accepted sense of national meaning and participation. National feelings can turn into a dangerous form of xenophobic nationalism, or be co-opted for ulterior motives against enemies within or without.

But there are international movements and moments as well, which transcend the national motives and views of individual states. And these, too, are communicated through their own forms of ceremony, which can be hugely impressive in their own way. The United Nations and the Olympic Games are perhaps the most obvious examples of this. Both have their own traditions, ceremonies, special events, codes and formulas for expressing and defending the values they stand for in the public eye, and on behalf of their constituent nations. Both can be used and misused by individual states for national self-interest. Both depend upon the way ceremonial organisation has developed to facilitate their activity and their international image and standards. Both use words and movement in their ceremonies. Both have developed traditions which have to be followed.

The United Nations ceremonially parades the flags of member States, as does the Olympic Games. Both rely upon a certain ceremonial design and ordering in the way their activities take place. The United Nations buildings themselves contain artistic and symbolic, ceremonial reminders of their origins, traditions and purpose. Even the way the UN Assembly and Security Council chamber is set out, emphasises the design and purpose of its reason to be[119]. There are procedures and protocols to be followed at every point, which are committed to maintaining its democratic principles of decision making, just as the Olympic Games preserves its own competitive principles of democratic participation based on merit alone. Both have rules which set out and implement those principles in practise, even though some countries, from time to time, seek to break them. Both organisations know that when they fail to protect those principles against the power of individual nations, they lose their credibility. Their public reputation depends on the quality of their internal integrity, and without that, all ceremony collapses into a meaningless, discredited, external show. The inside (values, traditions, beliefs) is betrayed by the outside (reported reputational damage), or vice versa.

In these examples, the public knows the value of ceremony as a way of expressing and externalising internal value and commanding public support. Put differently, people know when the public occasions of Liturgy in the World, and in the Church (at the service of the world), are working well and authentically (or not), with their interests at heart and at the centre of their realities (or not). They know when Liturgy embraces those realities even as it seems to transcend and transform them to give them a larger context and direction. If, as we have seen, the meaning of Liturgy came from the arena of public works, then "works" include cultural activities which carry meaning and benefit for the public good. Not just public infrastructure, but public culture and values as well, symbolised and represented by the way ceremonies are organised for special occasions and special remembrance; things the Church would want to

---

[119] I remember an occasion when I was a delegate for a Not-For-Profit organisation at a meeting in the UN building in New York. During a break, I went to observe a meeting of the Assembly from one of the galleries where I had a good view of proceedings below but was alone in the gallery. I suddenly had a massive nose bleed over a white shirt, just at a moment when Perez de Cuellar, Secretary General at the time, by chance looked up at the gallery. He must have somehow alerted security because suddenly the gallery doors opened and two guards, thinking I'd been shot ran in to help me out of the gallery.

offer to God as having a meaning which appropriates itself to something which transcends and transforms, as well as serves, public life and public value. This can be found in church services on special occasions, or in exhibitions held in churches or museums to explore urgent concerns, or in great State occasions when we challenge ourselves to be more than our usual selves. This can be found in great works of art, music and science, in performances and presentations which educate and inspire us. It can be found when groups or whole societies come to recognise something significant in a creative cultural, or political achievement, in the public, good work of an individual or an organisation, which merits public recognition and appreciation. And so often it is the work of inspirational individuals at a very local level, contributing their love and time and energy to the needs of others, which go unnoticed and unrecorded, but yet make the most difference to the wellbeing of society as a whole, in the Liturgy of the World.

## LITURGY THE GAP BETWEEN ESSENCE AND LIKENESS

The language of death and life, birth and rebirth is common in the arts, and often used to express the inexpressible about drastic situations and also the processes of transformation sought, or already involved. The idea of re-presentation might be one way of talking about a form of new life in another form or media. The ambiguity of this in the relationship between the previous and then the new form, might be seen as an echo of the contradictory reports of appearances of Jesus after his resurrection. He is the same, but different. The two contradictory things are both true at the same time. In the Gospel accounts, the "appearance" isn't, at first, recognised as Jesus. Mary, in her state of grief and desperation, assumes he must be the gardener before recognition takes place. The two disciples, on the road to Emmaus, see him as a complete stranger, and only recognise him when they invite him to share their table. He breaks bread and somehow, in that act, he is recognised, just before he disappears from their view, their sight, perhaps their understanding.

In the Liturgy of the World, the arts have explored so many different ways of re-presenting the image of something, in order to communicate the presence of something, or someone. In attempting to capture the representation, or resonance, or remembrance of something or someone, the idea of image can be useful in describing the gap between reality and the representation of reality, but in ways that also establish a connection in the senses, or the intellectual apprehension of the experience[120]. The combination of this connection and the ambiguity of the gap, together expresses something about the difference between very central Christian themes. Jesus is human and divine, both at the same time. The radical experience of suffering and death of Jesus is the radical source of the new life that appears as a resurrected Christ, who shows the holes of the nails of suffering as part of his appearance, which itself can suddenly come and then disappear again and retain an element of ambiguity in the disciples' recognition/perception of what and who he really is in his essence.

When artists paint self-portraits or the portraits of other sitters, they talk about capturing the *essence* of the person as being something different from "just" a likeness. There is here an acknowledged gap between the two things, although a *likeness* may communicate something of the *essence* of a person and the *essence* of a person can be conveyed or represented without their being a physical *likeness*. And, in every attempt at a likeness, there is huge variety in the look of the representation achieved, by the same painter about the same sitter, or in various portraits of themselves. No two paintings of anything, or anyone, are exactly the same, even though each may well communicate something about that thing or person that then becomes associated with it, or them. If a hundred painters sat down to paint the "truth", as they saw it, of a person's face, each would inevitably be different in some respect along a continuum that reaches from essence, through character, to a physical

---

[120] The public reaction to the intellectuality of art installations, for example, is usually mixed, particularly when the artist, although making a "work" which expresses her own intellectual interests fails to communicate what is involved inside her preoccupations and intent on the one hand and public perception/understanding of it on the other.

likeness. And observers may find it hard to distinguish the truth of the person they see in the resulting portrait, and the different possible combinations of balance between any of these categories within that spectrum. So, the truth of perception depends not only on the nature of the painter, but the nature of the observer of the painting.

Art has to navigate between different perceptions of the same thing, or different things, showing us something we've never seen before in quite that way, depending on how the artist sees it, and is able then to re-present what she sees. And, however much care the artist takes in looking at their subject/object, what they then create will only ever be an image of the person, but there are many ways in which an image can convey something about the person. And so the gap, the space between a person or thing, and an image of the person or thing, can be crossed, despite all the ambiguity involved which still remains. Some commentators believe that the image created reveals as much about the looker, the painter, the artist, as it does about the person or thing being painted. And then, some commentators believe we must add into the mix the influence of different ways of painting, schools and genre of painting, which have, in turn, influenced the way the painter looks and what she sees. But then, of course, we might want to stand back, and through the long hindsight of art history, comment on the influences involved in the person commenting on those different genres, and the points they wish to make, for whatever reason, about them. And there must be some truth in these claims, and if so, it is a truth that complicates even more what is really happening in the processes of re-presentation, and any observations made about it in our experience of it. In truth, there are many gaps and many ways of attempting to cross them in the processes of perception and representation. And this applies in the art and science of language, with all its cultural assumptions, as well as in the visual arts.

In the early accounts of resurrection appearances, we are dealing with the attempt by different individuals, in different times and places, and for different audiences, to remember and then describe what they recall of their then perception of those experiences, or what they have heard about them, and what they believe those experiences are attempting to say about the vision of the appearance and the physicality of the form of the appearance. Technically, because the descriptions by Paul of his vision of the risen Christ (asking why Saul/Paul is persecuting him) come first, chronologically speaking in our written accounts, it is tempting to say that the later and very different, contradictory (as well as similar and complementary) Gospel accounts are created in the spirit of that later experience (although probably based on earlier traditions passed on orally before any Gospel was written down) which yet includes none of their (Gospel) physical detail - the empty tomb, the stone rolled away, the different kinds of young men or angels or figures in white, giving different descriptions or instructions, the gardener, the stranger on the walk to the village of Emmaus, Thomas's need to see physical evidence of the suffering of Jesus. And each of these descriptions, whether or not they contradict or vary in their description of what happened, comes from the different experiences of the memory of what happened, as it was passed on by others to those who wrote down the Gospel account. And, sometimes, they might have been aware of other Gospel versions and sometimes not. And sometimes, particularly in the case of John's Gospel, their experience of the accounts and their belief in the risen Christ are infused into other parts of the Gospel, and not just towards the end of it. For example, in John (the writer may well have been a young man at the time of the crucifixion and resurrection), the Gospel is infused into the language he uses elsewhere about Jesus as the way, the life, the light, the truth....

And sometimes the "appearance" seems to point to what is going to happen in the future in another place (Galilee for example). Sometimes the power of the experience of not seeing an appearance, but seeing evidence that something completely unexpected has happened, is recorded as filling the witnesses with complete astonishment and fear. Here is the original end of Mark's gospel (Chapter 16). Early writers like Clement and Origen knew of no other version. Later versions were added in different texts. Chapter 16 begins with some common detail found elsewhere,

*When the Sabbath was over, Mary Magdalene, Mary the mother of James, and Salome bought spices so that they might go to anoint Jesus' body.*

**Mathew has Mary Magdalene and another Mary; Luke has Mary Magdalene, "other women" and Joanna; John has Mary Magdalene, Peter and the other disciple**

*Very early on the first day of the week, just after sunrise, they were on their way to the tomb and they asked each other, "Who will roll the stone away from the entrance of the tomb?" But when they looked up, they saw that the stone, which was very large, had been rolled away.*

**The same reference to the stone being rolled away occurs in Luke and John; in Mathew and John it is after an earthquake.**

*As they entered the tomb, they saw a young man dressed in a white robe sitting on the right side, and they were alarmed.*

**In Luke it is two men, in bright clothes; Mathew, an angel sitting on the actual stone outside the tomb. In John, Mary saw no one the first time but then two angels inside the tomb sitting on the stone bed.**

*"Don't be alarmed," he said. "You are looking for Jesus the Nazarene, who was crucified. He has risen! He is not here. See the place where they laid him. But go, tell his disciples and Peter, 'He is going ahead of you into Galilee. There you will see him, just as he told you.'"*

**Mark and Mathew; Luke referencing back what Jesus had already said while in Galilee about resurrection. In John, Mary is to tell the disciples what she had seen.**

*Trembling and bewildered, the women went out and fled from the tomb. They said nothing to anyone, because they were afraid.*

As any editor will know, this kind of ending can be very powerful and indicates the courage of the early church not to say anything more that might detract from the impact of this reality of fear and bewilderment. Because it is such a (unedited) human reaction to such an experience, it has its own credible authenticity. Something unexpected has clearly happened, but at this point no one understands it. Whatever the experience was like, it was enough to make the women flee from the tomb and say nothing, presumably in part because they thought no one would believe them, despite what the Gospel records say about Jesus's warnings. There are apocalyptic parts of Mark's gospel warning of future tribulation, hinting perhaps that the early church has already experienced some of the serious events of those times. So, there is fear in the air, certainly for those first witnesses and also in those who would have first read this Gospel account. The writer of Mark is wanting to locate Jesus's words within these wider struggles as warnings (Mark 13 gives a terrifying picture of the future including the destruction of the Temple, or a reflection of the reality which has already happened) or actual experiences (e.g. with Satan in Mark 3).

However inspired by the Holy Spirit these writers and writings were, we see, in these differing accounts, evidence of the real differences involved in witnesses' differing perceptions of the experience, in different ways of recounting the experience, as well as their own different backgrounds and focus on different audiences. Somewhere, in all of that, there are already hints at different ways of understanding the meaning of what is represented in the experience itself, as well as its recounting. None of this should come as a surprise, because of what we know from other dramatic events where eye witnesses, or later accounts of eye witnesses of the same event, differ considerably. The real surprise is that the accounts in the New Testament haven't been smoothed out to be more similar, and that we have as much contradictory detail as we have, much of which articulates the real theological problems involved in understanding what really happened. If Paul describes a Damascus Road inward vision of an external appearance, the Gospel writers describe physical details associated with different kinds of appearance of that same Risen Christ, and they do so with detail that in many cases does the disciples no credit at all. And, it has to be said, amazingly (given the attitudes of the times), these accounts give such a prominent role to particular women.

The impact of the thing represented, can be immediate and powerful in its own right. Further study of the re-presentation can reveal other layers involved in the interactions between the thing represented, and the ones doing the re-presenting; on what assumptions/beliefs did they observed and reflect on what they understood about it from different sources; the reasons they wanted to represent it, and to whom; the way they chose to describe it, and how different interpreters and commentators have understood what they described through the centuries and through different genres of historical and theological lenses. The layers accumulate, through time, about what has taken place in all these processes and what was at stake in the process.

In the interactions within, and between those things, we glimpse the way the human story is understood and told, about something which is more than a human story, one that transcends the human, however much it is perceived through its effects on human experience. We also see, looking back through the accumulated layers, how it affects the belief of those early Christians and then how their beliefs affect the way they understood it and told it. The new perspective creates, and then meets and intersects with, and flows from, the beliefs involved, as they themselves are affected in an ongoing way from within the Liturgy of the Church.

And then we discover or rediscover how all of that, in turn, affects the Liturgy of the World, and what is understood as being true and possible there, which in turn affects the way the Liturgy of the Church receives and processes what its beliefs stand for and imply, as they flow in and out of the different interactions and interpretations of this and other stories about our human condition in the life of the world. And those stories create their own paradigmatic myths about that condition, which are passed on and transformed as time passes. They interact with artistic, dramatic, linguistic, musical, cultural, political and other expressive re-presentations of them. For the outflowing and overflowing of Liturgical movement weaves its way back and forth, inside and out, of how we humans try to understand our condition, and the way we interpret it as a result. Like water, this Liturgical movement finds its own levels. It seeps unbidden or invited into our assumptions and beliefs, informing, inspiring and transforming the culture of our public, stories and our public works. It is therefore always part of the very waft and weft of the fabric of our universe and how we understand it, and interact with it, except that there are many more dimensions than two in the fabric of the space-time-matter of the universe. I have to believe that, in ways I could never understand, let alone compute, Liturgy is present in all of this, not just as another dimension or part but something involved and inhabiting the whole.

## LITURGY AS CITY DESIGN AND REGENERATION

In the Liturgy of the World, public works and public culture occasionally inform each other, particularly in city regeneration projects. The creative arts and creative industries can transform particular communities or the reputation of whole cities[121] and bring regeneration hopes back to areas of depression and degeneration which appear forlorn and forgotten[122]. The cultural industries are significant employers and economic generators, but also contribute to the transformation of how cities look and function, and how they are organised to encourage greater use of public spaces and performance areas. In cities which are forward looking, or desperate to lift community spirits, the local leadership will have invited creative architects[123] to take a fresh look at the environment, to upgrade or redesign it, democratising what isn't open to the public, creating new interfaces between public and private space, encouraging people to look in new ways at what they think they are seeing and experiencing.

In ancient cities, myths circulated as vehicles of relational significance and value within people's sense of the significance of their city. In exaggerated forms, they told the story of beginnings and ends, challenges and achievements, and how different cities, tribes

---

[121] Community arts in many parts of cities, but also the identification of particular art with whole cities not least bringing in huge tourist income e.g. Gaudi in Barcelona, the Guggenheim in Bilbao, Mackintosh in Glasgow, the Renaissance artists in Florence, Joseph Wright of Derby.

[122] As photographed for example in various parts of England, particularly the North East, by Bill Brandt (1904-83) at the time of the Yarrow marches of miners to London in 1936. He had read George Orwell's essays and J. B. Priestley's book an *English Journey*. After this, he returned to London and his photos of the Blitz have left lasting images of those times. His photos helped to motive post-war reconstruction.

[123] This became clear in Baltimore when a group of us from the Derby City Partnership visited regeneration partnership projects there, and in Washington and New York.

and ethnic groups had survived and conquered. These gave people a narrative about their own identity or where it fitted into a larger picture. At times, in the Roman world, it was common for an Emperor to call himself the Son of a God. The themes of these myths formed the subject of public art in public spaces such as baths, amphitheatres, and sports arenas, or domestic art, found, for example, in statues and frescoes in peoples' homes[124]. Through these cultural myths, beliefs embedded themselves in peoples' consciousness and their daily lives, as the early Christians would have known. Stories of different gods were prominent in these stories, in a world full of apocalyptic crises. The gods were meant to guide people through these crises and rescue them when disaster struck. It was a world peopled with heroes and heroines, and priests and priestesses, in cults with their own initiation rituals. Rich families and powerful women and men were responsible (as liturgists) for sustaining these cults, building Temples and public statues to honour their gods as part of the Liturgical life of their cities. In Pompey, influential women like Eumachia became a famous benefactor of the largest building in the Forum at a time of increased urbanisation. Wealth led to fame, reputation and social status. The female wealthy elite, like Eumachia, became priestesses of the gods and financially independent, capable of contributing to public works and public culture. She became at one time a patron of the city with a statue built in her honour. In truth, there are no cities in the world without any kind of public art, or public culture and values, however diffuse and dissipated they might be. Sometimes this happens through public monuments and statues, and in other cases, through public graffiti and wall paintings. Sometimes, often in fact, official public culture clashed, and clashes, with popular perception and popular art expression.

In modern cities, philanthropists and architects are the new liturgists, adding to the Liturgy of public value through innovative, public works and higher quality opportunities for enjoyment and pleasure in the development of the public good through cultural

---

[124] As can still be seen in Pompey and Herculaneum for example.

innovation. There are examples of this in many large cities. For example, the 2009 High Line in New York is a place where people can experience nature, art and design interacting with each other, safely protected from yet more building work obscuring it, attracting thousands of users and visitors every week. It is a good example of the greening of public life, adding a sense of transcendence of the normal city living experience, in the words of Liz Diller one of its partner designers.

## SEEKING THE SUBLIME

The language used to describe public spaces, public culture and public art in reviews and articles can be revelatory. In a world that has largely rejected any overarching meta-narrative, one still finds adjectives being used like sublime, transcendent, candescent, illuminating and inspirational, awe-inspiring, miraculous, adding a sense of mystery, and reaching for the "more' that is indescribable and unmeasurable within and beyond the human experience of ordinary things; ordinary things in nature, or in our art-full imagination of nature, or our design of things alongside and within nature.

For, in the Liturgy of the World, we find that Liturgy works within our attempts to aesthetically efficiently, and sustainably design our environment in ways that work with and complement nature. Artists and architects have gained much from looking carefully at the structures in the human body and in nature to learn their skills as they are inspired by shapes, forces and strengths. The natural philosophers saw in nature the design of God at the cosmologically and microcosmic levels. It was quite common for clergy (particularly those in rural parishes), later known as parson-naturalists, to lead the way in the intellectual pursuit of knowledge about the natural world, Their belief in a Creator, far from blocking such interests, stimulated a natural curiosity in the way things worked in the science of natural things.

Science and Art came together in Robert Hooke's (1635-1703) great work, "Micrographica" of 1665[125]. His scientific curiosity was enhanced by his ability to draw what he saw of natural structures under his microscope. At one time, it was the most popular book in Britain, if not in Europe. But he was also a great architect and city planner working as assistant to his university friend, Sir Christopher Wren (1632-1723)[126] on architectural surveys of London after the great fire of 1666. He was also Professor of Geology at Gresham College and an assistant to Robert Boyle in his chemistry experiments. He also looked at the stars, and built the first Gregorian telescope to observe Mars and Jupiter. And, during his work on light refraction in optics, inferred a wave theory of light. His is the first recorded theory that heat (which he saw as a form of energy) expands matter, and that air is composed of small particles. He challenged the current Biblical view of the earth's age, and argued that fossils found on the tops of hills and mountains had become forced up there by geological processes. In his observations of microscopic fossils, he contributed to the foundations of a theory of evolution. This indeed was the work of a great British polymath reminding us of the Italian, Leonardo da Vinci.

If his drawing or craftsmanship skills came from the inspiration of the Renaissance, his science came from the scientific revolution, including the work of Isaac Newton (who was jealous of Hooke's artistic skills) with whom there were tensions. Hooke had worked on planetary motion and a theory of gravity formalised by Newton's law. Both were unveiling their understanding of the secrets of the universe, and both carefully observed natural things to learn more about how they worked. Science has followed their inspiration, and today many artists seek a scientific understanding of their subjects to assist with their re-presentations.

And it is in the search for ways to do this, across different disciplines, that we might explore another level of liturgical relatedness; one that reflects the way divine relatedness incarnates

---

[125] And the first major publication of the Royal Society.

[126] Who was also an anatomist and astronomer. His great masterpiece, St Paul's Cathedral (completed in 1710) showed, in the construction of its dome, that the appearance of a thing isn't always the same as its actual structure.

itself in creation and humanity, and through our active participation of related connectivity within creation; our understanding of the implications, in science and the arts, for the claim that the image of the Word was made flesh. Rowan Williams, in talking about the *priestly nature of the community associated with Christ being taken up into the divine holiness through his self-offering included in his act of uniting earth with heaven. And so the sense that can be made of the world's raw materials through the culture of food preparation and food sharing is identified with the sense that is made of the whole human environment by the self-offering of Jesus to achieve reconciliation and absolution for the world. –* then goes on to say

*It is undeniably an intricate set of ideas, and in the history of theology different themes within this complex have emerged at different times; but here is a focal cluster of meanings that has remained fairly consistent, a cluster of ideas that has to do with the transformation of the material order as a dimension of what we are called to affirm and realize in worship. In this context Christian, anthropology has explored the notion of the innate "priestliness" of human existence, at least from the time of Maximos the Confessor. For Maximos, the distinctive role of the human is to be the mediating and uniting agent within creation in virtue of humanity's union with Christ in whom the division and oppositions that characterize creation as we know it are decisively overcome.*[127]

I am daring, in my inside-out understanding of Liturgy, to apply this idea of *priestly* role as the *mediating and uniting agent* to those who are courageous enough to work within nature, art, design and science; priestly as if they are human co-workers and co-operators within the ongoing task of understanding and developing attentiveness to what really matters in those things. The place and skills of engineers, builders and artist has varied in the way these roles overlap with the responsibility and experience of design as a *mediating* experience *overcoming divisions and oppositions* in the *transformation of the material order.* If this took place within the narrow confines of worship alone, within the Liturgy of the Church, we may well include such tasks within our definition of being priestly. Accordingly, as they take place within the Liturgy of the World, we

---

[127] *Looking East in Winter.* p 132

might well include such tasks as having their own priestly quality, even though that language has been lost over time, or was never applied in that sphere. But perhaps it is useful to reflect on its possible application now, even though few outside of the church would recognise or accept its relevance.

Rowan Williams goes on to write an intriguing and tantalising sentence, where he challenges the idea that *humans are free to exercise power over the material world as if it were not already the carrier of grace – existing in relation to God before it exists in relation to us humans.* He writes, *And our capacity to disclose this pre-existing truth and bring it to speech and meaningful action, to bring it to "culture" is the exercise of our priestly calling.*[128] Perhaps then, we have reached an appropriate point in human history when we can again, or, in most cases for the first time, bring into our ideas and language, and the *meaningful actions* of our culture, a vision of a priestly calling in the Liturgy of the World. And perhaps it is the priestly task of priests and Christians in the Liturgy of the Church to call upon this to happen by first affirming this priestly role in the Liturgy of the World, and then working in partnership with it. This would certainly apply to anything to do with the design and delivery of public art, public design, public works and public service, and all the specialisms which have accrued around these things and amongst the people responsible for the quality of their existence and development. In my view at least, this would be far more worthwhile than another Archbishops' call to evangelise secular society. In this sense, it is we Christians who first need "converting" to see what is already there, *existing in relation to God* and the calling it inspires for recognition, affirmation and investment in *meaningful action to bring it to "culture"*, as Rowan puts it so powerfully. And all this as the *exercise of our priestly calling.* And if that, then it should be centre stage in priestly training and the task of every parish church congregation in the country!

Definitions of this kind of public art (works) and public works will vary from age to age in response to changing needs. As we have seen, design is ubiquitous in human activity and the environment of

---

[128] Ibid 133

social development. The best architects pay attention to the details inside buildings as much as their outside appearance. The best planners work close to the ground with local communities. The best organisers of meetings and events listen carefully to every stakeholder's concerns. The best design combines visions and dreams with what is practically appropriate, necessary and possible at a particular time, looking to the past and the future, paying attention to clients, customers and users. Mistakes can easily be made in development and regeneration philosophies and fashions, as can be seen from the brutalist concrete architecture of the 1960s. Many architects see the city as a significant public resource for the development of a better human experience in large groupings. They recognise how design can change how space is shared, and question how comfortably people can be living in high density, space limited structures. They use language about it that stretches back to the early history of urban development. They show that ideas can change lives for the better or the worse[129]. Cities can attract more criminality and chaos, the density only magnifying the worst of human behaviours. They can isolate individuals into anonymity and powerlessness in the sheer size and scale of their spread. They can also develop talent and skills, ambition and aspiration making the most of a variety of positive role models, the provision of cultural, educational, and employment opportunities, social and commercial facilities, and a variety of cultural expectations. The best designers know that design is everything but that design has its limits and must be convincing enough to set clear templates and flexible enough to pay attention to ongoing use and need.

And good public art can enhance the public spaces of our cities and towns. This can be to memorialise people killed in war and other

---

[129] On a partnership visit to Baltimore, Washington and New York organised with my friend John Forkin OBE, the mayor of Baltimore told the story of its regeneration. He brought in three top private architects to live in the city and oversee all design proposals. When told that the city already had a department of architects and planners he allegedly replied, "and that is the problem". Investors had to commit to building local housing or infrastructure projects as part of their contract.

tragedies, to celebrate great achievements with statues of the leaders involved, or to use abstract art to beautify a public square or garden or enhance the approach to a corporate building. From Roman and Greek sculptures to the Renaissance and then to Auguste Rodin, Jacob Epstein, Henry Moore or Barbara Hepworth to Robert Smithson's outside artworks, Louise Bourgeois, Anthony Gormley, Anish Kapoor and the installation and performance artists and beyond, artists have turned the gallery space inside-out to locate art in publically accessible places to enhance that environment, cityscape and landscape.

Public works and public buildings can be used in different ways. But, in one crucial sense, they are public, even if built by private investment and for private companies. Why? Because people walk past them, see them as part of their environment, and even take them for granted, however controversial their design had appeared at first. If the building is a library, school, university, hospital or museum, then the public will at some point see inside as well as outside. In the first case of a private building, the inside design and activities aren't seen (except by employees and visitors) but can be understood from an outside perception of their effect. In the second case, they are understood from the inside as well as the outside. Outside-In and Inside-Out then, so many buildings are public works even if that only works from their look and design. We cannot but be affected by public works in our environment. There is only rarely no utility value at all, however indirect, in the activities and existence of public buildings, but even public art and monuments contribute their aesthetic quality and content to the value of our surroundings. Good architecture pays attention to detail as well as overall design, knowing that a beautiful shape can be spoilt by small details that let a building down.

Some architects strive to bring the inside of buildings outside or vice versa in their design. In such cases, a building isn't just a closed box hidden from the public, but generates a two-way interaction. Atriums and lobbies can create an outside-in or inside-out feeling. And this can lead to a merging of architecture and the nature of landscape. Building and public work design affects our perception and experience of the public realm, not least environmentally, but also aesthetically and behaviourally. And that seems to matter. Areas where buildings have been neglected or badly designed, soon deteriorate. They appear to attract graffiti, litter and criminality of their own accord. They seem to reinforce the message that nothing matters and so we can do what we like to our environment and to each other. There may even be some kind of correlation between a deteriorated and neglected environment and human violence within it. Sadly, terrorism has necessitated the need for architects to design more secure barriers between inside and outside. As a result, access has become more restricted and monitored. We are forced to go through barriered security checks to enter a public building. Checking in and checking out becomes an arduous process and it reinforces the division between outside and inside which previous architects had sought to soften in their designs.

## LITURGY AS PERSONAL CULTURE

In the Liturgy of the World, all of this and more is part of how we bring order out of disorder, creativity out of chaos, beauty out of ugliness, hope out of lostness, learning out of ignorance, altruism and cooperation out of selfishness and egotism. And this applies to the very small and very local and personal, as well as to great public settings and occasions when we sense a public connection with something bigger than our own personal lives. As we sit around the "table" of everyday life, using things, eating and sharing the food that has been produced through human work, we are experiencing hints of the presence of something more in the work done, relationships and culture formed, and bodies spiritually refreshed, renewed and transformed. It was at a meal we call the Last Supper, full of tense internal and external reference points and meaning, that Jesus gave of himself through the ordinary things of life made special by his presence. As he poured himself into these things, he was leaving us a sense of his presence, right at the heart of the Liturgy of the very, and sometimes, all too human World. "Do this," he said, every time you eat and drink it, and do it in remembrance of me. Do it to re-member my presence with you and in you, and for you, in many, many others, and through these things shared among you, things that you make and give and receive. Those are a stretched out, extended version of his words of course. I could be wrong to imagine that kind of meaning involved, in my attempt to draw it out. In fact, he used very simple words, and, as far as we know, very few words, certainly those recorded for what was said at this moment, in that particular meal, which has become the central point around which everything else turns in the Liturgy of the Church.

As we move from the Liturgy of the Church into the Liturgy of the World, I like to take, from the former, a possible interpretation of the meaning of those words, and anchor them in the Liturgy of the World, where a shared meal is central to our understanding of the relational and physical needs of every human on the planet. I believe they live, in their own way, in that wider context, just as they live within the Passover themes of that Last Supper meal. And, given the real, physical and spiritual hunger and thirst of too many on the planet, and given the continuing need to re-create and re-member a sense of his presence everywhere, I believe it makes sense to talk about the spiritual meaning of that presence, right at the heart of our physical and relational lives and our shared human activity in the Liturgy of Public Works in the World.

So, we get to the Liturgy of the World, via the maximal meaning and reference points of Liturgy itself, as used, that is, within the Liturgy of the Church to hold the meaning of worship, particularly in the Eucharist, and its reference points sacramentally in the potential meaning of all meals, and all matter in creation as mediated through the relational human and their potentially priestly role. So, we pause now to focus for a moment on that pivotal word "sacrament" and how it might be used in its maximal sense, its Liturgical sense, understood in a maximal way. We have already attempted a brief discussion about the nature of things, in themselves, as seen in art and design as part of the outworking of Liturgy in the World, a cultural part, that is, of its public works. But what if things in themselves, before and after they are designed and fashioned for use in public works, had a potential, symbolic, or real quality to them which partook of the quality of a sacrament? And what if the priestly role of mediating the sacramental significance of material things was applicable in the Liturgy of the World, as we are used to believing it is in the Liturgy of the Church?

The sacramental question, related to art and design, and the organisation of people, processes, and the production, delivery and consumption of things (with all their ethical implications) is "what is their true *significance*, their true standing within the nature of things in their own right, and then in their state of transformation affected by our handling? This takes us immediately to a question about how we perceive the intelligibility of their *significance*, and our relationship to it, our responsible part in it. Is it, or are they significant, only because of their utility to me and my desires and needs, or are they significant in themselves, as existing parts and dimensions of creation, or through our human, fabricating part in it? We might be used to asking ethical questions related to our *fabricating* role, not to mention our consumption, but what about the *in themselves* question? Isn't this ontology important for our understanding of a priestly role? And don't both then have sacramental implications and hence significance? This is clearly a question that matters to every person struggling with questions of fulfilment and purpose in their daily work. In which case, and in that sense, is that *significance* a constituent descriptor of something we might also know and name as a *sacrament* of creation? Rowan Williams has these words to say about human perception of the significance of things,

*We may perceive objects either as related to the unreconstructed needs of the human self or as related to the single intelligible purpose of the creator....seeing the things of the world in their true -that is, symbolic – significance and using them accordingly (cf., for example, Maximos, "First Century on Love" 92, 11, p63). This is a natural state in that it relates human consciousness to the real significance of things. And this allows us to say that the world as it is has nothing in it that is intrinsically evil, whether in soul or body; everything has the capacity to convey the divine intelligence and so to be related to human intelligence in its proper state (Maximos, "Second Century on Love" 76ff., 11, pp78-9). For the human intelligence – and thus the life that intelligence organizes – to be natural is to perceive the world as comprehensively significant; and because the world is significant in relation to God, it cannot take its significance from its potential for self-directed or self-serving human use.*[130]

If things in the world are *comprehensively* significant in relation to God, who are we to reduce or hinder their significance? Who are we to assume that significance only signifies for the purpose of *self-directed or self-service human use*? Is it not the case that the delineation of *comprehensive*, relational significance is a priestly calling and responsibility? If so, haven't we, in the priestly role of the church, been failing in that very responsibility? If so, doesn't that make it even more urgent for that priestly task to now be re-discovered in both the Liturgy of the Church and affirmed in the Liturgy of the World?

## LITURGY AS SACRAMENT

"Sacrament" was derived from the Latin, sacramentum, meaning an oath with "sacro" meaning to hallow or consecrate. A sacramentum, as used, for example, in the Roman army, was an oath of allegiance. Tertullian, a third century Christian writer compared the sacrament of baptism, as an initiation into the Christian community, with a soldier's oath at the beginning of his new life in the army.

Now, in church circles, we talk of receiving the sacrament, meaning the Eucharistic sacrament of communion, or we talk of the other sacraments of the Church of which the Eucharist is deemed the most significant. So, in between then and now, much has happened. Sacraments are commonly seen as the means or outward signs and symbols of God's special and inward grace, so a symbol of God's presence through e.g. the bread and wine, the water of Baptism, or the oil of anointing. It is revealing that most Protestant churches in the Reformed tradition, only recognise two sacraments (baptism and Eucharist) and some Anglicans don't see confirmation, holy orders, marriage or penance as sacraments. Some, like the Quakers, see

---

[130] *Looking East in Winter.* pp 14-5

sacraments as reminders of common practice or ordinances which are part of the Christian faith. While some Orthodox would affirm seven major sacraments and some would see the sacred mysteries as including the church itself. The Catholic Church sees the sacraments as necessary for salvation though not every sacrament is necessary for every individual. And in its Canon IV, it asserted that "anyone who suggests men may obtain of God through faith alone the grace of justification, let him be anathema" and in the process condemned most of the theology of the Reformed Protestant Tradition.

The Orthodox Church, while talking about seven sacraments, seems to believe that anything the Church does, as Church, can be sacramental, and, above all, they resist the temptation of classifying and coding the validity of sacraments and prefer to use the phrase sacred mysteries. The mysteries, they claim, are an affirmation of the goodness of created matter, and a declaration of what that matter was created to be. This different approach moves into the broader understanding of liturgy as having to do with all of creation, which, in its ontological nature, partakes as created matter of the loving action of a creator, which/who is part of the very nature of the mysterion in and of God.

The Orthodox Church uses language in this way because they hesitate to affirm definitively, or exclusively, anything that restricts our understanding of God to our human knowledge or perception of God. Their instinct is to remain open to what we don't know, as part of the *mysterion* of God, and so they, instinctively, prefer apophatic, or not-knowing, theology as a way of relating to that mysterion. When talking about the Roman Catholic way of thinking about God the Orthodox humbly, or sometimes arrogantly, suggest that its mistake has been to risk reducing that mysterion by talking cataphatically, or positively, about what we know, as if by our doctrinal definitions we can control, order, or encompass the nature of God's mysterion. One Romanian Orthodox monk said the following to me as we talked one night, sitting on a balcony in Putna monastery, high up near the Russian border, as the sun disappeared behind the hills behind us.

*If the first chapter of a book of Catholic theology starts with "What*

*God Is", it is bound to finish with "What God Is Not"*[131]. *We start the other way around, but don't believe we can ever arrive at What God Is in any chapter.*

Anyone familiar with quantum physics will know that Heisenberg and Schrodinger perceived the dogmatic certainties of some science to be blocking the way forward. Heisenberg, in particular, argued that his *Uncertainty Principle* was part of the very make up of the physics of the universe and not just our knowledge of it. It had ontological significance, and so that which was unknowable, at the quantum level of reality, couldn't be known with any certainty whatever measuring instruments were used. Uncertainty was part of the nature of everything. Both these physicists had read some philosophy and knew the significance of what they were saying to the scientific establishment, including the great Einstein, who allegedly summed up his doubts about this in the famous phrase, "God does not throw dice"! There are, then, parallels to a theological *via negative* to be found in the mainstream world of physics, both at an epistemological and ontological level and those levels of knowledge are connected and not connected at the same time.

So the relationship between what is, and how it appears, or can be known, continues to haunt our questions about the nature of (created) reality. There are warnings from science and theology that this is never a simple question. It lies behind what the church has tried to articulate about the relationship between creation and a creator through the centuries. To what extent can we say we believe in the presence of God in the world of things? How is this presence to be demonstrated? For centuries theologians used various scientific understandings of the world as a kind of proof of God as Creator. Eventually science itself turned on them, and bit them, or just turned its back and moved away. Sometimes, theology tried to keep up, or just gave up, or resorted to defending last ditch positions that had already been declared untenable[132].

---

[131] At the time "God is Dead" thinking from writers like Nietzsche was more in demand.

[132] Having spent ten years or more writing my trilogy Love's Energy on cosmology,

And then within all those questions, comes the issue of sacraments. Schmemann and others ask us to look again at the idea of sacrament in relation to the whole world. Rowan Williams talks about the significance of material reality in relation to God. I suspect it is time in Anglican and other, Western church circles, to have the courage again to use such language and consider the sacramental significance of ordinary things, and then to reach out from the Liturgy of the Church to the Liturgy of the World with a new offer – one that affirms the value of ordinary things in daily life and work, so that people outside the Liturgy of the Church can find new significance waiting there to be discovered in the Liturgy of the World. But even if, and when, that were the case, right at the heart of the affirmation and the discovery, a certain ambiguity of perception and of choice would still rightly remain. For nothing here is being or should be, imposed, and, in its appropriation, nothing here should claim to be actively true at the level of certainty. And in whatever way it might be offered as a truth to explore, it would only be a disservice to the nature of its truth, if we were to apply dogmatic categories of knowledge to its nature. The world may indeed have sacramental significance way beyond the limits of the church's usual understanding of sacraments, but that must remain a matter of perceptive choice by free agents, wanting, in their different ways, and from within their different cultural assumptions, to make sense of the world and its significance to them. At the same time, those who perceive this sacramental significance to be the case, have every right to live their lives and pursue its meaning, following its implications in the decisions they make in the handling of things, as if it were indeed the truth. And both can of course be true at the same time.

As we look back at the early mystics, we find a certain wisdom in their insistence on an apophatic approach when it comes to exploring a theology of the nature of God. Pseudo-Dionysius, Maximus the Confessor, and the Cappadocian theologians, in their understanding of the transcendence of God, maintained the truth of

---

quantum and evolution, I know how difficult these questions are but how worthwhile facing head on.

unknowability from a human perspective, even as they claimed the knowability revealed in Jesus. Both were true at the same time. Within that unknowability, they set out their belief in the limitless capacity and horizon of God beyond our understanding. They also developed a creation theology to fit within that scope of unknowing, and at the same time affirmed a connection between the Logos of God present in creation. and the Word of God who was Jesus. They seemed able to move from broad, cosmological questions to the place of the heart as the dwelling place or Temple of the "nearness" of God. In our own times, we might turn to the writings of Olivier Clement, *Dumitru Stăniloae (also known for his work on the Philokalia)*[133], Alexander Schmemman and Vladimir Lossky[134]. The latter two have written formative and inspiring books on Liturgy which emphasise its importance and re-orientate our understanding of its scope within creation itself. All of them draw upon the early theologians we have mentioned. St Maximos the Confessor (c 580-622), for example, said this about creation in his work intriguingly entitled "Ambigua".

*If by wisdom a person has come to understand that what exists was brought out of non-being into being by God, he intelligently directs the soul's imagination to the infinite differences and variety of things as they exist by nature and turns his questing eye with understanding towards the intelligible model (logos) according to which things have been made, would he now know that the one Logos is many logoi? This is evident in the many incomparable differences among created things. For each is unmistakably unique in itself and its identity remains distinct in relation to other things. He will also know that the many logoi are the one Logos to whom all things are related and who exists in himself without confusion, the essential and individually distinctive God, the Logos of God the Father. He is the beginning and cause of all things in whom all things were created, in heaven and on earth, visible and invisible, whether thrones or dominions or principalities or authorities – all things were created from him and through him and for him (Col. 1:15-17,*

---

[133] I had the privilege of sitting in his doctoral seminars in Bucharest during my year there in 1967-68

[134] See his *The Vision of God, The Mystical Theology of the Eastern Church, Orthodox Theology; An Introduction, In the Image and Likeness of God.*.

*Rom. 11:36). Because he held together in himself the logoi before they came to be, by his gracious will he created things visible and invisible out of non-being. By his word and his wisdom he made all things (Wisdom 9:1-2) and is making all things, universals as well as particulars, at the proper time.*

Equivalents to the Orthodox apophatic way, with its profound humility in the face of what can and cannot be known or said about the nature of God, are to be found in Western history where we also find an emphasis on Liturgy as a dimension of creation. Notable among many writers are St John of the Cross, Julian of Norwich and *The Cloud of Unknowing*[135], a fourteenth century, spiritual classic on contemplation. In more recent times, there are notable figures who have enriched our own contemplation of Liturgical breadth and depth relating it to the whole of creation, Teilard De Chardin, Karl Rahner, and Rowan Williams. But they are not the only ones to do this. There have been many monks, nuns and others who have pursued this approach in their own spiritual life and writings.

The French philosopher Simone Weil (1909-43) was an ascetic and mystic, a teacher and factory worker, labour activist and political militant, who believed spirituality and theology are connected on the deepest ethical levels. In the face of existentialism and post modernism, she insisted on using terms like "truth," "reality," "the sacred," "justice," "soul," and "God." The American, Trappist monk, theologian, mystic, poet, social activist and scholar of comparative religion, Thomas Merton (1915-68) taught that contemplation and political struggle complement each other and go properly together. Many witnessed to the same integration in South America. Archbishop Romero of San Salvador (1917-80) was martyred for his social and political witness while celebrating the Eucharist. In Africa, Bishop Colin Winter of Namibia, Bishop Trevor Huddleston, and Archbishop Desmond Tutu illustrated how a profoundly spiritual life could be combined with dedication to those suffering under

---

[135] which may draw on the work of Pseudo-Dionysius from the 5th or 6th century A.D. and John Scotus Euiugena 815-877. Some compare it to some of the spiritual writings of Nicholas of Cusa 1401-1464. It's influence can be seen in the inspiring poetry of the Four Quartets by T. S. Eliot.

Apartheid, as did countless numbers of less well-known Christians.

The way we do our theology and the epistemological assumptions behind it, is related to our choice of certain key ideas and their meaning. I have chosen "sacrament" and 'mystery" as significantly relevant ideas, given a certain orientation in their use, with implications for our understanding of "liturgy" in relation with all we know as creation. And the meaning of those key words has clearly changed over time. This has happened through developments and influence in various, separated parts of the Church which then, having come to the cross roads of division, move on to create their own new ways. Yet. all still claim to be faithfully following what can be found in the Gospels and the traditions inherited and passed on from the early church. Their understanding of those traditions, and the process of passing on, varies according to their theological viewpoints, and it is a matter of intense, academic debate as to what exactly has happened historically as a result.

Some would say that the cross-road points of history were truly that, and others that they didn't matter that much. But the point is that no Christian can easily stand aside from these questions, as if on some kind of neutral ground from which to survey the directions taken. We can study and research them, and then develop our own critical self-awareness about the place from which we ourselves view the world. We may never fully see that in any total perspective but that "place" tends to produce its own narrative about the world. If true about us and those we observe and study, then it was ever thus even from the beginnings of the early church.

So, saying that words change their meaning as the meaning of the Gospel is encultured in different ways of understanding those key words, is perhaps obvious, but clearly not to everyone. Many take their present Christian understanding of the Gospel as itself the Gospel! And, as a result, they risk reducing or expanding Gospel and Tradition into ways that may not always be helpful. But because we are all involved in the same process, consciously or unconsciously, it is worth censuring any judgements of others that we might too easily arrive at, but, at the same time, openly question the assumptions behind the different and often conflictual positions that have been adopted and then developed. There may well have been good reasons at the time why certain new movements appeared in reaction against the existing tradition or beliefs of the church. Perhaps that has always been the way. But then, later, it is quite possible that the new movement enshrines its own objections into a new ideological or fixed position of certainty, that then, itself, becomes the tradition of belief in its part of the church.

I am all too aware of these dangers and don't see an easy way out. I was brought up an Anglican and came to respect its claims to be inclusive even though that lead to mostly uncomfortable, internal relationships across quite profound differences. So, I have mostly chosen to look at the theological thinking about liturgy taken from the Orthodox Church. This is for two main reasons. First, that when I first came across it during that year spent studying in Romania, it seemed to be something entirely new and alien from my experience of church. Secondly because, over time, I came to appreciate the way they insisted on such a broad and inclusive approach to our theology of God which was at the same time so maximal, and so spiritually cautious and humble.

But within that maximal, spiritual orientation, when it comes to understanding the meaning of things, in themselves, there is also the question of an underlying foundation for that approach. And here again we have to base what is being said on the central belief in the incarnation. If we wanted a key biblical passage we could do no better than to use, *And God loved the world so much that he gave...* It is a salutary reminder about incarnational orientation and direction. We are so used to the church being the focal point of our concerns and our starting point for seeing the world, that we miss how radical this incarnational emphasis really is, with its basis in three key words. "God", "love", and "world". We are so used to "going" to church, as part of our direction of travel for Christian nourishing and focus, that we might easily miss the possibility that we are invited by the movement of love in the opposite direction. If the church building stands for anything as a physical symbol of where God is, then we have to re-orientate ourselves away from the church in the direction of the world, which God loves so much, in order to encounter the direction of the gaze of the incarnational God. Yes, we "go to" church to be with and part of the Liturgy of the Church, to experience something that has the intensity and direction of love to move us back out of the church in the direction of the world, to people, things and situations in it. And as we do that, perhaps it really does matter if we can rediscover its sacramental significance in relation to God.

Sometimes, in some traditions, what has followed is the assumption that the movement towards church, is also a movement away from the world. There is perhaps only a subtle difference in these two approaches but a difference nevertheless with profound implications. It is one thing for us to be drawn into the Liturgy of the Church in order to find the presence of God in the Liturgy of the World. It is quite another thing for the church and its worship to become the bastion of escape against all that is happening in the world. To say this is not to underestimate the problems, dangers and faults of any person's experience of being in the world. It is to remember the reason for the Incarnation in the first place as the revelation of God's love for the whole world to which the church bears witness and becomes the place of new perspective based on the New Person Jesus and the radically new creation established in him over the Old Person of our humanity. In Liturgy, the worship of the church restores and refreshes and makes possible again our participation in that act of new creation in Jesus. If liturgy is more than worship, then it embraces all that is often thought of as being "outside" of the church or even over, and against it. And the evidence is clear that there have been, and still are, times when the world really is over and against what the church stands for, and what the church is, in its representational nature.

## THE LITURGY THE MOVEMENT OUTSIDE-INSIDE

And we might pause at some point in the Eucharist of our worship to remember who we are, because of where we've come from, and to where we are going "after" our worship. As we leave a service quietly and respectful of others' needs, or as we go over to talk to certain people with those needs, or as we socially reconstruct our relationships with each other since last we met and talked, we might pause before leaving the church building. We might do this not just to admire its sense of peace or beauty, or to notice the architecture or hear the end of an organ voluntary. We might do this to register that what we are about to do has its own significance. We are about to leave the church to be the church in the world. We are about to return to our normal, every-day lives. We are about to move from the ambit of worship into liturgical time as experienced in and through those lives.

Something of this is caught at the end of every Eucharist in the Western Catholic or Anglican traditions, when we hear these words. "The mass is ended. Go in Peace." Or we might add the words of blessing at the end of the Anglican Eucharist. "to love and serve the Lord", with their implication that we move away from the centre, that the church represents, to discover the world as its own sacramental centre and not just on the edge of something. The Orthodox I've met and certainly Alexander Schmemman, think of it like this - we leave the liturgy of the church so that the liturgy of the world can begin. It's as if, when the Eucharist finishes, our first step is not only away from the church, but is part of the steps that will bring us back into the Eucharist of the church in a sacramentally circular movement, which includes everything else in between, in the meaning and scope of its liturgical processes. We leave the church and the Eucharist by taking the first step that will lead us back into it a week or so later. In the process, we are taking the first step into the Liturgy of the World, informed by the meaning of the Liturgy of the Church. It is an inside-out and an outside-in kind of world when seen through the perspective of Liturgy. There is no artificial border between the sacred and the secular in God's eyes, if we dare to believe that kind of metaphorical statement without too much presumption and arrogance.

In this liturgical inside-out and outside-in, liturgical reality, there is only the different phases and tones of two overlapping frameworks; each giving the proper template for the other, the appropriate perspective on the other. It's up to us to adjust our way of looking, and, from that will come the perspective we choose to adopt.

So long as we choose to see the world as evil or secular in order perhaps to emphasise the church as the sacred space we live in, then that is how we will see it. I am suggesting that is not how God sees it, but who am I to ever use such presumptive language? If we choose, on the other hand, to see everything as potentially and latently sacred as a sacrament of God's love and presence, then our attitude to everything will inevitably be different. The following words illustrate this other way of thinking and looking. They come again from Alexander Schmemann.

*When we see the world as an end in itself, everything becomes itself a value and consequently loses all value, because only in God is found the meaning (value) of everything, and the world is meaningful only when it is the "sacrament" of God's presence. Things treated merely as things in themselves destroy themselves because only in God have they any life.... The sin was not that man neglected his religious duties. The sin was that he thought of God in terms of religion, i.e. opposing him to life. The only real fall of man is his non-eucharistic life in a non-eucharistic world. The fall is not that he preferred the world to God, distorting the balance between the spiritual and material, but that he made the world material, whereas he was to have transformed it into "life in God", filled it with meaning and spirit.. Religion is needed where there is a wall of separation between God and man. But Christ who is both God and man has broken down the wall between man and God. He has inaugurated a new life, not a new religion... In Christ, life - life in all its totality – was returned to man, given again as sacrament and communion, made Eucharist.*[136]

And in those short words, we might well see the calling of the future priestly task in relation to the wall broken down between God and "man" in Christ, in a world given again to be understood as sacrament in relation to God.

## THE LITURGY OF THE GREAT WHITE SHEET

There is a revealing incident in Acts 10 and 11, which illustrates the struggle the early disciples had with the tension between the sacred and secular, the clean and unclean, the pure and impure, the holy and the profane. Peter has a vision. This is how one

[136] The World as Sacrament.

translation puts it (Phillips)

*"I was in the city of Joppa praying," he said, "and while completely unconscious of my surroundings I saw a vision—something like a great sheet coming down towards me, let down from heaven by its four corners. It came right down to me and when I looked at it closely I saw animals and wild beasts, reptiles and birds. Then I heard a voice say to me, 'Get up, Peter, kill and eat.' But I said, 'Never, Lord, for nothing common or unclean has ever passed my lips.' But the voice from Heaven spoke a second time and said, 'You must not call what God has cleansed common.' This happened three times, and then the whole thing was drawn up again into heaven.*

Other translations have *"do not make unholy the things I have made to be holy,"* or *"What God hath cleansed, that call not thou common."* Or *more revealingly "what God has cleansed and pronounced clean, do not you defile and profane by regarding and calling common and unhallowed or unclean."*

So, if a sacrament is somehow a visible re-presentation of something invisible, a physical symbol of something spiritual, nothing God has made clean should be defiled by us calling it profane, or unhallowed, or unclean, or impure, in a religious sense. And there were all sorts of laws and codes and rules that separated off the clean from the unclean and the sacred from the profane in Judaism then and now. But, in this vision, we get more than a hint of a different orientation and direction of travel based on the incarnation, which, in turn, reflects a movement of God in the direction of the other which is creation and God's presence in our understanding of creation. Peter then sets off for Caesarea, gentile territory, and when later he has to defend himself against criticisms from the Jerusalem church, he ends up saying *who am I to hinder God*. We may not understand how circumcision could have caused such a fuss, but we have our own issues to face in relating Christian belief to different values in Public Culture, in this as in previous generations. And who are we to hinder God by putting blocks in the way of such relationships by imposing things of only penultimate significance.

It is interesting that, at Easter, when the Orthodox celebrate the feast of the resurrection, the ceremony of the Light of Christ begins *within* the church and is then taken in procession *outside* and around the church, as if to symbolically and liturgically include the whole world around the church as the locus of the direction of travel for the meaning of resurrection. Those Western churches who have a ceremony of the Holy Fire, usually begin with the lighting of the fire in a small brazier outside the church, and then bring the holy light of Christ into the church. They are movements in opposite directions. And you may be thinking, what is in a movement? What's the big issue here? Well, in Liturgy, the movement of actions in the choreography are symbolic, but depending on what we mean by that word, something else as well. It's as if they are also "real" and not just standing symbolically for something else that is real. That is, they are representing in the sense of re-presenting what they mean and stand for. There is a dynamic and close relationship between the symbolic meaning and what it re-presents in reality, at least within the framework of liturgy as understood in the maximal sense.

And we might say, well that's all very well, but do people get it, really get it? And that's almost impossible to answer accurately or authoritatively. Whatever the statistical answer might reveal, the point is that many people do, enough at least to pass on this meaning behind the tradition, so that others will understand what is happening in the future. Yes, such an understanding depends on its own kind of philosophical idea about liturgy, for the theology to make any sense. But for people I've talked with in Orthodox countries, this is very real indeed. Things are done for a reason, they would say. This is why we do things like this. Because it means.... This is far more than a church service. This is something that affects and is part of the ontology of everything when that everything is understood within a belief in the mystery of the incarnation and its sacramental implications. This movement is part of that understanding. And it moves from the within to the outside of the meaning of church, as if the Liturgy of the Church is purposed in the direction of the Liturgy of the World; as if it is following the very orientation and movement of the Incarnation itself.

## AN EXAMPLE. THE INTERCESSIONS

A key moment in the Eucharist, or any form of worship, is

when we turn our heads and thoughts in the direction of others. In most, if not all churches, the intercessions come after the readings, sermon and Creed, and before the pronouncement and sharing of the Peace. It's as if we cannot speak of peace in our hearts, in the lives of others, and the life of the world, until we have turned in its direction through the intercessions. We think of others before we move into the anaphora or offertory prayer. And that is surely the right position. We are, as a church community, gathering together all that needs to be offered as part of that offering of ourselves to God, in that moment and meaning of God's offered presence to us in bread and wine.

We imagine the early Christians thinking of others not present with them in different kinds of need; prayers for different situations and people, for healing and for their enemies. Prayers where individuals have brought the names of those in need and named the need, or just the person, so that all present could reach out to them. I imagine that prayer originally developing in a natural way, and then inspiring individual commitments to do what was possible for those in need, and for the Deacons to visit the people prayed for, where it was possible of course.

We use the word intercessions for this pivotal moment, and, in many churches, those intercessory prayers will be taken by a lay person who will have prepared carefully, to make sure they know about those who have asked for prayer, and those who need the church's prayer. It is a recognition of the ministry of lay people to know each other, and other others, well enough to be able to do this on behalf of us all, and not only to bring prayers for, but to give thanks for as well. It can be a very moving part of any service, as we focus on the names of real people and their real needs in our relationship with God. For that relationship is not just about ourselves as isolated, or separated off individuals. It is about us as a community, a liturgical community in the sense we are talking about here. A community, however varied and scattered, or online, that is part of the Liturgy of the Church, and also part of the Liturgy of the World, even if many or most don't know the church in any meaningful sense, or the connection between the two. And yes, it is about a community that can be fractured, and in which individuals can feel isolated and separated off for all sorts of reasons including disability, illness, social isolation, mental health problems, lack of transport, poor mobility, and the vulnerabilities of old age. And there are far too many with such needs who feel forgotten, unnoticed or unloved.

And the Intercessions are more than just a list of names to be rushed through. Each person is precious, and we feel each need as if it were coming from a member of our own family, which of course in one way it is! I remember a well know Russian Archbishop, Metropolitan Anthony Bloom saying to me once that he was in awe at Anglican intercessions. This took me by surprise. There was something about the way he'd used the word "awe" that hinted at something else. So I asked him what he'd meant. He said something like this,

*you always add the words 'all those' suffering from…as if you are praying for thousands of thousands of people throughout the world in that kind of need or trouble. It's not possible is it, for that prayer to be truthful even if it is sincere. You cannot know 'all those' people or what it is like to be them and so how can you be praying for them?*

Just as I was about to say, *but God knows them*, and very much as if he knew what I was going to say, he looked at me with those piercing, knowing eyes of his and said something like this.

*'To intercede' literally means to go between, inter – between; cede from cedere - meaning to go. If you are to be the go-between between these people and God, then you are putting yourself in the eye of the storm when it comes to the things you are praying about or for.*

It was a lesson well learnt for my own private prayer as well as public prayer. Another wise priest said to me, *Don't turn intercessions into a list because then you will read them out like a list, and they are people who deserve far more than that.*

Somehow over time, in my prayers, I found another way. Firstly, I never said in my head, "let us pray for…." followed by a name. So often in church the intercessions are a list prefaced by the rubric "let us pray for…." without ever really praying for them. Instead, I found myself addressing God directly, missing out on the rubric and going straight to the heart of the need and turning that into a prayer for God to be with that person, to give courage, strength, hope, guidance, or whatever I thought, in my ignorance and clumsiness, that person most needed at the time, because of their situation. Then I found myself focusing not so much on the name, but the person through the name, bringing that person into my thoughts in the presence of prayer, in, dare I say it, the presence of God in Christ through prayer. That led to the next stage, which was to hold myself in prayer next to that person in my spiritual imagination, sensing that being next to them prayerfully brought me closer to them in the prayer for them. And then it didn't seem necessary to ask God for particular support for that person, but just to very quietly and slowly let my prayer turn into a meditative relationship with that person in their relation with a God who was and already with them. And then I felt as if the words of prayer turned more into the nature of prayer, as if I was entering closer into their world in the presence of God. I would use their names only through the quietest of whispers, followed by a long enough pause for that to mean something more than I could know. Perhaps this doesn't make much sense, but then just reading or praying a list of names hardly felt that meaningful either, valuable though it can be in a church context.

When possible at a weekday, said Eucharist, I would first ask the congregation who or what they were thinking about, concerned and anxious about, and slowly turn that into the intercessions, bringing as it were those persons to be along side us in the offering of the Eucharist. It took longer, but felt not only more participative, but less like the recitation of a prayer catalogue. That way of being the spiritual go-betweens, isn't always possible of course. And sometimes, as the spiritual go-between, we have to accept that we cannot possibly cover 'all those who…..'

Sometimes, holding people in prayer is all we can do. At other times, it is the liturgical moment, the turning point, when we know prayer and intercession for people can lead to organising practical help for them. Sometimes, it's not just them but their carers, and the caring agencies, who need our prayers and so prayer can spiral out into the networks of families and communities. Through them we are taken straight into the realities of the Liturgy of the World and then back through them straight into the praxis of the Liturgy of the Church. Sometimes, their names are put on a list, not for anything specific or easy to define, but because someone senses that person's name needs to named, and so brought from the Liturgy of the World into the ambit of the Liturgy within the Church. So, the intercessions are an obvious point, in any worship, when we realise how close those two things are within the presence of the Kingdom of God, and when we feel ourselves at the go-between point of their overlap.

## AN EXAMPLE; THE GOSPEL PROCESSION

Let me give another example. In the Western, Catholic and Anglican churches, at least some of them, there is, or used to be, something in the Eucharist called a Gospel Procession. In some churches we can now only find remnants of its original meaning, because the movement or rather the meaning behind the movement has been reduced. It used to be a high moment in the first part of the service with a crucifer leading a small procession down into the very centre of the church where a server holds the Gospel book between two candle holders for the priest to read and sometimes incense the book. Now it seems perfectly normal for the Gospel to be read, along with other readings, from a lectern at the front, following a Gospel or Gradual hymn, but with no procession or "fuss". The change may not have been noticed much, partly because people don't know, or didn't know in the recent past, that there was a meaning to the movement of the Gospel book from the altar through the sanctuary area, right down into the nave of the church. The procession which began with the Gospel book on the altar, was symbolically, or we might say liturgically, moving it down into what? The nave represented the place where the *laos* gathered in church outside the sanctuary, which used to be, in some cases, part of a monastery building, or certainly that Eastern end of the church building where the "holy things" happened and where the priests officiated.

And one can see the rationale in the architectural model behind this which probably drew on at least two things. First, in the Temple in Jerusalem the Holy of Holies was separated off from the sight of the people by a curtain to protect them from its holiness.

Only the high priest was allowed into that Holy of Holies, and only once a year at the Feast of the Atonement (where blood from the sacrifice was scattered all over the walls and then onto the "scapegoat" who was sent off into the wilderness to carry the people's sins far away from them). At least one of the Gospels and the letter to the Hebrews (with its profound exploration of the metaphor of Christ as both victim and priest) is at pains to say that this barrier was rent in two at the crucifixion.

Secondly, the early use and development of Basilica type buildings or their design as a model for the first churches. The Basilica was originally the large building in which the local governor or ruler held court, sitting at one end of the building, reserved just for him (and it probably was mostly a him) and his entourage, who held court and gave out legal judgements and notices and no doubt other kinds of pronouncements and speeches. These kinds of buildings are to be seen in various parts of Italy or throughout the Roman Empire. So, it was probably a fairly obvious design for the early Christians to have used. One end of the large building is reserved for where the special, holy things happened, and where the priests were situated in their court as it were. The rest of the building was reserved for the community. And so, over time, the basilica/Temple model developed after Christianity was formally and publicly institutionalised in the fourth century. And how different that architectural setting must have felt from the small group gathered in a house, perhaps sitting on the floor or around a table for a meal.

So, in the liturgy of the Eucharist, according to Orthodox praxis, the Gospel which is a book, but stands for the Word of God revealed in Christ, is on the altar (table) behind the screen of the iconostasis separating the altar which represents the holiness of Heaven from the world represented by the rest of the church building. The senior priest blesses the Gospel book and senses it. The Deacon then carries it sometimes around the altar before processing it out of that area through the screen (tent of separation) down into where the laos are, right into their midst, right into the thick of things in the world. Because that is how they understand its rightful place and movement, to echo the movement of the incarnation itself. And the people represent the world into which the Word came and dwelt among us. There the Gospel book representing the Word of God is again incensed to acknowledge its dignity and holiness as the people are incensed to acknowledge that they carry the image and likeness of God because of the action of Christ who is the perfect image and likeness of God, the Word made flesh in the world. And that means that just as the Gospel book is censed, so whenever the laos are censed something important is being said that has a meaning in reality. And it is an ontological reality, not a moral one. It is not saying this or that person deserves to be acknowledged or singled out in this way for any ethical reasons, but that all people are part of this ontological relationship which the whole world has with God.

This is significant, and, in many ways, unexpected. It also goes against the grain of assumptions in much Western Christianity that people are naturally sinners and need to come to church to be repaired, or spiritually fixed. It is the reverse of that. It is a recognition of the latent image and likeness in everyone (not just those in church) and the latent sacredness of all created reality into which the Gospel comes to proclaim the incarnation, to tell the story of Jesus within the life of the world (the congregation). It is a witness that all humans are made in the image and likeness of God, and, at the same time, calling them to know and live out the full and abundant potential of that image and dignity. So, yes, it has profound meaning for how we understand the nature of the person, every person, *per se*, whoever they are and whatever they believe and wherever they come from. It is a statement that whatever their sex, gender, colour, age, disability, work, language, beliefs there is something more about them which both transcends all these things, and is more basic about than any of them. They are incensed as individual persons and as members of the gathered community, both being true at the same time and both being vehicles for the sacramental presence of God in the Liturgy of the Church which in this case represents the Liturgy of the World.

And so the Gospel is brought down right into their midst, not only for them as individuals within a particular congregation and community, but to symbolise the movement of the One who is the Gospel, incarnationally, into the very midst of the flesh and humanity of the world God loves so much. It is sacramental in its essence. It is risking and making a statement about the presence of that holiness of God, incarnationally and sacramentally present in the world. The *laos* of God, assembled in church, represent all people everywhere, for whom the Gospel came into the world in the person of Jesus, as the re-presentation of God's love in their midst. And that movement re-presents the movement of God in the incarnation into the world God loves so much, bringing them the gift of the words and meaning of the Gospel about that same incarnation.

And do all Orthodox understand what this symbolic movement re-presents in reality? I suspect many do and some don't. And many would understand it in slightly different ways. In some places this is so much part of their spiritual orientation and their understanding of the meaning of what is happening, liturgically, that it has become encultured in their expectation and worldview, and so now naturally but implicitly understood. And as you stand in an Orthodox service as this procession comes "down" through the icon screen into your midst, you feel a frisson of responsibility for taking its meaning out with you into the community you come from, bearing the message and meaning of the Gospel as part of the Liturgy of the World.

As of course, this, or a version of it, also happened in the Western Catholic tradition and the Protestant branch that broke away from it. The Gospel procession in the Anglican Church has somewhat slipped in the way it is done, and what it means for many Anglicans who aren't part of the Anglo-Catholic or other traditions that still use it. But I suspect even those who include a Gospel Procession may have lost touch over time with the meaning given to this movement in the Orthodox or older churches. The Gospel is not just the third reading to be read. It is not just some part of one of the Gospels being read. It is something that moves symbolically and dramatically amongst us as representative of the movement of the Gospel of Good News who is the Christ in the world. It has an almost physical symbolic meaning as conveyed by the physical movements involved.

To honour this in Western churches where people mostly sit for the service, except for the creed and the hymns, and increasingly part of the Anaphora or Eucharistic prayer, they stand for the reading of the Gospel to honour its importance. In Orthodox Churches, they are already standing. The Orthodox believe that they stand through the whole service because they can do so in the full dignity of the image and likeness they bear, rather than feeling they have to sit or kneel in shame and guilt at their sin, which can be a dominant emphasis in some churches. Those who need to sit because of their frailty do so. In the free movement of people standing, we see individuals moving to kiss icons, light candles, move to particular parts of the church as if they are in the open market place of a spiritual agora, where it is natural to move freely and not always stay in the same place, let alone in the same pew. And not having pews, this freedom of movement is easy and natural as it is in and out of the church space.

Pews only came into worship buildings in about the 13th century and then only for a few important people. "Pew" came from the Old French for a balcony or elevated seat or hill, which in turn came from the Latin podia, the plural of elevated place, or the front balcony in a Roman theatre where the more distinguished sat. We still use the word podium where the speaker stands, or a panel of important people sit. In some Anglican churches, the pews weren't simply there for seating, they also divided the aristocracy, or employers, owners and benefactors of a church from everyone else. Everyone knew their "place" and sat in their pew places accordingly. Even today, it is common for people to sit in the same place by habit, and the front pews are often unused except on special occasions for visiting dignitaries or guests. The only movement, in a traditional Anglican church service, was that of the collection being taken and the wine, water and collection plate taken up to the altar, visually symbolising the gifts we offer to God in the Eucharist. It is a surprise therefore for a visitor in an Orthodox service to see the almost charismatic and natural movement, as people enter and leave the church, moving from the back to the front to kiss an icon, light a candle and then back again. And it is into that maelstrom of free movement, and an atmosphere of spiritual devotion that goes with it, that the Gospel Procession moves liturgically from the altar into the very essence of the people of God to symbolise more than just a Church congregation, and to be part of the people's work in the service of the kingdom of God.

# CHAPTER THIRTEEN

## 13    INCARNATING THE MESSAGE

*Religion is needed where there is a wall of separation between God and man. But Christ who is both God and man has broken down the wall between man and God. He has inaugurated a new life, not a new religion.* Alexander Schmemann

As we have seen, the idea of *Leitourgiea*, in the maximal sense, has largely emerged in an Orthodox Church context of worship and from the writings of recent, 20th century, Orthodox theologians, rediscovering and recapitulating earlier meaning in the mystical writers of the early church. This maximal meaning is about more than the meaning of the words of worship. It includes the theological architecture and choreography of liturgy and what its main constituent moments and movements might have meant and still mean to many Orthodox today, although many Orthodox have commented that there is still a huge task of education to be done in many Orthodox countries.

Clearly, I am not a liturgical specialist in any academic sense. I struggle with understanding lectionaries, which are supposed to express the themes of the liturgical year within what I have called liturgical time. I struggle with understanding any of the historical details within the broad sweep of doctrinal divisions taking place over the first centuries. What I offer in this book has been learnt from conversations in Orthodox countries and monastic communities, as well as my reading and reflection on what I have heard and seen. For those interested in any of the detail, there are better researched studies to pursue than this. My task has been to raise some questions about a different perspective and orientation on the meaning and importance of Liturgy in the life of the world today. And I do this out of a concern which may reveal an underlying arrogance, as well as ignorance. But that concern is, put simply, as we saw at the beginning of this piece, that, in some places, we might be unwittingly reducing the horizons and reference points of the Gospel's revelation of the meaning of God, in the way we frame and perform our worship. And that, in turn, might mean that our worship no longer communicates anything like that sense of Liturgy as theological "public works" out of which it partly sprang. If, and where, that is the case, we might be losing a crucial connection between the Liturgy of the Church and the Liturgy of the World. The more that happens, the more the theological and psychological distance between Church and World will increase with negative implications on either side. So much has already been lost in people's views of Christianity - not least through the scientific revolution that has stepped so far ahead, intellectually, of contemporary theology, and of course profound social and cultural changes - that it would be a great shame if the church's rejection of the world took place in ways that blinded it to the Liturgy of the World, and only increased the distance between the Liturgy of the Church and the Liturgy of the World.

## THE WORD IN THE REAL WORLD

There are many theologically appropriate and realistically understandable reasons for the way this *distance* has developed, been experienced, depicted and even advocated by the churches. There are moments in the life of Jesus when he is prompted to talk about a distance between the things of Caesar and the things of God[137]. His answer - that we must give unto Caesar the things which belong to Caesar and to God the things which belong to God, certainly implies a separation and even a distance of God from the former. It can alas be seen as a both/and, rather than an either or. But there are other parts of the Gospel which speak of a real *distance* which undermines much of what I've been proposing, for example statements about the world which rejects Jesus and those who follow him. The Gospel of John opened with these powerful words about creation,

*In the beginning was the Word, and the Word was with God, and the Word was God. He was with God in the beginning. Through Him all things*

---

[137] Taxation was highly controversial at the time given the atmosphere of rebellion against Roman contraventions of Jewish customs. Pilate had in recent years erected images of the Emperor on the fortress Antonia, adjacent to the Temple. The question was clearly intended to trap Jesus in a political dichotomy between his obedience to the Jewish law (inc thou shall not make any graven images..) and obedience to Rome.

*were made, and without Him nothing was made that has been made. In Him was life, and that life was the light of men.* But then comes the next sentence, *The Light shines in the darkness, and the darkness has not overcome it.*

So, yes, there is of course darkness present in the world in which all things were made by Him. And the darkness is like a shadow on the lung of the world and our humanity within it. But more needs to be said about this darkness, in its various manifestations. A few lines later we find this,

*The true Light who gives light to every man was coming into the world. He was in the world, and though the world was made through Him, the world did not recognize Him. He came to His own, and His own did not receive Him. But to all who did receive Him, to those who believed in His name, He gave the right to become children of God— children born not of blood, nor of the desire or will of man, but born of God.*

The world is loved so much that God gives of himself (John 3.16) in His Son, but there are those who did not *recognize* or *receive* him. Indeed, the *world* itself which was made through Him, did not recognize Him. There is, then, both a "true light" which gives light to every person coming into the world but at the same time, a world that rejects Him in the context of its own darkness. Those who responded received the possibility of a new kind of relationship with God. But even some of his "own" did not receive him. Later, in the same Gospel, we also find the following words in that wondrous chapter 17 of the "Farewell discourses' between Jesus and God (Chapters 15-17).

*But now I come to You; and these things I speak in the world so that they may have My joy made full in themselves. I have given them Your word; and the world has hated them, because they are not of the world, even as I am not of the world. I do not ask You to take them out of the world, but to keep them from the evil one. They are not of the world, even as I am not of the world. Sanctify them in the truth; Your word is truth. As You sent Me into the world, I also have sent them into the world. For their sakes I sanctify Myself, that they themselves also may be sanctified in truth. I do not ask on behalf of these alone, but for those also who believe in Me through their word; that they may all be one; even as You, Father, are in Me and I in You, that they also may be in Us, so that the world may believe that You sent Me.*

This passage starts with a surprising and inspiring statement about the divine joy being "made full in themselves". It then moves into a profound note of realism, a clarity about how the world "hates them" (disciples and followers) because they are not "of this world" just as Jesus describes himself as being "not of this world". Then the turning point comes, which is about being "sanctified" in the truth. It is hard to know what that really meant when first written and heard, at least in its fullest sense. We know quite a lot about the background to the word in Jewish and Greek thought. But what was being said here that was new or different? Did this mean more than something we'd expect to find in the Liturgy of the Church? Was this germane to what we have been claiming for the Liturgy of the World in the light of what the Gospel has said about creation and recreation? As Jesus was sent into the world so he sends them into the world, protected by this same sanctification in truth which applies to all who believe in Him, leading to the climactic prayer that they may all be one even as *You, Father, are in Me and I in You, that they also may be in Us so that the world may believe...* To achieve that quality and kind of being "one", is another extraordinary, prayerful longing, claim and vision. It is one that surely takes us well beyond its usual context of inter-church unity and reaches out into all the needs of the world, locally and internationally.

This is a dense and profound statement which ends with a vision of a divine unity as the model for human relationships. In the Sistine Chapel, one part of the different frescoed panels, that attracts much attention, depicts that creation moment when the Father's pointed hand almost touches the hand of Adam. Almost! There are many ways of describing or articulating the nature of the gap between our sense of human nature and the nature and being of a holy, transcendent mystery in the being of God. As we have seen, Rahner insisted on two things at the same time. First, the absolute transcendentality of God and, second, the freedom given in the gap between God and creation for humans to receive or reject any kind of relationship with God's self-communication across that gap. So, however understood, that gap of ontological difference, which can only be bridged by God, is the context for all gaps, including any difference we perceive between the sacred and the secular, or the church and the world.

But just as we assert that context, so comes the need to affirm what is claimed in Christian belief for the way God has crossed that gap in the experience of the Incarnation into our human condition. There are many aspects of the gap which remain, not least in our lack of recognition and acceptance, and our continuing proclivity towards making the wrong choices and failing each other and God's love amongst us. But, according to John's Gospel at least, there is a sanctifying of that which is prone to such failures and faults. There is, in the cross, the hope of a salvation, flowing across that gap and its realistic implications. So, the cross remains as the gap-bridging point between the distance, understood as being either small or large between the meaning of God, and our ways of reaching out towards it.

## MOVING FROM ONE MEAL TO ANOTHER MEAL

But here is another thing that Schmemann says about Liturgy that might be relevant and helpful to this discussion.

*Once more, the joyful character of the Eucharistic gathering must be stressed. For the medieval emphasis on the cross, while not a wrong one, is certainly one-sided. The liturgy is, before everything else, the joyous gathering of those who are to meet the risen Lord and to enter with him into the bridal chamber. And it is this joy of expectation and this expectation of joy that are expressed in singing and ritual, in vestments and in censing, in that whole 'beauty' of the liturgy which has so often been denounced as unnecessary and even sinful... Unnecessary it is indeed, for we are beyond the categories of the 'necessary.' Beauty is never 'necessary,' 'functional' or 'useful.' And when, expecting someone whom we love, we put a beautiful tablecloth on the table and decorate it with candles and flowers, we do all this not out of necessity, but out of love. And the Church is love, expectation and joy*[138].

He moves outward from the joyful character of the Eucharist to the beauty, joy and love which can be experienced in any meal. This is a constant theme in his book and a reminder of the kind of connections that can be made between the act of preparing, eating

---

[138] *For the Life of the World*

and sharing a meal, any day of our normal lives, and what we come to Eucharistically in the Liturgy of the Church. So, if we could find no other connection between the Liturgy of the World and the Liturgy of the Church, this might well be enough. Elsewhere, in the same book he writes,

*The world as man's food is not something "material" and limited to material functions, thus different from, and opposed to, the specifically "spiritual" functions by which man is related to God. All that exists is God's gift to man, and it all exists to make God known to man, to make man's life communion with God. It is divine love made food, made life for man. God blesses everything He creates, and, in biblical language, this means that He makes all creation the sign and means of His presence and wisdom, love and revelation: "O taste and see that the Lord is good"…. Centuries of secularism have failed to transform eating into something strictly utilitarian. Food is still treated with reverence…To eat is still something more than to maintain bodily functions. People may not understand what that 'something more' is, but they nonetheless desire to celebrate it. They are still hungry and thirsty for sacramental life.*

This way of looking at material things in our ordinary lives encompasses the whole world and its sacramental significance. It resonates with the way many of the early mystics viewed creation and links with many contemporary Orthodox and other writers. It asks us to re-evaluate our understanding of matter in nature and in creation. The Catholic priest, Gerard Manley Hopkins, wrote about nature being shot through with the glory of God. Poets and scientists have discovered the "burning bush" in their own different ways as they turned aside to look more closely at it. Rahner talked about every day mysticism pointing us in the direction of a daily way of living that could be essentially spiritual in its own right. Rowan Williams, as we have seen, in his latest book, writes *Liturgical action is, we might say, "saturated" with the meaning God gives to the material process of the world.*

The challenge is how to facilitate and support that same sense of "saturation". For centuries, Orthodox Christians used the Jesus Prayer as a way of integrating spirituality into their daily lives. As we have seen many monastic communities lived within a daily framework of prayer and work. Many Christian groups and movements throughout the world have lived a daily pattern of spirituality and communal prayer. Many individual Christians have discovered the importance of living and offering the activities of each day in prayer. While there have been many attempts to link the ministry of the church with the workplace (worker priests and Industrial Chaplains[139]), there has always been a certain distance between the workplace and the Church, at least since the Industrial Revolution onwards. Work takes many forms and its cultures are changing all the time, not least because of Britain's slow adjustment to Brexit and the implications of the Digital Revolution. Covid has forced new hybrid working patterns and Government subsidies. Strangely, we live now with low unemployment, high inflation, high energy and food prices and increasing anxiety about poverty, food insecurity[140] and climate change.

This is as good a time as any for leaders of the Churches to engage more actively with policy issues and their implications, and to find ways of helping people at work (paid and unpaid) to rediscover the intrinsic and spiritual value of work *per se*, as well as to challenge some of its ethical failures. The churches need to rediscover or find a language to proclaim the significance of work, in its most general sense, for its contribution to Public Works and Public Culture, its goodness, and the many ways that goodness is blocked or undermined. Imagine then that the Liturgy of the Church could again be the signpost to the Liturgy of the World in convincing ways. Imagine that it could consciously set out new directions and help people navigate their different pathways through their different responsibilities. Imagine if it equipped people to rediscover their identity and purpose within the mysticism of daily life through a new perception and valuing of what they could contribute. Then we might be making a profound difference to the way people sensed

---

[139] I was one in Southampton for a time, based in the local parish. One of my predecessors, Julian Eagle had famously pioneered a ministry in the Docks and with the unions. My focus was more on Retail, Local Authorities, Chambers of Commerce and Partnerships,

[140] New post Brexit agricultural regulations seem more focused on wild life diversity than food production.

their involvement within that Liturgical experience, where all public and personal works played their part in turning away from what mars the beauty and truth of creation, and their part in turning in the direction of the things which enhance it. Wouldn't that sense of purpose and responsibility be a firmer basis for individual and community wellbeing? In the Liturgy of the World as well as the Church this might indeed be a formative breakthrough moment and pivot point about which new creative things might happen. This is what Schmemann said about such breakthrough moments.

*The Eucharist of Christ and Christ the Eucharist is the "breakthrough" that brings us to the table in the Kingdom, raises us to heaven, and makes us partakers of the divine food. For eucharist—thanksgiving and praise—is the very form and content of the new life that God granted us when in Christ He reconciled us with Himself. The reconciliation, the forgiveness, the power of life—all this has its purpose and fulfillment in this new state of being, this new style of life which is the Eucharist, the only real life of creation with God and in God, the only true relationship between God and the world.*

If the Liturgy of the Church, focused in the meaning of the Eucharist as the sacrament of the world, is to be understood as present within the Liturgy of the World, as created and redeemed by God, then new theological and practical connections can be made and existing ones affirmed. Of course, many Christians make that connection naturally and instinctively, as they engage with local need in projects and programmes. But a new understanding of liturgy might provide a helpful orientation, bridging back into our experience of daily life and work. And there are many places of work where that is urgently needed because of a sense of lost purpose or hope in jobs that don't satisfy specific, or wider human aspirations. And there are many places of work where individuals are dehumanized by this lack of human fulfillment, or by other ways in which the behaviour of employers or colleagues affects them negatively.

A bridge across the gap provided by this maximal understanding of *leitourgia*, straight from the liturgical values of Christian belief and worship, might prove its special contribution to other ethical debates about work. It might add something more profound that touches the ontology of work, and its place within human responsibility as priests of creation, handling the sacrament of created things within the Liturgy of the World. It might return to the world a sense of the sacredness of this sacrament in material and physical forms, as well as in the emotional and spiritual intelligence of human relating for the sake of the other, particularly the alienated or needy other. It might help to restore the meaning of our human "image and likeness" in relation to the image and likeness of God given freely as self-giving gift in Jesus.

## THE LITURGY OF HUMAN IDENTITY

This wouldn't be about Christian intervention in the lives of others to convert them. It would rather be about the Christian facilitation and discovery and unveiling of what is already there, in the ontology of human identity and the autonomy of human agency. For discovery and rediscovery are sometimes closely related, if we respect the image and likeness of God in every human being, however covered over, or marred, or distorted and damaged by different aspects of living and choice making. That respect for the integrity of the other, given by God in God's prior relationship with all humans within the otherness of creation, can then be the starting point and framework for any discipleship learning and development which honours the theological mystery of human nature and identity per se.

This identity is a primal, ontological one and should not be confused or reduced to current discussions of certain aspects of human identity. This ontological understanding of human identity, within a wider and sacramental view of creation itself, has many practical implications. As we have seen, the zeitgeist of our times has been to divide up the human race around language, skin colour, sex, gender, ethnicity, culture and countless other categories of labelling and definition which seem to increase all the time. Each has its own changing history and approach, but altogether they contribute to a massive fracturing of human identity and risk a breaking down of any real "solidarity". And that is, of course, in certain EU and political circles, a key idea and sometimes all too rhetorical a construct, compared with the ontological gap we have been discussing. It is so tempting for tribal identities to surface – whether of family, group or nation – and create a sense of emotional difference and division. However understandable and powerful they are within those groupings, if they erect perceptual boundaries which separate humans from other humans, then they are truly dangerous. And we have seen ample evidence of that danger in history, leading to hatred and violence. It is one thing for our national identity to instil a sense of belonging, loyalty and even pride,[141] but that can so easily morph into something far more sinister as we saw with National Socialism, or Serbia's dream of a Greater Serbia, or a Putin's vision of a Greater Russia, which all led to horrific wars, and to a justification of the massacre of other others.

Also, there is a new language about human identity in what is sometimes called the digital or online world. Some now even use the phrase "offline world" to distinguish our real lives from what is happening digitally. Some are warning that we now have a digital identity that is closely monitored in the "meta-verse", where shopping choices and gaming are platforms for a marketing of our consumer identity, passed around various digital networks known or unknown to us, with or without our permission. And this is because our consumer potential has become our "identity" in these networks. It can be quite accurately defined, the more we participate in them. More, description becomes categorization, which in turn becomes type, and presupposes certain personality profiles based on accumulating online data. And this of course can be manipulated for good and bad reasons.

This is being called the "attention economy", but it operates without transparent governance. Apparently, we are influenced by

---

[141] For example, the cultural and political nationalism of Johann Gottfried von Herder (1744-1803) who warned that, despite Enlightenment confidence in human reason, tribal instincts can still come to the surface. Or see the way Chopin incorporated Polish folk tales in some of his compositions written in Paris after Russia had swallowed up Poland and taken away his mother and sister. When the Nazis invaded Poland, Chopin was banned and his monument destroyed.

what attracts our attention. Tristan Harris, the President and Co-founder of the Centre for Humane Technology[142] points out the subtle influence of the attention economy on our choices and thinking. This is not searching for better public good or value or social fabric, but what he calls "maximum attention/engagement to suck people down internal rabbit holes" – to reward addiction, polarisation, narcissism, extremism, divisiveness..." This economy turns societies into addicted machines for profit. More users and more hours per day means more profit. Tristan warns that software is running the world, but it cares little about the individual wellbeing of its consumers, apart from their online commercial needs, creating many new ethical dilemmas. And, he reminds us, the Five largest tech companies in the world are like giants eating up profit from our *attentiveness* and addiction to their products. This is not to undervalue the usefulness many people find in being part of this digital revolution, nor to ignore the more obvious dangers of being caught saying or doing the wrong things within social media networks.

But the point is that we are contributing to a new identity which might be called our data identity, and it is largely true that we are identified by a combination of that and other personal and accessible details about age, address, national insurance number, driving license or passport number, NHS number, bank account, credit record, police record, not to mention so many and often forgotten passwords which become the portal through which we can access our online identity or not. And if we forget a password, then even we cannot access our own online identity, but others might be able to hack it! And the faster and more efficient technology becomes, the more dependent we are on it for our relationship with that online meta-verse of identity profiles. And the more we might begin to self-identify with those identities and even create them for ourselves!

These are but two examples of how our identity is being shaped not only in cultural and consumer market places, but through ~~our own active involve~~ment, even where we didn't realise what that

---

[142] Who used to be the Design Ethicist at Google.

activity was creating. Such identity identities give the easy impression that we live in a more joined up connected world and that must be good, mustn't it? And yet, doesn't it all, at the same time, only function as something partial and incomplete leading to a more banal and fractured understanding of human nature.

As I write this, some Russians are being interviewed on the streets of Moscow about President Putin's invasion of the Ukraine, which the Kremlin denied as an "invasion" or war. Putin had repeatedly announced he was never going to invade - but only mount an exercise triggered by neo-Nazi terrorists in the Ukraine. Many Russians couldn't understand it. How, they said, can you invade your friends, your relatives, your neighbours? And they are right. Putin himself had been drawing on a Russian Church understanding of national Orthodox patriotism and spiritual/cultural identity. One might say that the Russian Orthodox Church, under Patriarch Kyril, has turned nationalism and patriotism into a kind of idolatry that blinds itself to the harm being done to fellow Orthodox in Ukraine, the home of Russian Christianity.

But what is it in the political systems and assumptions of the world that undermines this basic solidarity of friend, neighbour, relative? Clearly many things do this, but they are all transgressing the basic, primal truth and ontological solidarity of the human race. And that transgression undermines the underlying nature of human beings and sacrifices it on the altar of penultimate truths about alienating human divisions and separations which are not the ultimate, primal, or complete truth we could be nourishing and espousing. Any reduction of our complete humanity can result in a distortion of the way we see people and therefore a distortion in the way we think of them, react and relate to them, and behave towards them. A category mistake of this kind has existential implications that can accumulate quickly. The evidence of its results is easy to find in human history. So, when we collude with its imposition or influence, or create it consciously or unconsciously ourselves, we need the cry to go up. No, we are more than that! And we need then to live from within that truth and discover its depths for ourselves. One remarkable thing about the New Testament, as shown in the letter to the Galatians (Gal 3.28), written centuries ago, is that early Christians could say something truly profound in the midst of their tensions and divisions. *For, there is neither Jew nor Gentile, neither slave nor free, nor is there male and female, for you are all one in Christ Jesus.*

So, something is seriously wrong as a by-product perhaps of the way we now view identities and identity rights. A return to an understanding of the New Testament insight about our human nature might go some way to re-orientating our worldview and self-understanding. I might be from Russia, or from the Ukraine, or anywhere else, but those identities are secondary to the one which really matters, and which would prevent me ever turning on my friends, neighbours, and relatives and treating them as enemies. All humans are my relatives, even though my family members are relatives in a more specific sense. This reorientation will require its own new clarity about the language we use to describe other others in the human race.

This understanding of diversity within a common identity, as part of creation, will take seriously all that we know from science about the evolution and development of human nature and personality, as well as a theological orientation based on an understanding of the world as sacrament, and sacrament as part of the Liturgy of the World. And this is not a dogmatic understanding of identity, because it takes seriously the work of the Holy Spirit, leading us constantly into greater truth, and that means closer union with the source of creation in the perfect image and likeness of God in Jesus. And that truth includes the best of all kinds of scientific knowledge, and the theological knowledge that is beyond our usual understanding of knowledge. As we have seen, this is what has been called apophatic knowledge, which functions well within any *cloud of unknowing* - that cloud like place where ambiguity and uncertainty are part of the givenness of human experience within creation, and part of nature as perceived by our human experience of it. And the best of science recognises the truth of that cloud as the place where physics confronts its own *Uncertainty Principle*. And, in this cloud, we draw closer through the way in which we are not, in order to discover ourselves in our fuller, human potential. And in that process of discovery, we need others to know that we too need their help, as they might need ours, for human identity is part of the otherness of creation, in which other others evolve their own autonomy and discover their own interdependency.

Spiritual growth can affect and be part of all other kinds of growth within the Liturgy of the World. And it is no simple, predictable or predetermined thing. It draws us closer to the place where we might encounter our own, but inevitably partial perception of the mysterion of God's self-giving, in order for us to participate more fully in that human image and likeness potential given and restored to us in Christ. And, therefore, our experience of the Liturgy of the World can bridge us back into the Liturgy of the Church as well as the other way around. The one can lead to the other, or inform the other with its own orientation and understanding. We might even discover that the one is, in fact, part of the other. But this is only possible if the connection has been made clearly enough for individuals to catch sight of it, and to experience or experiment with what it might mean for them. Its meaning is intensely personal as well as intensely social, just as the nature of the divine life of the Trinity is supremely both at the same time, in ways that are fully beyond our understanding. And if there is a movement of *theosis* in the divine self-giving, emanating from the Trinity of the society of God in our direction, so our humanity can know and respond to that self-giving; so there is a movement of *theosis* between the Liturgy of the Church and the Liturgy of the World. And because of Jesus, both partake of each other and overlap on each other's templates and reference points in our humanness in relation to God and to creation. And this is why the cross can be said to be at the heart of creation, because the once-for-all, self-giving of Jesus outside the walls of Jerusalem, on the Roman cross of a first century Calvary, touches the very suffering of real human experience present within the life of the world. If this is true, then it must be true within the causes and cycles of violence and the cycles of pain and the way pain is passed on in acts of wounded revenge on others, or self-harm on ourselves.

## A LITURGY OF SUFFERING NORMALITY

And there can even be suffering in our experience of normal, everyday life, not just through serious illness, disability and pain, not just through misunderstandings and hurt, but lost hope and purpose, loss and longing, or that strange, non-specific sense of alienation, ennui, and despair over small, apparently normal things. At times of crisis and pressure, people of all ages are vulnerable to mental health anxieties and real life can be very hard indeed. Nor should we take for granted the smooth running of National Health Services for they too are subject to pressures of change, resource allocation and oscillating political policies. Their staff must be as vulnerable to overladen, bureaucratic and managerial complexity as its customers are!

Normal things in normal times can be a wonderful source of discovery and fulfilment, if we but stop to examine them and value them more closely. But, "normality" isn't always as consistently normal as the word implies. It will include a wide spectrum of different perspectives and experiences. Sometimes, those who have good things or good experiences don't always appreciate them as much as those who haven't had them, but long for them. Clean drinking water and modern sanitation, or enough good food, for example, might seem, for the majority in many parts of the world (including the basement hiding places of the bombed-out cities of the Ukraine), as quite extraordinary and well beyond their grasp, while others consume these things as if they are quite normal, unnoticed expectations in the passing of everyday life. But from within the perspective of the Liturgy of the World, that which is normal can be a wonderful thing in its own right. Lives can be changed exploring the taken for granted existence and appearance of normal, daily things. How did they come into existence? Why do they look as they do? How do they work? Who makes them work? How would the world be without them? What would our lives be without them? Once we stop to see and perceive what is under the surface of what we are looking at, or using, then a whole new world unveils itself. It was always there, even when we took it for granted. When it's not there, we might stop and really look, and wonder how we could have possibly missed its significance in the first place.

In all lives, there is, or has been some kind of suffering. Even the wonder of a new birth involves an amount of pain, sometimes a great deal of danger and uncertainty. Watching a rugby match or taking part in any active support we marvel at how strong, flexible or resilient our bodies are, that is right up to the point when we injure ourselves and then spend months recovering. Something that can happen in a split second, like a fall, can change our lives for a long time until, if we are lucky, we slowly see our body heal itself from the inside out. And it is a miracle that so much of our body, especially our skin, can replace itself through its own, normal cellular and biochemical processes. But suffering seems to be always and everywhere present, in its different forms, caused not only by the inevitability of human frailty and entropy, but by our human fallibility and foolishness, our failure to follow the ways of love in the way we treat other others. And yet, because of that cross in both the Liturgy of the World and the Church, the ways of love continue and are offered to us as redemptive of our human fallibility and failures, if we chose to receive and follow them as best we may, and as inspired and helped by the life-giving Spirit of God, everywhere present in creation as the life-giver.

Some of this language, as used in this approach, may imply a logical connection or process between the Liturgy of the World and the Liturgy of the Church. But real life is not like that. This is no flip chart exercise! The dots don't always join up in any simple linear way. And it is partly a matter of perception and how we choose to understand the world. That which we might think of as the epiphany of discovery and rediscovery is given as graceful, unexpected, undeserved gift in the sacramental experience of ordinary, daily life and its work and relationships. And this is a gift which can break down many barriers to perception and the experience of Liturgy within daily work and living, hard as those things often are. And it's important not to ignore or dismiss the possibility of this gift too lightly or arrogantly; for the truth is that we just don't know. The Glory of God hidden within the cloud of our not-knowing shines its own light, even if it be one of a dazzling darkness that blinds us all.

This kind of language is obviously densely packed and very different from the transactional sounding language of some conversional discourses and expectations, which can come across as superficial or simplistic by comparison. We are, after all, talking here of a mystery of spiritual unveiling that is beyond our knowing or control, and yet invites our participation and further searching. It is not to be reduced to a simple equation that might be described as in the following. Input A, from conversion intervention B, produces Output Z, from any converted person Y, in a linear and expected way. Two plus Two may equal Four in our mathematical systems, but the meaning this theological language stands for might be far more subtle. Sometimes in human experience, Two plus Two can equal either Three, or Five. In other words, less or more than it theoretically promises or indicates, in the way we calculate it. For there is something unpredictable and uncertain at the heart of our certainties, at least there is, if we take seriously real human experience of how things can work out, in ways that seem to go wrong or right well beyond our control. And although we may actively pursue our calling and hopes, our skills and potential, this may still be the case.

Spiritual unveiling, discovery and growth will be different for every person, because God respects the precious uniqueness of every person and loves beyond our calculations, hopes, measures and limits of love. And this is part of the sacramental mysterion of God's Love. Its nature may not be ever fully knowable, but it has been known because of the divine presence in Jesus in ways that take us closer to the place where we can glimpse something of its true mysterion. And that takes us back to what happens sacramentally in the Liturgy of the Church, as understood in this maximal way, and what happens in the Liturgy of the World, as we discover its sacramental significance. And once we do that, once we orientate our thinking into the possibility of this maximal and inclusive understanding, then our assumptions will change along with our perception of the sacramental value of the things we call nature in creation, and our experiences of them in daily life, and our relationships with other people. And, slowly, we might find that our horizons are widened and our understanding deepened, and, within them, nothing can separate us from the love of God in the world God loved and loves so much. And when that happens, we may find that we don't want to think of the world as secular any more, because mysteriously it has been returned to us as sacred in its creation, its creativity and its potential. And then we might look around and, in the words of T. S. Eliot, "know the place for the first time."

# CHAPTER FOURTEEN

## 14 TOWARDS A CONCLUSION - BACK TO THE BEGINNING

*We shall not cease from exploration*
*And the end of all our exploring*
*Will be to arrive where we started*
*And know the place for the first time.*
*Through the unknown, remembered gate*
*When the last of earth left to discover*
*Is that which was the beginning;*
from "Little Gidding" T.S. Eliot, Four Quartets[143]

In the Liturgy of the World, as in the Liturgy of the Church, exploration leads us to a new perception, and an exploratory arrival at a new beginning. And it happens through the unknown and unknowable, but sometimes remembered gate, though we sometimes travel into confusing and difficult territory where trust is as important a route as knowledge.

*If you came this way,*
*Taking any route, starting from anywhere,*
*At any time or at any season,*
*It would always be the same: you would have to put off*
*Sense and notion. You are not here to verify,*
*Instruct yourself, or inform curiosity*
*Or carry report. You are here to kneel*
*Where prayer has been valid. And prayer is more*
*Than an order of words, the conscious occupation*
*Of the praying mind, or the sound of the voice praying[144].*

*Little Gidding* is overflowing with fertile images about the nature of things in themselves, and how we perceive them. It is its own liturgy and has its own liturgical truth to tell, though not always through straightforward assumptions and sensory perceptions, even though there may be the sound or silence of the voice praying.

So now we come to the heart of the matter and its obvious

---

[143] Gardners Books; Main edition, April 30, 2001. Originally published 1943.

[144] The end of Part 1 of *Little Gidding*

dilemma, that is, if we want to draw some kind of conclusion or consider some kind of implication from what has been said so far. There may, of course, be no conclusion possible, if we are to take seriously the nature of faith. Also, there may be implications for how we look at the world and try to understand it in the light of the Liturgy of creation and incarnation. Simply thinking of it as being part of the Liturgy of the World might be a good start, and that will begin to change our perception and understanding of its meaning.

If we believe that which is "Liturgy" really is part of the nature of things; that the ontology of things is part of how they were created as part of the movement of God in our direction, then we cannot step back from the claim we've made about Liturgy being a truth about the nature of things, whether we agree with that or not. If this claim is true, then it doesn't matter whether we perceive it to be true, believe it to be true, or even what its epistemology might be. From that perspective, we all stand in the same place, whether we identify it as the Liturgy of the World, or of the Church.

On the other hand, there can be no certainty within the ontology of things, and the ontology will include its own ambiguity, otherwise we are being untrue to the nature of reality as we know it, scientifically and theologically. Therefore, the claim being made about Liturgy "being a truth about the nature of things" must allow for this uncertainty as part of its truth.

So, the dilemma is to find a way of speaking about both at the same time, as if both apply at the same time, although in different ways. To believe in the liturgical dimension of reality, and that liturgy has its own effect on reality, we have to insist that it is part of the nature of things, whether or not it is encountered or known as part of that reality. But, on the other hand, to believe in the liturgical dimension of God, or a relationship with God in that reality, is to insist that faith in that belief remains uncertain, because it is not forced, or proved, or provable, in the usual ways. We believe that liturgy really does affect the nature of reality, because it is the same reality that God created and is "part" of, incarnationally. But we accept that our belief is a reflection of our perception, and that includes the subjectivity of the human condition in relationship to what is knowable. And we also believe that the nature of God is essentially and ontologically unknowable. And this must be true, even though God has moved in our direction so that, in Christ, God is knowable in a human, visible sense, but one that can still only be known apophatically, not cataphatically. For the very nature of the holiness, the wholly otherness of God, even as revealed in the human otherness of Jesus, is transcendent of our full understanding, even as it is immanent within it. Sometimes, it is important to recognise that two apparently opposing things can be true and have to be true at the same time.

We are forced to admit, therefore, that we cannot stand in front of others others, and proclaim that we have a provable proof of the ontology of liturgy, or rather of the effect of Liturgy on the ontology of things. And this is true, even though we insist it is part of the nature of things, and therefore, that must be true, even if it is not perceived to be true. And we must admit, epistemologically, that our nature lies on both sides of the perception that is part of our fallible nature on the one side, and the nature of God whose being and nature is "unknowable", on the other.

So, while I want to say to fellow Christians that their worship is more than just worship, but makes a liturgically, ontological difference to the nature of reality, I also feel compelled to insist that this remains a dimension of my human perception as mediated via my belief. Liturgy is "more" and makes more of worship, but not in a way that bypasses the nature of reality, with all its ontological uncertainty, nor the fallible nature of my participation in it, and of it. But if Liturgy is "more", in the way we have been describing, I believe how we sometimes understand worship is a reduction of that "more" to something less than it could be, and something less than has been glimpsed by those Christians through the ages who have taken Liturgy seriously in its maximal sense. And this was particularly true in the early era of Christian developments among the mystical theologians. I am grateful to them, though I am unworthy of ever pretending I fully understand their insights, which flow from a profound encounter with the incarnational "mysterion" that meets us sacramentally in the life of the world. And the more we look for the meaning and presence of the "Liturgy of the World", I believe we will find more that makes sense to us in the Liturgy of the Church, and vice versa. And perhaps then, the question and orientation within the Liturgy of the Church, won't be so much about people's church going, but about the way they look at the Liturgy of the World, and participate in it. But as Eliot said, there are many routes, and many ways of exploring, and then arriving at the thing which really matters. And I would add – there are many ways of coming to the intersection between the overlapping Liturgy of the Church and the Liturgy of the World and finding or making a connection between them.

There is, then, a significant moving space in the connecting gap, somewhere in between where the Liturgy of the World and the Liturgy of the Church begin and end and overlap each other. And that space has been perceived in different ways over time in different parts of the history of the Church. As Christians we believe that the gap was bridged by the kenotic, ek-stasis of God, reaching out to make possible the being of the Other. Ever since, we have surely been struggling to understand how, and when, and why, we humans have lost that sense of connection, preferring instead to create our own kinds of inherited, or newly assumed boxes or gaps. Perhaps we are living in another time and space now, when it is possible to believe in the significance of this moving, dynamic space, and, if so, to proclaim it as territory worth inhabiting[145].

We will have our different places from which to reach out and perceive what is on the other side of the Liturgy of the World and Liturgy of the Church gap-connection, and from that place to proclaim what we see as the significance of our perception. To proclaim a truth, means to claim it, or represent it, on behalf of someone or something. Perhaps we feel we can claim it for ourselves, in order

---

[145] I've borrowed this phrase from Richard Parry the Director of *Coleridge in Wales* and now The *Company of Ideas* which is engaged in the pursuit of a new Public Culture. In my role as Chair of this organisation we have been working together for some years on the theological underpinning of the exploration of new ideas which find traction in the debates of our times.

to make it accessible to others, and that has been the purpose of this book. Or perhaps we find ourselves somewhere on the edge of the gap reaching out across it, either towards the Liturgy of the World from the perspective of the Liturgy of the Church, or the other way around. Or, we may find ourselves already moving deeper into the connection and context evoked by the meaning of *Liturgy* in and of itself, in the way we've been speaking of, which largely makes the gap between the Liturgy of the World and the Liturgy of the Church redundant. Wherever we find ourselves, I hope the pro-clamation of this book is helpful to your navigating, as you explore this territory from within your own maps of the world.

Liturgy can be seen as the movement from the inside to the outside. It can be an experience of Outside-In, balanced by Inside-Out perceptions. It is the transformative movement from something to something else; from disorder towards order, incompletion towards completion, unfulfillment towards fulfilment, lostness towards purpose, disconnection towards connection, all expressed in physical ways, but implying and carrying a spiritual significance. In all these movements, it is the direction "towards" that is important. The idea of movement towards something is always relative to where we are, at any one moment, in our journey from here to there. And the paradox is that the closer we get to "there", the further away it might seem, for that is its very nature, from the beginning, wherever we start from. For the artist, this is the very stuff of their exploration and interrogation of their artistic interest and perception. For the scientist, it is something similar, though rarely articulated in this way. For the social scientist, it is again similar though understood and expressed in the different language of politics, the political economy, social structures and services. For the person doing the daily household chores, making and mending, all these movements, from here to there, apply as part of the managing of the needs of the home, the family and its wellbeing.

For Liturgy, in its maximal sense, covers the whole range of public work from the *oikumene* to the *polis* to the *oikos*, the meta-physical to the physical, even, or especially, in its most mundane and material senses. That is its surprise and its secret; a secret that is hidden in plain sight within the ordinary things of God's creation. We do not need to articulate its presence everywhere, if the doing of ordinary things is done as an offering of our humanity to that which is more than our humanity. When we begin to articulate and annunciate its presence, then we begin to discover how it is present everywhere. Then, in all our exploring, through the depths of our ordinary and extraordinary world, perceivable in both those ways, sometimes at the same time, we will arrive where we started, and know that place for what it truly is, for the first time.

# OTHER BOOKS BY THE AUTHOR

The Virtual Apocalypse (the devices call our bluff)
The Playground (Kate remembers Geneva and a Russian interpreter)
The Photograph (a photograph, assassinations, the Vatican, Cold War)
Shadows of Memory (Harry, a spy, remembers Vienna and Prague)
One Leg is Both the Same (UN and Middle East)
The Lawn in the Mud (a WW1 soldier and banker; a discovered letter)
Cobwebs (Beirut assassination, archaeology and Hezbollah)
The Spider (stand alone sequel to Cobwebs set in Boston)
The Circus (a murder mystery; Eastern Europe)
Myfanwy (A literary tour, Lake Geneva. Frankenstein to Chaplin)
The Bottom of the Garden (Pakistan, Africa, shadows and light)
The Secret Trial (stand alone sequel, involving Jack and Taliban)
The Falling Shroud (continuing the story of Jack)
Going Back (the final story of Jack, terrorism and Afghanistan)
Chloe's Time (Who is she and where does she come from?)
The Virtue of Vulnerability (China, Russia and the gender debate)
The Recreant (Tom, a civil servant; beginnings and ends)
The Intimacy of Strangers (Bosnia and London)
Cross Talk (A writer and artist meet in Australia)
The Glow Within (based on a real experience in Romania)

POEMS. 'Finding a Way.' Collected Poems 1970-2015
PLAYS.  Various.
LATE NIGHT MEDITATIONS. Different themes.

'LOVE'S ENERGY.'  A Trilogy on science and theology.
*If creationism is untenable and dangerous in Christianity and Islam,*
*how can we talk about a Creator, or Source, in a universe that 'makes itself'?*
Part 1  Pattern paradoxes in cosmology and quantum: the Big Bang.
Part 2  Pattern paradoxes in the theology, inc autonomy and freedom.
Part 3.  Pattern paradoxes in evolution: the Big Birth.
                *Available from Amazon and other online stores*

Printed in Great Britain
by Amazon

81064318R00181